Faster, Fitter,

Faster, Fitter, Happier is the first book to bridge the gap between the practice of psychology in both professional and amateur sport, and the theoretical foundations on which the science is based. Author Tony Westbury has been working alongside coaches and performers across a range of sports for over 25 years, during which time he has been asked everything from the best methods to combat nerves to developing that elusive 'will to win'.

Here he provides the answers to 75 questions that encapsulate some of the most important issues he's faced. From motivating yourself to stick to a training programme to taking a high-pressure penalty or getting back in the saddle after a fall, the book offers guidance and advice across a range of sports for both professional and amateur alike. Its accessible style is ideally suited to performers, coaches, teachers and parents, while each question also includes a summary of the theory – an invaluable resource for students and early career practitioners.

With a foreword by British Lion and Scottish International Jason White, this is a unique overview of how sport psychology can support us in our everyday sporting endeavours. Engaging, insightful and practical, it will be essential reading whether you're training for the Olympics or just losing confidence after yet another missed putt.

Tony Westbury, PhD, has worked as an applied sport psychologist for the past 25 years, working at all levels from novices to Olympians. He is the course leader of the MSc in Sport Performance Enhancement at Edinburgh Napier University, UK.

Faster, Fitter, Happier

75 Questions with a Sport Psychologist

Tony Westbury, PhD

With a foreword by rugby union international Jason White

Routledge
Taylor & Francis Group

LONDON AND NEW YORK

First published 2018
by Routledge
2 Park Square, Milton Park, Abingdon, Oxon OX14 4RN

and by Routledge
711 Third Avenue, New York, NY 10017

Routledge is an imprint of the Taylor & Francis Group, an informa business

© 2018 Tony Westbury

British Library Cataloguing in Publication Data
A catalogue record for this book is available from the British Library

Library of Congress Cataloging in Publication Data
A catalog record for this book has been requested

ISBN: 978-1-138-69612-9 (hbk)
ISBN: 978-1-138-69613-6 (pbk)
ISBN: 978-1-315-52533-4 (ebk)

Typeset in Bembo and Myriad
by Swales & Willis Ltd, Exeter, Devon, UK

MIX
Paper from
responsible sources
FSC
www.fsc.org   FSC™ C013985

Printed in the United Kingdom
by Henry Ling Limited

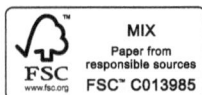

Acknowledgements

Mum. Always.

My brother Patrick and my best mate Jon Graham – everyone should be blessed with friends as good as you.

Ian Campbell – the best psychologist I've ever met. Your gentle inspiration has carried me up many literal and metaphorical mountains when my body had long given up.

I have been privileged to work with amazing colleagues, coaches, students and performers – there really are too many to mention. I have to keep quiet about this but often my work doesn't feel like work at all – you are the reason!

The late John Syer: when the student is ready to learn, a teacher will emerge.

I would like to sincerely thank Russell George, Alex Howard and Julie Willis for their patient and professional help in the production of this book. It is greatly appreciated.

Contents

Foreword

FIGURE 0.1 Jason White with Calcutta Cup. (Courtesy of David Gibson of Fotosport.)

Jason White has 67 Scotland caps, is three-times winner of the Calcutta Cup and was British Lion 2005.

I was studying at Edinburgh Napier University trying to juggle the demands of being a professional rugby player and the university time-table when Tony and I first met. He was one of my lecturers on the Sports Science degree programme and therefore had the unenviable task of keeping me engaged and fully on task when my mind would naturally wander to thoughts of my weekend's upcoming game.

Tony introduced me to sport psychology in a way that engaged my interest and invited me to explore the potential benefits it could have when applied to my performance. We formed a relationship that enabled me to develop a toolbox of mental skills and resilience that helped me problem solve and identify solutions to challenges I faced during my career.

Elite sport, to me, is a complex puzzle with the ultimate aim of producing influential performances time after time. With Tony's help this became a clear and achievable goal for me.

As a performer there is nothing better than feeling full of confidence and ready to perform on the biggest stage. However the reality of sport by its very nature means that there is always an opponent or team trying just as hard as you to win the battles that happen every second and minute of a match or competition.

During a game of international rugby when your performance does not go to plan it can be very hard to stay on track when any mistake is seen by over 60,000 people in the stadium and millions watching on TV. Every time I played against the greatest team in the World, New Zealand, it would without doubt ensure I was tested both mentally and physically to the limit.

Part of my toolbox was finding a routine that would allow me to prepare mentally for a match. This routine took some time to perfect and I had to try different things to find out what worked for me. I would go for a walk on the morning of the game to do some visualization of my core skills, listen to a certain play list to increase my energy levels and again practise some mental imagery. This routine became a key part in my week and allowed me to feel prepared mentally to perform.

During a match it was critical to get myself into the 'here and now' straight away, being ready to play from the first whistle. This started with my routine during the team warm-up before the game when I would follow specific drills that allowed me to match my mental preparation with my physical preparation. Having the balance between the mental and physical was very important.

There will be bits of advice and learning in this book that will strike a chord with you and allow you to take ownership of your sporting performance. Tony gave me the toolbox to do that and I know there will be parts of this that will be of benefit to you no matter where you are on your sporting, coaching or parenting journey.

Jason White

1

Why do we need a psychology of sport?

What's this book about?

This book answers questions. For the past 25 years I have had the privilege of working as a sport psychology consultant with teams and individuals at all competitive levels, and in many different sports. Performers, coaches, parents and teachers ask great questions. Questions about the mental side of sport they encounter in the course of their sporting lives. They are about motivation: why it is so difficult to maintain; about emotion: why they get sick with nerves before they perform; about concentration: why they lose focus at the vital moment. These are questions about psychology: it is my purpose in this book to provide answers.

People in sport tend to focus on and prioritize the physical side of their performance – getting stronger, faster and more skilful, until they hit a challenge or setback – then they begin to appreciate the complexity of what they are doing; they see that being fit, strong and skilful often isn't enough. This is when they tune into the mental dimension of performance.

Throughout my sporting career and into my work as a sport psychologist, my first thought has always been about the mental side.

- ♦ What does it feel like to take a free throw to win a play-off game?
- ♦ How does a pro golfer stop her hand from shaking when she putts for a career-changing title or large cash prize?
- ♦ Why can't that football coach control his anger when a referee makes a decision against his team?

All of these are 'headline' questions. I'm just as concerned with processes:

- ♦ How do we stop the judgemental voice in our heads, saying 'you're not good enough'?
- ♦ How can we make sure children stay active in their sport and enjoy it more?
- ♦ How can we ease the mental challenges that players experience at the end of their careers?

This is not a traditional textbook. There are many excellent recently published academic sources and I do provide a list of the ones I consider to be the most useful. Textbooks tend to be focused on the theory rather than the practice and usually do not address the types of questions raised by performers, coaches, teachers and parents. This book has grown from my work with performers, as clients, attending educational workshops or in 'teachable moments' such as conversations at training or games, in dinner queues or waiting for 'warm downs' to be completed. In every case the identity of the 'client' has been protected, maintaining the confidential relationship I have established with each one.

The questions have determined the structure and content of this book

Most textbooks offer an overview of the current knowledge from which readers have to answer their own questions. This book is the other way around – I have gathered questions and these have informed the content. Each chapter begins with an accessible overview of what we currently know about a central topic in modern sport psychology. I then move on to the questions. I set out to do two things with each. Firstly, I answer the question asked. I outline my approach to understanding the issue and how I would go about designing and implementing an answer. The second part of the answer goes deeper. It is designed to give readers an insight into my thinking process behind the answer I offer. I have included the second part for two reasons: firstly, I think it can help if people understand the complexity of the question they are asking, and secondly, to offer a resource for students and those undergoing professional training, learning to think like a sport psychologist.

When I supervise students undergoing professional training in applied sport psychology techniques I advise them not to fall into the trap of lecturing their clients about the research evidence behind an intervention. A minority are interested and want to know, but as a general rule clients are more concerned with the 'what' and the 'how' than the 'why'. The background provided here can inform a developmental dialogue with their tutors and supervisors.

What type of questions will I be looking at? An example is one of the first questions I noted down – about 25 years ago. I was asked to do a pre-season mental skills workshop for professional cricketers. I worked my way through my overhead projector slides (that's how long ago it was!). At the conclusion, I sat back thinking I'd done a great job when the coach fired this question at me:

> We spend about 200 days of the year in each other's company, often in stressful conditions. There is a lot of banter between us. Do you think we should take the "mick" out of each other as much as we do? (Only he didn't say 'mick')

It's a 'trapdoor'-type question. Banter can affirm membership and status in the group; when we banter we can acknowledge that we are a cohesive group. Equally, banter can severely undermine individuals and drive a team apart. Can we establish a line beyond which banter doesn't go? I groped for an answer and all I could manage was, 'It depends'. It is scenarios like this which give me the subtitle for the book – 'It depends'. You will be pleased to know that I've thought more deeply about this question since and offer a more detailed answer in the text!

It depends!

The answer to almost all the questions posed in the text is 'It depends'. It depends because it's complex: the individual and the unique context are central to how I have framed my answer. It is therefore important to clarify that my answers are not *the* answer. The answers presented here are *an* answer, a starting point: absolutely *not* a definitive or perfect final word.

Clients are often surprised by my pause before answering the seemingly simple question they are asking. There are usually layers of complexity providing a backdrop to the presenting issue. This highlights the importance of the second part of my answers. By presenting a deeper theoretical commentary the reader gains a sense of the evidence I am bringing to bear on the question. I draw on the theory because I aim to practise in an evidence-based manner: this is a key aspect of the professional code of conduct which psychologists operate in accordance with. Psychologists are required to keep up to date on the most recent research to ensure that their practice is as effective as possible. Staying current can be challenging. The evidence base in sport psychology is rapidly growing; there are now more peer-reviewed professional journals and other sources than ever. However, there is a fundamental challenge in the application of much of this material to the 'real-life' context.

Evidence-based practice vs. practice-based evidence

Most research studies don't use elite performers. Why would world-class athletes risk their performance by volunteering as 'guinea pigs' for psychological research?

Psychological research data are most likely to be collected from studies recruiting recreational performers, from a wide variety of performance levels. The data are also frequently collected from a narrow range of the most popular sports. Therefore a great deal of applied work, including the work I do with my clients, stretches the evidence base to, and perhaps beyond, its limit. Often studies are not replicated. Can evidence generated in a recreational population be applied to the elite of performance? Can evidence generated in one sporting context be translated to another? There are important differences between the motivations and motivational climates around youth sport in different parts of the world; can we apply evidence from research in the United States to the European context?

The applied practitioner is often faced with a conundrum which is more persuasive in the case I have in front of me: *evidence-based practice* – the peer-reviewed literature – or *practice-based evidence* – my experience and structured reflections? This is a dilemma faced by practitioners in a range of areas. In this I concur with the comment made by Terry Orlick in the seminal *Consultant's Guide to Excellence for Sport and Performance Enhancement* (Halliwell et al., 2003) that, for many years in his work with individuals and teams, he felt he was taking more from them in terms of knowledge and understanding than he was giving in terms of mental training exercises. Evidence is important and serves as a starting point; practical experience and reflection are also vital in framing and delivering a performance-enhancing service to clients.

Is sport psychology really psychology?

Psychology is the scientific study of mind and behaviour. In common with all sciences, psychology aims to observe, describe and explain natural phenomena, in this case around human behaviour and the limitations of performance. Once these steps have been achieved the theory can be used to design interventions which can optimize and enhance thinking, feeling and behaviour and ultimately functioning. Historically, psychology has been most usually applied to understanding and reducing human distress. This is why psychology is most usually associated in people's thinking with pathology – a loss of function and mental illness. Recently a new approach in psychology has turned this on its head. The positive psychology movement has shown that psychology also has the potential to observe, describe, explain and intervene to enhance function.

Sport psychology is a relatively new area. Prior to 1990 there were few people looking at the mental side of sport performance in a systematic way: at that time pioneering psychologists in the UK and North America were becoming involved in both research and working with high-profile sporting teams. Both academic and applied development increased at a pace over the next two decades to the point now where sport psychology has received unprecedented media and public attention. High-performing individuals and teams have become as willing to discuss the mental factors associated with performance as they are their physical, technical and tactical training. It is no longer considered to be a sign of weakness to consult or work with a sport psychologist. Indeed, the work done by Professor Steve Peters with the GB Cycling Team and Team Sky has cemented the role of psychology in the comprehensive preparation for performance at all levels of performance, but especially at the highest level.

Despite the increase in awareness, there is a gap between the practising sport psychologist and the players, coaches, teachers and parents involved in sport and wanting to know more about the mental side of performance. Research tells us that there is an appetite for more information but that all sport scientists have a bit of an image problem to many in the sporting community. They are viewed as outsiders, often more concerned with doing research than contributing to the development of individuals or teams. From a young age modern sports performers will be exposed either directly or indirectly to a multidisciplinary team of support staff. Often they have a broad understanding of the role of the coach, the strength and conditioning specialist, the nutritionist and the performance analyst, but the work of the psychologist is still viewed as a bit mysterious. It is my aim in this book to lift the lid on the work that the psychologist does to prepare individual performers and teams for performance. In this text I will be inviting the reader to see the world through the eyes of a sport psychologist and to examine the ways in which we conceptualize and approach the kinds of practical questions we are faced with in our work with coaches, teachers, parents, other sport science and sports medicine practitioners and also with the performers themselves.

Where does sport psychology fit into preparation to perform?

I encourage those I work with to think about sport performance in four overlapping areas – physical, technical, tactical and mental.

Physical training concentrates on the strength, power and endurance challenges of different sports and activities within sport. Sport science has generated a great deal of knowledge about the most effective methods of developing these building blocks of performance. However this is a rapidly evolving area of research and many strength and conditioning specialists are wedded to ideas and techniques which are not necessarily supported by the 'leading-edge' research. Efficient physical preparation is not just about hard work in the gym or training field. It is about specifically preparing for the demands of performance in a particular sport or event, balancing the optimal stimulus to ensure that the body adapts fully to training whilst also ensuring full recovery between bouts, through adequate rest and nutrition.

Technical training is concerned with developing the requisite movement skills to perform. Skill is the ability to bring about specific outcomes with the maximum of certainty and the minimum of effort and/or time. Clearly skill is an essential aspect of preparation to perform, however skills are of little value if you are not physically fit enough to compete. In common with physical preparation, technical training should be specific, developing skills which will be challenged in actual performance. In some sports, skills are typically developed in a way which is different to competition – for example, a golfer practising at the driving range, or a cricketer practising in the nets. Effective coaches understand this point and work hard to create practices which develop skills under identical or near-identical conditions to those which will be met in competition. This has the additional benefit of 'inoculating' performers to the pressure of competition and helps to build the confidence that you can execute the necessary skills whatever the situation.

One of the characteristics of consistent high-level performers is the ability to do *exactly* the right thing at *exactly* the right time. This is the *tactical* area of sport performance. Some players have an intuitive understanding of space and timing. They appear to have a 'game intelligence' which ensures they anticipate what will happen ahead of others. The coaching community is divided as to whether you are born with this type of tactical awareness or it is learned: there is probably a bit of both, but my own view is that one of the key attributes of effective coaching is to create learning experiences which help players learn and practise decision making under pressure.

Sport is 100% mental!

All of this brings me, at last, to my point – obviously, as the author of a book about sport psychology I believe that all sport is 100% *mental*. No matter how much you know about and develop physical, technical and tactical aspects of sport, none of these explains why you get up out of the chair and do it to the best of your ability, day in and day out, under the pressure of competition, taking the peaks and the troughs in your stride. That answer is 100% about you and your personal performance psychology.

You may answer the question differently and I'm not dodging the issue. If you believe that your golf performance is 80% mental then you are correct; equally, you are correct if you believe that it is 20% mental. As a practising sport psychologist my question to you is whether you believe your performance is 20% or 80% mental, and what are you doing to develop the mental skills required to perform consistently to your potential in your chosen sport?

The $64,000 question: does sport psychology work?

You would expect me to say yes – I've spent 25 years of my life skilling myself to be an effective sport psychology practitioner! However, I think it is important to address the question in a little more depth.

Firstly, what does 'work' mean in this context? Does it mean that everyone who uses a sport psychology intervention will enjoy continual success in performance and constant psychological well-being? If so, then *no*, clearly this is not achievable. Sport performance is more complex than that. There are many factors which impact on the outcome of any event – not least the physical, technical, tactical and mental performance of an opponent, a factor which is outside the personal control of the performer. This is why I am sceptical of any coach or psychologist who offers, or worse still guarantees, a 'winning formula'. There is no formula – there are things that you can do which make that outcome more likely, but there is no 'magic'. All aspects of preparation for performance 'work' when they systematically develop a platform which eliminates areas of weakness and polishes areas of strength. Even when you are the best in the world at something, you may still have areas of weakness – albeit these are relative. The systematic elimination of weakness is one of the main reasons that all sport performers, from the beginner to the world's best performers, continue to work hard in training.

Secondly, effectiveness is often difficult to demonstrate in sport psychology. In other areas of science, it is much easier to present comprehensive evidence showing whether a treatment or intervention actually works. You can set up a study where a sample of people are given a treatment and a matched control group either receive a placebo, a treatment that participants believe to be effective, or there is no treatment at all. These studies are common when developing a new drug treatment or in sport, to develop a nutritional supplement. In sport psychology interventions, this type of design is almost impossible. In my work with athletes and teams, I do not have a control individual or team, matched in every possible way to the person I'm working with. Even if I was able to do this, it would be ethically dubious to deny one athlete an intervention I believed to be effective, in order to say with more authority what I already considered to be true.

Thirdly, the evidence I rely on most strongly to answer the question about the effectiveness of my work is that of the clients themselves. Sport psychologists recognize that case studies are towards the least compelling end of the scale of scientific evidence and would certainly not constitute a strong enough case if we were testing a new drug. However, practically, in the absence of stronger evidence, case study material is valuable in both informing practice (i.e. what you should do) and also providing evidence of effectiveness. I accept there is a publication bias: textbooks and journals are more likely to publish case study material which shows that sport psychology interventions have been effective, rather than ineffective. However, there are many more cases, published and unpublished, where performers report benefits rather than problems from working with a sport psychologist.

Fourthly, sport psychology may also 'work' in ways not directly aligned with improving performance. I have worked extensively with performers towards the end of their careers, coming to terms with retirement and the transition out of sport. This can be an extremely challenging time, when performers face a change in patterns of behaviour which have carried them through adolescence into adulthood. Retirement dramatically alters how they view themselves and how they interact with others. Retiring well is not about performance: it is about an adjustment which maintains or enhances psychological well-being. This is another context in which the effectiveness of sport psychology is highly personal – and in research terms, it would be impossible to control or for there to be a placebo.

Ultimately, whether sport psychology 'works' is down to how you frame the outcomes.

A philosophy of practice

I was trained in a humanistic tradition. The central ethos of this approach is that the role of the psychologist is to 'hold the mirror' up to the client's thinking, feeling and behaviour. This is a questioning process which enables clients to gain self-awareness and helps them to understand the choices which lead them to think or feel or behave as they do. The job of the psychologist is to guide individuals to see their options and help them to develop skills which help them grow and develop. In sport psychology, growth and development may be related to gains in performance, but this is not always the case. A central idea in this approach is the quality of the relationship developed between the psychologist and the performer. Paraphrasing Carl Rogers, a founder of the person-centred approach to counselling and psychotherapy, in my early work as a sport psychologist I tortured myself with the question: how can I *change* how this person (my client) thinks, feels or behaves? With greater knowledge and experience I now phrase the question: how can I *provide a relationship* which my client can use for his or her development and personal growth?

Importantly, this is a non-directive approach. The role of the psychologist is to listen actively, summarize and reflect – not to solve the client's' problem. This is how I work with my clients face to face. However it would not be possible to write a book like this if I remained steadfastly attached to this approach. I have used the word 'advice' throughout my answers. The advice is humbly offered.

My clients are often surprised that when they work with me on performance enhancement issues I will not give them a 'prescription' or advice. Many sport performers, even at the elite level, have a surprisingly passive approach to their performance. They are often told what to do by coaches, and other sport scientists, and they passively just do it without really thinking about why they are doing it. Performers may find it strange to be treated rather differently by the sport psychologist. Rather than being *told to do* something or think something, they may be invited to consider options. There is a good reason for this. If the psychologist is directive in approach, the client doesn't own the new strategy. If the client tries and initially fails with a new strategy, s/he will probably blame the psychologist or dismiss sport psychology as ineffective. With a non-directive approach the work with the performer becomes more collaborative, an alliance of growth. Seeking, testing, trying out, with the purpose of gaining understanding of what can work to enhance the individual's performance. This is the bit that's missing from the many self-help books on sport psychology. They are often excellent books but they tend to be highly directive and fail to recreate the essential rapport between psychologist and client.

Myths and misconceptions

Working in applied sport psychology, the practitioner rapidly becomes aware of the many myths and misconceptions that performers, coaches, teachers and parents have about the mental side of performance. I have already addressed some of these. I am going to address more of these and others will be picked up in more detail in specific questions later in the text.

'Miracle cures'

In my first meetings with clients I explicitly address some of the biggest myths. The first myth is that sport psychology offers 'miraculous' and transforming changes in thinking, feeling and behaving. Occasionally, there are simple plans or interventions which yield dramatic benefits, but this is rare. Usually there is a small, incremental straightening out of faulty thinking which impacts positively: this requires hard work on the part of the client. In this way developing mental skills is similar to enhancing physical ones.

One would not expect to improve fitness dramatically in a single gym session. Often changing established but faulty patterns of thinking needs effort and patience. Some performers are looking for a 'mental aspirin' – there are none!

Working with a sport psychologist – you must be mad

Another myth is the misconception that psychology and psychiatry are the same thing. Psychiatrists are medically qualified and study, diagnose and treat mental disorders. Currently the highest-profile sport psychology practitioner in the UK, Professor Steve Peters, *is* a psychiatrist. This is an exception. The majority of sport psychology practitioners have a background in psychology – the study of mind and behaviour. Different countries have different criteria for the training and licensing of psychologists. I strongly encourage those seeking psychological support in sport to look carefully at the professional standards and codes of practice under which the practitioner is operating. This can be confusing as there are a range of other titles used by practitioners, for example, mental skills coach, performance consultant, Neurolinguistic Programming (NLP) practitioner. All of these will have different skills and experience, but may be less accountable to a professional body in terms of professional codes and requirements for developing practice. To confuse the consumer further, there is a range in the quality of the services provided under the banner of 'sport psychology' and a definite *caveat emptor* – buyer beware. I advise those seeking the services of a sport psychologist to speak to other clients, where this is possible, to find out if the practitioner and his or her experience and approach are a good match – this is another issue I develop further later in the text.

This is confidential – right?

Confidentiality is a guiding principle

A concern that many clients have regards what is done with material discussed in meetings and consultations. In the UK, practitioners registered with the Health and Care Professionals Council or accredited by the British Association for Sport and Exercise

Sciences (BASES) are required to practise under a professional code of conduct. The code is clear about material discussed in meetings: it is confidential. It can only be disclosed to a third party with the explicit consent of the client. The only circumstance where this can be overridden is if there is a concern on the part of the psychologist that the client has disclosed information which makes him or her a danger to him- or herself or others. Psychologists disclosing under any other circumstances are in breach of their professional code of conduct. I become concerned when psychologists appear in the media discussing the work they are doing or have done with clients – unless consent has been sought and given, it is a breach of the profession code. When it does happen it often reveals more about the motives of the practitioner than the client.

Sometimes coaches will ask questions about what has been discussed in meetings with specific players. Ethically again, this is clear cut, unless explicit consent for partial confidentiality has been given. Including the coach in meetings would change the nature of the relationship between the psychologist and the client, probably not for the better, and would make the practitioner's work with the client less effective.

An important corner to the issue of confidentiality is the work of the psychologist with young performers. My preference is for parents or guardians to be in meetings with young performers. As I will pick up later, sometimes it becomes necessary to have a meeting with a young performer without parents being present. This requires special management but privacy and confidentiality remain paramount concerns.

A psychologist who hasn't experienced sport at the highest level cannot fully grasp what it's like, therefore can't help

Many performers and some coaches believe that only people who have been through what they have been through can fully understand what it's like, and therefore offer advice. This is common but flawed logic. We don't demand that clinical psychologists have experienced depression or anxiety or that orthopaedic surgeons have to have experienced knee reconstruction. A key basic requirement for effective sport psychology work is empathy – the skill of developing an understanding of the experiences of others. Walking with them through their challenges. Empathy is a highly complex process and one which I work to develop in those I train. Without it, sport psychology is sterile and ineffective.

My team doesn't need a sport psych – they can all talk to me

The final myth I'd like to address at this stage is the question of whether sport psychology specialists are a necessary element of a support team. As sports coaching becomes more professionalized, coaches are becoming exposed to postgraduate-level sport science. They have an excellent knowledge of psychology, but can they deliver sport psychology interventions? Without doubt some of the most effective psychologists I have worked with are not formally trained. They are coaches, parents and teachers who appear to interact intuitively with their performers, pupils and children in highly skilled ways to develop effective mental skills. However, there is an important issue here around 'wearing too many hats' – the coach as psychologist is particularly problematic as there is a clear clash of interests. The coach is required to be objective and dispassionate, whilst the psychologist builds a rapport based on a warm, empathetic and non-judgemental relationship. Many performers prefer psychological support outside the immediate team environment. It provides a safe sounding board and a place to offload, without fear that material will ever come back metaphorically to bite them.

My invitation

In a sporting world where access to psychological support remains sparse, the onus often falls on the coach, teacher, parent or individual performer to develop mental skills without expert direction. The sport psychology practitioner community has become skilled at peer-to-peer professional dialogue; we are good at talking to our academic colleagues. I believe that to remain relevant it needs to be much more proactive in reaching out and sharing its knowledge and expertise. Sport psychologists need to listen to the everyday questions that people in sport have, accept the complexity of the real world and provide answers. It is in this spirit that I offer the book.

Bibliography

Halliwell, W., Orlick, T., Ravizza, K., & Rotella, B. (2003) *Consultant's Guide to Excellence for Sport and Performance Enhancement.* Zone of Excellence.

Hemmings, B., & Holder, T. (2009) *Applied Sport Psychology: A Case-based Approach.* Wiley.

Rogers, C. (1995) *On Becoming a Person: A Therapist's View of Psychotherapy.* Mariner Books.

II

Do I need sport psychology?

The simple questions are the hardest to answer.

Introduction

> You used to be considered odd and slightly suspect if you
> went to see the sports shrink, now you are odd and slightly
> suspect if you don't.
>
> (Bradley Wiggins – Tour de France winner
> and five-times Olympic gold medal winner)

Most sport psychologists are used to being described in unflattering terms – 'psycho', 'head shrink' or 'boffin' are among the nicest! The point is that now most sport performers recognize the role of psychology and are comfortable with the idea of 'mind coaching' – whether it is by a psychologist, psychiatrist, mental skills coach or other type of practitioner.

It is appropriate that this chapter begins with a quote from one of the most successful British cyclists of all time. The history of British cycling can be used as a barometer of change in the culture of sport, particularly high-performance sport, not only in the UK but across the world.

In the early 1990s Peter Keen, a cycling coach with an academic background in sport science, was appointed as British Cycling's performance director. He transformed the process of preparation for elite riders, establishing a culture of benchmarking performance on hard data. His approach achieved unprecedented success. However, the rest of the world rapidly caught on . . . and caught up.

Prior to Keen's innovation sport in the UK tended to have an ethos of 'If it ain't broke, don't fix it'. Some sports remain in this mindset. The next phase in the development of British cycling turned this conservatism on its head, and as a result transformed the process of training and performance preparation of many sports in the UK and across the world. Two influential coaches working in different sports, Sir Clive Woodward in rugby union and Sir Dave Brailsford in cycling began to examine every aspect of preparation with a view to finding the areas of marginal gain. They rightly reasoned that no single factor would take a performer ahead of the competition and to the top of the podium. Instead they looked for the tiny marginal areas which enhanced performance by 0.1%. If ten increments could be found, their accumulated sum gives a clear performance advantage.

Both Woodward and Brailsford were convinced of the value of sport psychology: Woodward employed a mind coach, Yahuda Shinar. Brailsford appointed Professor Steve Peters, a psychiatrist for two Olympics cycles, and continued on to form the Team Sky road team, which led to the first British rider to win the Tour de France in 2012. It is worth noting that, whilst Shinar and Peters are not sport psychologists, Shinar is a life coach and Peters a psychiatrist. The techniques they use draw heavily from areas of applied psychology, in particular sport psychology.

Despite Woodward and Brailsford being convinced of the benefits of working on mental skills, many of their performers were rightly sceptical. They wanted proof that working on their mental game would result in clearcut improvements in performance. Providing this kind of proof can be challenging: it's not the same as being able to run faster, lift a heavier weight or reduce the number of putts taken per round. Gains in mental skills are often subjective and tied up with other performance indicators. However, the type of attitude change summarized by Sir Bradley Wiggins was enough to demonstrate the value of psychology. Many teams and governing bodies of sport began to offer psychology in some form as a normal part of the comprehensive training and support systems for players.

As the profile of sport psychology has grown, many coaches and performers have come to view it as the 'final frontier' of sport performance, but still may find it difficult to get a clear sense of what psychology offers. The mental side of sport becomes clearer when we examine some of the psychological challenges faced by performers:

- ◆ High standards of excellence – motivation to excel:
  - ✓ mental skills around motivation and striving for excellence over a long period

  ✓ skilling the performer to balance thoughts and emotions to strive for an achievable optimal rather than unobtainable perfect level of performance

◆ Competition – wanting to win:

  ✓ competition between performers – the drive to beat other competitors is a defining feature of sport

  ✓ competition may be against others or one's own personal standards

◆ The part played by emotions – optimizing the mental 'temperature':

  ✓ understanding the impact emotions have on performance and developing skills to regulate and optimize them

◆ Being in the moment – keeping your eye on the ball:

  ✓ sport demands optimal attention – doing the right thing at the right moment under pressure of time, fatigue, opponents and other environmental factors

◆ Performing with an evaluative audience:

  ✓ audiences tend to increase physiological arousal – engaging the 'fight, flight, fright, flee' response. Skilling performers to cope

◆ Thriving under pressure:

  ✓ pressure is created by internal factors such as personal goals and expectations or externally by the expectations of others. These are compounded by the variable performance of others, such as opponents or officials. Performers require mental skills to thrive in these conditions

◆ Managing the consequences:

  ✓ the ability to manage emotions and learn from the outcomes of performance.

◆ Career management:

  ✓ sport involves transitions from junior to senior age groups, possibly also from senior to elite, into retirement and these may present profound psychological challenges

  ✓ managing periods of injury and rehabilitation.

The mind and body fallacy – if you are fit enough, you must be mentally ready

Because most sport performers, coaches and parents tend to focus primarily on the physical and technical aspects of a sport, there is often an assumption that if individuals are technically good and physically fit they must also be mentally ready to perform. This is often not the case. I frequently encounter performers who cannot understand why they are inconsistent in performance or that they perform really well in events which don't really matter but underperform in the big, important matches. These are usually signs that their mental skills are relatively undeveloped. Often in sport we encounter scenarios where we have beaten a stronger opponent because we were more committed, or lost a game because our opponents maintained their composure better than we did. These are the times when we begin to get a sense that the mental side of sport is valuable.

I have worked with performers who have gone through their whole career with a feeling that there was something missing in terms of their preparation. They reflect on what they have done in their careers and are left with uneasy questions: 'why did I do that?' or 'why didn't I take that opportunity?' These performers are often diligent trainers – they prepare well physically, technically and tactically – but they have a nagging doubt that they have not fully fulfilled their potential. It is often because the mental side has been neglected.

Equally I have met and worked with performers who have limited physical ability: they are told they are not big enough, or they are not fast enough, or they are told they lack the skills to perform at the top level. Yet, despite these apparent flaws they achieve at the highest level. These performers often bring a mental game, which is either innate or has been learned, which enables them to outperform their seemingly more gifted peers.

Sport psychology is a major part of the performance equation. Developing mental skills to support other areas of development offers an opportunity to prepare comprehensively, to leave less to chance and to address those questions in anticipation of what is to come.

In this chapter I am addressing some big questions. These are all questions which have come from parents, teachers, coaches and performers, and they set the scene for what is to come later in the text.

Q1

Will sport psychology help me win?

No ... and yes!

Why no?

I'm afraid that if you are looking for a secret formula to ensure that you defeat Geoff from Accounts every time you meet on the golf course, sport psychology will disappoint you. There is no secret formula. The problem relates back to one of the central principles of applied sport psychology – control the controllables.

Sport performance is highly variable; ultimately whether you win or lose is critically dependent on a range of factors outside your immediate control. The most important is the performance of your opponent; if you regularly lose to Geoff, but on one great day, he is slightly off his game and on the same day you play well – you win! On another day he might be slightly off his game but you fail to raise yours – he wins! This is why sport is exciting – the unpredictable can and often does happen.

The complex match of performance levels on a given day often makes it difficult to assess how and why outcomes have happened. You may play better than you have ever played before, but on that day, an opponent is fractionally faster or more skilful than you. Again you lose, but you are also left not knowing whether to be pleased or upset. This is why most elite performers combine aiming for specific outcomes (a tournament win or place) with an even greater emphasis on processes which make winning more likely.

Why yes?

Sport psychology can play a crucial role in developing the processes which make winning more likely. Note the subtle difference: it's not a guarantee. It's about making those days when you are able to raise your game more frequent. The processes are aimed at ensuring that your preparation for performance is comprehensive and that you have a clear plan to ensure that you are as *ready* as possible to play Geoff. For example, it may require you to do additional practice, which you dislike doing and avoid whenever possible. It might require analysing your game more: where do you tend to drop shots? From this you can develop a plan which puts him under pressure; all of this is under your control. *But* bear in mind: Geoff doesn't want to be beaten, and your development as a player may nudge him to develop his own game in order to maintain his edge over you.

This feels like sport psychology is *not* working, but it is; you have developed, but ultimately the outcome is determined by uncontrollables.

Going deeper into the theory

Performers and coaches are often sensitive to the process-vs.-outcome paradox in sport. Good performances are frequently not rewarded by a winning outcome. Equally, poor performances can result in a victory. Practitioners need to be keenly tuned into the fact that, particularly in elite sport, they are in a results business. If teams are not consistently winning there is a strong likelihood of unwanted consequences – coaches fired, players replaced and a generally negative atmosphere. Despite this, the psychologist is required to act as a role model for keeping winning into perspective; processes really are more important than outcomes.

Winning occurs when preparation has been comprehensive and opportunities are exploited. Winning can look pretty, but this is not an essential requirement. A scruffy win is a win and can actually have a more powerful impact on an individual or team. When teams show that they can win games they shouldn't, they make attributions about their ability to demonstrate a resilient 'win ugly' mentality. Players are encouraged that optimistic, gritty thinking keeps them working hard and committed to the struggle. This is a motivational issue which I develop in more detail in a series of questions in Chapter III.

Bibliography

Burton, D., Naylor, S., & Holliday, B. (2001) Goal setting in sport: investigating the goal effectiveness paradox. In R. Singer, H.A. Hausenblas, & C.M. Janelle (Eds.), *Handbook of Research on Sport Psychology*, 2nd edn. Wiley.
Gilbert, B., & Jamieson, S. (2007) *Winning Ugly*. Simon and Schuster.

Q2

What percentage of sport performance is mental?

An impossible question! Nike has to lot to answer for! Many people in sport have responded to the instruction to 'Just do it', and presume that the only important aspect of sport is getting physically fit enough to do what the activity challenges them to do.

People don't stop thinking, feeling or behaving when they lace up their shoes, and often what they think, feel and do will have an impact on their performance in, and enjoyment of, sport.

If you were to walk into a locker room ahead of a game at any level of sport, from beginner to elite, you would find a whole spectrum of personalities and emotional responses to the upcoming game. At one end is the performer who is struggling to 'get herself up' for the game: there are no nerves, but that isn't good. At the other end, there is the player who is routinely physically sick with nerves ahead of the game. This may be equally damaging. Somewhere between these extremes is the player who is at the ideal 'emotional temperature': she is excited and her thoughts are on task – she cannot wait for the game to begin.

It is this diversity which makes the question impossible to answer. All players in the locker room have a unique behavioural response to their thoughts and emotions prior to and during their sport.

What I can assert with confidence is that the higher up the performance ladder you get, the more important the psychological component becomes. At the elite, Olympic level, everyone will be physically, technically and tactically extremely well prepared. The outcome will come down to the tiniest of margins and the ability to operate at or close to your physical, technical and tactical potential as possible. This will probably be down to mental factors rather than any other aspect.

One final point: I frequently ask performers, irrespective of performance level, 'How much impact do you believe your mental game has on the outcome of your performance'? The majority will report that over 50% of the outcome is determined by mental factors. Even if you believe it to be less than this figure, 5% is a big percentage, one that could make the difference between winning and losing. My follow-up is 'Which mental skills do you believe to be important – which ones will give the biggest 'bang for buck'?

This is where the work of the sport psychologist begins.

Going deeper into the theory

Frequently performers, coaches and particularly journalists are keen to ascribe values to different components of sport performance. Modern sport science has established that dividing sports by how 'mental' they are is unhelpful. The interesting and useful applications of sport science occur at the interfaces between the physical, technical, tactical and mental. For example, performers and coaches may perceive fatigue to be a purely physical phenomenon. However they would also report that their perception of fatigue can depend on mental events: for example, fatigue in an athletic event such as cycling is different when you are winning as opposed to when you are struggling, despite the fact that physiologically the two states are identical. The work of Noakes et al. (2005) work on the central governor model of fatigue aimed to acknowledge and integrate the mental dimensions of fatigue. This is a controversial approach which has generated a great deal of positive debate and research. This type of multidisciplinary challenge is positive and highlights the importance of collaborative research and theory development.

There are many other examples of the interface between the physical, technical tactical and mental. Anxious performers often move in less efficient and effective ways, undermining their ability to execute movements skilfully. Decision making is frequently affected by stress and fatigue.

What this highlights is that effective preparation for performance should transfer on to actual performance in as complete a way as possible. Skills should be practised at full intensity and under the types of stress you will encounter. If you don't do this, you will always be unsure what will actually happen in competition.

Bibliography

Noakes, T.D., St Clair Gibson, A., & Lambert, E.V. (2005). From catastrophe to complexity: a novel model of integrative central neural regulation of effort and fatigue during exercise in humans: summary and conclusions. *British Journal of Sports Medicine 39* (2): 120–124.

Q3

From a psychological perspective, what are the hardest sports to excel in?

My short answer to this question is simply, no sport is harder than any other. There is trained and there is untrained – if you are untrained, you are unprepared, therefore you will find the sport hard.

Success is the science of perfect preparation!

The question is more about how to ensure that physical, technical, tactical and mental training is comprehensive and aimed at preparing performers for *every* possible challenge they will confront. If all the 'boxes are ticked', performance is easier than training! This is why we train, comprehensively and exhaustively.

The longer answer is that sporting life isn't as simple as that. We need to know a little more about the challenges posed by different types of sporting activities before we can really get to grips with this question.

There are lots of ways of dividing sports up into different 'families' on the basis of the physical, technical and tactical demands they place on performers. The most basic distinction is between gymnastic sports, athletic sports and games. Each category can be divided further, but it is a useful framework.

◆ Gymnastic sports, e.g. diving, gymnastics, dance: performance determined by how well you learn and replicate a pattern of movements.

◆ Athletic sports, e.g. track and field, swimming, rowing, triathlon: performance determined by short- or long-term power production.

◆ Game-type sports, e.g. soccer, hockey, tennis: scoring more points than opponents through retention and skilful exploitation of possession.

The key point from this type of analysis is that different sports challenge performers in a range of different ways – physically, technically and tactically. But mentally the challenges are similar.

The approach many sport psychologists adopts is to look at the five C factors – concentration, commitment, confidence, control and communication. In assessing the psychological demands each of these is challenged in a different and unique way according to the sport, the performance context and the performer.

TABLE 2.1 The five C factors

	Demands in training / preparation	Demands in competition
Commitment	For example, marathon runner needs to run over 100 mpw	Sub-3-hour marathon: sub-7-minute miling for up to 3 hours
Concentration	For example, quarterback having to learn and execute plays	Effective decision making under pressure in a 'limelight' role
Confidence	For example, cricketer maintaining confidence in preparation during a period of poor form	Maintaining belief in skills when opposition are dominating for a long period
Control	For example, a climber maintaining emotional control under conditions of boredom doing repetitive training	The same climber may have to control anxiety and negative emotion in competition
Communication	For example, positively interacting with coaches, team mates and more broadly with officials and the media	In competition, the performers have to interact minute by minute with the officials, the opponents, their own team mates and the audience, whilst managing their own physical and psychological effort

Going deeper into the theory

Having established a framework for understanding the type of sporting challenge, we need to think about the level of psychological challenge inherent in each. A useful framework is to think about the mental challenges of sporting in terms of the five C factors. (Table 2.1).

I am inclined to add a sixth C factor in *coping* – a topic I will develop more fully later in the text.

Hopefully, what this conveys to you is that every sporting event places profound psychological challenges on the performer, in a variety of different ways. Making a definitive judgement about which sport is the 'hardest' is impossible. The key take-home message is that what makes sport 'hard' is when a challenge of an event or opponent is not met, or a demand exceeds the preparation capacity of the performer.

There are no 'easy' sports, I'm afraid.

Bibliography

Harwood, C.G. (2008). Developmental consulting in a professional youth soccer academy: the 5Cs coaching efficacy program. *The Sport Psychologist 22*: 109–133.

Q4

Do I need to work with a sport psychologist?

I accept that I'm biased but I believe that every performer, at every level of performance, could benefit from working with a sport or performance psychologist!

The aim of applied sport psychology is to help performers gain mental skills which enable them to perform consistently at or as close to their physical, technical and tactical potential as possible. Given this knowledge, why would someone *not* want at least to find out what a sport psychologist could offer?

There are three main formats that work might take:

1. An educational approach, where the work will aim to raise awareness in coaches, parents and performers about what sport psychology is and how it can be applied. This often takes place in a one-off or short-course format in a group workshop setting.
2. Working with a sport psychologist as the performance consultant. This is focused on individual or small-group work, where there is a period of assessment of the main psychological needs and then ongoing work to develop a training package aimed at developing mental skills.
3. Short-term, critical intervention format. Players and coaches sometimes have a significant or unexpected event for which they feel unprepared or overwhelmed by, and may seek support from a psychologist.

The role of the psychologist may differ depending on the level the client is at. At grassroots level the role may be more educational, raising awareness of the key mental skills to work on to support other areas of performance development. At the elite level the psychologist and performer will work on more specific aspects of performance, perhaps areas which have been identified in performance or in collaboration with other support staff, such as the coach, physiologist or performance analyst.

Work with a psychologist ranges from a brief meeting to reflect and review on an event or a season's performance all the way through to indepth and detailed work aimed at systematically developing a narrow and specific aspect of performance. Some sessions can be timetabled into relatively formal meetings in an office, but often sport psychologists do effective work in 'teachable moments' actually out on the practice field, or even in the corridor or lunch queue. In these moments an opportunity can be seized to make an observation or offer a suggestion at a time when it can make the biggest impact.

There are many self-help sport psychology books and online resources now, many of which give the impression that sport psychology is a toolbox of mental skills, such as goal setting, self-talk, managing nervousness and imagery. These are important skills and a performer may work on them alone or with help, however the thing that really makes a difference is the rapport developed between the psychologist and the client. This creates a supportive environment which fosters the growth and development of the performer.

Going deeper into the theory

Work with a sport psychologist takes many forms. Broadly there are two main aims of the work – performance enhancement and maintaining or developing psychological well-being. Mark Andersen presented an interesting response to a debate that occurred between Andy Lane and Stephen Mellalieu around the validity of the claims that sport psychology has a performance-enhancing role in elite sport. This is worth following up (Andersen, 2009).

An important question clients ask is whether sport psychology is effective in improving performance and psychological well-being. I have looked at this in the opening chapter. My experience is that many sceptical performers have inaccurate ideas about what working with a psychologist entails and how it can fit into their overall preparation to perform. Case studies such as those presented by Hemmings and Holder (2009) tend to support this.

There are many models of delivery used in applied sport psychology. The service delivery heuristic presented by Poczwardowski et al. (1998) and refined by Poczwardowski and Sherman (2011) identifies key elements of the process and is a valuable starting point for discussion. Within these models I would highlight four key stages: initial contact, professional philosophy, the consultant–client relationship and the management of the self, on the part of the client.

Initial contact refers to the process by which the client becomes aware of sport psychology and is either referred to or makes contact with the psychologist. Initial contact is a first impression in both directions and sets the tone for future work. I advise students and supervisees to treat these early minutes with care and heighten their observation and listening skills. Often key information is given and received in these moments. The client's motives for coming to see the sport psychologist should be explored. An important early question is, 'what are you aiming to gain from speaking to a sport psychologist?' This can be further developed into, 'What would you view as a successful outcome from working with me?' With skill and experience, the psychologist can build rapport with the client and begin to formulate an assessment of the client's needs in the early stages of work.

Applied sport psychology is a human-to-human interaction. Sport psychologists must recognize that to be effective in their relationship with the client they must become the agent of change in thinking, feeling and behaviour. Behind this interaction should be a well-understood and organized professional philosophy informing what they say and how they behave with their client. This philosophy is partly driven by professional ethics and partly by the choice of approach adopted by the psychologist. The majority of sport psychology interventions have been developed in other 'helping' contexts, such as clinical, counselling, educational or occupational psychology. Many of the techniques are based on a cognitive-behavioural model. However, there is a danger in this type of approach. Often I see inexperienced or untrained practitioners adopt a mental skills intervention, such as goal setting, in a formulaic way, as if they were lifting a tool from a toolbox. They use it clumsily and don't understand why it isn't effective. It is often the case that *what* is done with a client is less important than *how* it is done. This reinforces the importance of developing a warm, empathetic and non-judgemental relationship.

Sport psychologists are human – they can experience a range of emotions in their work; we enjoy working with clients who respond to our work and become frustrated when our work fails to help our clients. Applied practitioners rarely have the benefit of an identical twin acting as a control to determine whether their work has been effective. There is an obligation on the part of the psychologist to engage in this highly personal reflection in order to ensure that they are developing the experiential hinterland that improves them as practitioners. In other areas of applied psychology, this process, called supervision, is formally embedded in practice. In sport psychology it is often informal but this does not make it any less vital.

Bibliography

Andersen, M. (2009). Performance enhancement as a bad start and a dead end: a parenthetical comment on Mellalieu and Lane. *The Sport and Exercise Scientist 20*: 12–16. Retrieved on 26 April from: http://www.bases.org.uk/pdf/The%20SES%20%2820%29%20web-part1.pdf.

Hemmings, B., & Holder, T. (2009). *Applied Sport Psychology: A Case Based Approach:* John Wiley.

Poczwardowski, A., & Sherman, C. (2011). Revisions to the sport psychology service delivery (SPSD) heuristic: explorations with experienced consultants. *The Sport Psychologist 25* (4): 511–531.

Poczwardowski, A., Sherman, C., & Henschen, K. (1998). A sport psychology service delivery heuristic: building on theory and practice. *The Sport Psychologist 12* (2): 191–207.

Q5

A couple of the players have suggested we should appoint a psychologist. Do you think it is a good idea? What should I be looking for in terms of qualifications and experience? And how will I know if the psychologist is being effective?

I think every team should have sport psychology support in some format. The decision for you is to decide what form the support should take and how much time and money you are able to invest.

Firstly let's get the issue of qualifications and experience out of the way. The title 'sport and exercise psychologist' is legally protected. The British Psychological Society (BPS) maintains a registers of chartered psychologists with expertise in sport and this can be your first port of call: http://www.bps.org.uk/bpslegacy/dcp.

However, life is more complicated than that! You can also find practitioners with a great deal of knowledge and expertise in sport psychology interventions who are not chartered by the

BPS. Officially these are not psychologists and should not advertise themselves as such. They might be practitioners in other areas, such as Neurolinguistic Programming (NLP) or counselling or may be accredited by the British Association for Sport and Exercise Science (BASES) as sport scientists. There is a register of these practitioners on the BASES website (http://www.bases.org.uk/Consultants).

It is worth noting that many high-profile teams don't have formal sport psychology support on a day-to-day basis. They have staff 'mental skills' coaches working with the team and then bring in specialist psychology support as and when it is needed.

My suggestion is that you informally meet several possible candidates. Outline what your needs are and open a dialogue. Find out what they think they could offer and get an idea of how they would develop the players and coaches. At this stage I would ask the possible candidates to give you a CV and contact details of a client who has agreed to act as a referee. Find out some practical information, about fees and whether, if you feel this is necessary, they are available to travel with the team. Coaches often feel that it is important for the psychologist to have first-hand experience of the sport. In my view this is *not* necessary, and in fact may become a distraction, as they may offer technical or tactical advice which can confuse the coaching message. It is more important for the psychologist to be a good listener and willing to find out about the sport and its culture.

In terms of the CV, there are a few essentials. Firstly, whether you are interested in having the psychologist working with juniors or not, candidates should have a Protecting Vulnerable Groups (PVG)/disclosure statement. They should also have public liability insurance. After that my advice is that you look more closely at the applied experience than the academic qualifications. You are aiming to appoint someone who will make a difference to the team, not someone who will be aiming to conduct research.

Don't appoint a sport psychologist as window dressing. My advice is to spend time with the psychologist to develop a programme of work for him or her. Too often coaches appoint psychological support and then let the psychologist get on with it. Clarify what you want the appointee to do and make sure that you give the individual time to do it. You may want to run group sessions on mental skills. If you do, schedule them in advance, give the psychologist time to prepare and resist the temptation to cancel at the last minute to do some additional skills training. This sends a clear message to the players that mental skills are not important. Bear in mind that group sessions are efficient ways of raising awareness of topics, but the real benefits come with one-to-one work and small groups. Programme these.

Don't expect sport psychology support to be free of charge. If resources are tight, some coaches offer access for research purposes in exchange for fees being waived. Ethically this can be problematic. Coaches cannot consent on their behalf for athletes to participate in research: athletes are required to consent themselves. There are often issues of confidentiality as well. I prefer the two roles to remain separate – either you are an applied practitioner or you are a researcher. Both parties have clarity and awkward ethical issues are avoided.

Going deeper into the theory

There are two sides to this question. On the one hand, the client is seeking a practitioner who is qualified and competent to deliver the service required. On the other side, there is a practitioner who is aiming to deliver the service. On issues of qualification and training I have already touched on the types of academic and training profiles you would expect in someone providing performance enhancement support services. On the broader issues of practical and ethical aspects of service, Hays (2012) has condensed some of the key aspects into three areas: training, role and ethics. Ongoing professional development of practitioners, both formal and informal, is important. Practitioners should act as role models to their clients in their desire for constant improvement.

The role of a sport psychologist is defined by both what is done and how it is done. Developing as an effective practitioner requires reflection on both aspects. The process of professional reflection is critical in this.

Ethically practice is driven by the professional code established by governing or regulating bodies. Reflection on ethical aspects of practice and developing a positive approach to ethical aspects of day-to-day work are part of being a developing and reflective practitioner.

There are many challenges in this. A prominent one is how to present and publicise yourself as a sport psychology consultant. Is it ethically legitimate to ask for endorsements from clients, as I have suggested? Is it legitimate to wear kit from a high-profile client in consultations with other client? Personally I think this is ethically problematic.

Bibliography

Hays, K.F. (2012). The psychology of performance in sport and other domains. In Murphy, S. (Ed.), *The Oxford Handbook of Sport and Performance Psychology* (Chapter 2, pp. 25–45). Oxford University Press.

Q6

Is there a sport personality or type of person who is more likely to succeed in sport?

(Asked by a national martial arts coach who also works in person-nel management and has an interest in psychometric testing.)

In the UK, every December there is a TV show hosted by the BBC. It reviews the sporting year and at the end of the show awards are given to the performers in various categories – team of the year, coach of the year, amongst others. The main award is called Sports Personality of the Year, which is unfortunate, because it gives viewers a false and misleading view of what the word 'personality' means in the context of performance psychology.

To the psychologist, personality is defined as the characteristics which make an individual unique. These should be stable over time and consistent over different situations. The question you are asking is whether there are any stable and enduring characteristics which can be accurately 'captured' and can reliably predict success in sport.

There *are*, but there are also challenges in applying this know-ledge in sport. I'll run through the characteristics and then put them into the context of your question.

There is evidence to suggest that successful performers at every level of performance are conscientious, which means they are organized, systematic and driven to achieve goals. They also display optimism, hope and a positive form of perfectionism. This type of perfectionism is based on the ability to keep performance in perspective and view every performance as an opportunity to learn. There appears also to be a less positive aspect of personality associated with high-level performance: evidence at the non-elite level suggests that narcissism, a strong but unrealistic level of belief in one's own ability, appears to help promote high levels of performance under pressure. It should be noted that this evidence is not conclusive.

Moving to the context of your question: psychometrics is a branch of psychology which aims to measure accurately psychological skills and abilities. Psychometric tests are generally online or 'pencil-and-paper' questionnaires which have been developed to profile the qualities and attributes which are thought to be important for a particular role, job or career. With your background in personnel management you will have been trained not to base any decision or appointment on a psychometric test alone. The recommended approach is to use triangulation, making sure that you use other sources of information as well. My concern is, what will you do with the results of your testing? Given the lack of conclusive data, what type of personality would you consider to be the best fit in your team? Would you really give those identified as having the 'right' psychometric profile more attention than others on your team? I accept I'm biased against psychometric testing. In my view it poses more questions than it answers.

Going deeper into the theory

This is a controversial topic!

Personality has been an important research area in psychology for decades. There are many lines of theory which have aimed to describe and explain how the stable and enduring characteristics of individuals form habitual patterns of feeling, thinking and behaving. In the space available it would not be possible or wise to try and present an overview. Currently the literature is dominated by the Big 5 model proposed by McCrae and Costa (1987).

This approach identifies 30 lower-order characteristics which can be drawn together into five higher-order factors: extraversion, neuroticism, conscientiousness, openness to experience and agreeableness. There is some developing evidence of a link, albeit a weak link, between aspects of the model and sport performance.

Personality theorists aim to identify the ways in which people are similar, based on stable and enduring characteristics. This 'type' approach to personality is based on the idea, not accepted by all researchers, that people have a stable psychological core – their true character. The opposite view has been proposed, that people behave in ways which are shaped by the environment they are in.

A comprehensive model of this approach to personality was proposed by Hollander in 1971. This integrates the 'type' and the situational approach together and explains how the two may interact. This is a useful approach in the context of sport, where people may have to take on different roles, some compatible and some incompatible with their psychological core.

Psychometric testing has not been extensively applied in sport. There are some sport psychologists who strongly advocate the use of questionnaires as an assessment tool in applied work, however the majority of the development has been in the sphere of research. Some of the earliest empirical work in applied sport psychology was based around some flawed notions of using psychometric tools to 'predict' sport performance. The work of Morgan (1980) is an example of this. Using a questionnaire which was developed from a clinical assessment tool for the diagnosis of depression, Morgan claimed a strong link between aspects of mood and actual sport performance. However, subsequent work identified so many caveats and qualifications to this prediction that it became no more than a weak observation that in some people, in some sports, the absence of negative mood helped them perform well.

People who use these tests extensively believe that that are valuable in ensuring that people are effectively matched for the role they are being appointed to. It is exactly this reason that makes them difficult to use in sport. If you are aiming to recruit a new player for your squad, could you write down the main psychological characteristics you are looking for? You want someone who is committed, confident, resilient and able to fulfil a range of roles. Currently there is no test which could identify this blend of characteristics.

Most sport psychologists would place two other assessment techniques above psychometric testing as a way to gauge the psychology of the players and teams they are working with. Firstly, careful and systematic observation opens the way for detailed conversations about specific performance-related behaviours. Secondly, skilful interviewing of players develops an understanding of the thought process behind behaviour and their emotional reactions.

Personally, I am not a great fan of 'pencil-and-paper' tests. I have objections on the grounds of poor validity, particularly predictive validity – my own notes and observations have proved to be stronger. Also, it is often difficult to create conditions where tests can be completed to give an authentic picture. Tests administered in a locker room or team bus are of little use. Players collaborate or 'flick and tick' to get through the test quickly. But ultimately, such tests tell me nothing that I didn't know already from talking with and watching the players I'm working with.

Bibliography

Hollander, E. (1971). *Principles and Methods in Social Psychology*. Oxford University Press.

McCrae, R., & Costa, P. Jr. (1987). Validation of the five-factor model of personality across instruments and observers. *Journal of Personality and Social Psychology 52*: 81–90.

Morgan, W.P.(1980). Test of champions. *Psychology Today* July: 92–108.

Q7

If personality doesn't predict success, what does?

Follow-up question.

In 2009 UK Sport commissioned a piece of research to answer exactly that question. This project has just reported and I would strongly advise you to have a look at it (Rees et al., 2016). There are some surprises! It presents evidence that genetics, the practice environment and physical factors are linked, albeit in a complex fashion, to the achievement of elite or superelite status in sport. The indication was also that there were key mental skills and attributes which characterized performers at the higher levels of performance.

Mental skills are not the same as personality characteristics. By mental skills I mean patterns of thinking, feeling and behaving that can be learned and developed. They are not 'wired-in' parts of a person's character.

Motivation is a key predictor of success. I am going to develop this further in the next chapter; at this point I'll just highlight that motivation in sport has two basic forms: task orientation, which is motivation to improve, and ego orientation, which is motivation to demonstrate dominance by winning in competition. High-achieving performers typically report high levels of both.

In addition to the motivational orientation of performers, the more successful tend to have higher levels of self-belief, control, mental toughness and resilience. They also display better coping skills under pressure and greater resistance to 'choking' – indicating that the high-performers have the skills to thrive under pressure rather than see their performance levels drop. Finally, successful performers present with a well-developed range of performance-related skills: goal setting, managing nervousness, use of mental imagery, self-talk and effective decision making.

The clear message from the research is not that mental skills are an optional extra; more certain is that you probably won't achieve your physical, technical or tactical potential without them.

Going deeper into the theory

A key publication in the historical development of sport psychology was a paper by Orlick and Partington in 1988. This study collected evidence from Olympic-level participants on the mental links to excellence; they found that the more successful performers demonstrated the following characteristics:

♦ commitment
♦ coping with pressure

- focus and distraction control
- goal setting
- imagery
- planning and organizational skills
- quality practice
- realistic performance evaluations
- self-awareness.

Andersen (2009) condenses the list to five main psychological skills – relaxation, self-talk, imagery, goal setting and concentration – and describes these as the psychological skills training canon. In applied work this type of approach can be challenging as practitioners can miss key contextual information through trying to fit what their client is telling them into this framework.

The Great British gold-medal project published in 2016 has highlighted the following mental skills as being associated with high-level performance: motivation, confidence, perceived control, mental toughness, resilience, coping with adversity, resistance to 'choking' and well-developed mental skills. This study reported these findings to be consistent, but based on research of moderate quality (Rees et al., 2016). To strengthen this evidence further much more specific questions about specifically what types of motivation are causally linked with gold-medal performance are needed. Interestingly, findings around personality factors such as conscientiousness, hope, optimism and perfectionism were inconsistent.

Bibliography

Andersen, M.B. (2009). The 'canon' of psychological skills training for enhancing performance. In K.F. Hays (Ed.), *Performance Psychology in Action* (pp. 11–34). American Psychological Association.

Orlick, T., & Partington, C. (1988) Mental links to excellence. *The Sport Psychologist 2* (2): 105–130.

Rees, T., Hardy, L., Güllich, A., Abernethy, B., Côté, J., Woodman, T., Montgomery, H., Laing, S., & Warr, C. (2016). The Great British medalists project: a review of current knowledge on the development of the world's best sporting talent. *Sports Medicine 46* (8): 1041–1058.

Q8

I've heard a lot of performers talk about 'getting into the zone' – what does this mean and should I be working towards it?

Anyone who has played sport will have days when everything seems to go perfectly. Kimberly Kim, who at the age of 14 became the youngest ever US Women's Amateur Golf champion, captures it clearly and simply: 'I don't know how I did it, I just hit the ball and it went good'.

This is the 'zone' – a psychological state where conscious control of movements is reduced and normal perceptions of effort and time are suspended. It feels like everything you try works and, better still, it just feels effortless. When people talk of getting into the 'zone' they are striving for this state, although there is a paradox here – the harder you strive to get into the zone, the more difficult it is to achieve.

The zone is linked with both high levels of performance and also a deep sense of satisfaction about performance. This is why most sport performers try to repeat all the things they did to get into this special state. They can become quite superstitious about it.

Coaches often tell players to 'get their heads in the game' and tell them off for 'not wanting it enough'. Paradoxically, this can be the worst advice if you are aiming to get into the zone, particularly in sports where complex skills or a high level of thinking are required. Conscious effort and trying hard encourage us to think about what we are doing and *try* to do it harder. In fact, to regain the zone state we need to think less about what we are doing – to allow the unconscious 'autopilot' to execute well-learned skills and to minimize the conscious thought impacting on their execution. Worry, distractions and conscious effort are the three main factors which bring people out of the zone.

What are the best ways to get into the zone? Firstly, find a task which best matches your ability and skill levels: if it is too difficult you will be overwhelmed by fear or fatigue; if it is too easy you will become bored. Next, adopt a playful approach, not trying, not instructing, not judging – just moving. Then, allow your senses, vision, hearing, and 'feeling' of the movement to wander and fix on the most relevant part of the task – the stripes on the tennis ball, the feel of the surf beneath your canoe or the texture of the basketball as you bounce it. Finally, do what comes easiest. Ignore the critical voice in your head, saying that you *should* do this or you *must* do that or *ought* to do something else. By filtering this voice you allow yourself to become immersed in what you are doing.

For most of us this is a completely alien approach to sport – instruction, effort and striving are essential. If we strictly adhere to this, we will probably not experience the zone often.

It is called 'playing' sport for a reason – when we truly play we make the 'zone' experience much more likely.

Going deeper into the theory

Optimal levels of performance is an umbrella term for a number of subjective states – flow, peak performance, the zone, peak experience – all of which share some common characteristics – high levels of performance, total immersion in the activity, high satisfaction, clarity of thought, merging of self and action. The literature often fails to discriminate between these constructs and it is important that practitioners are clear about their distinctions. Harmison and Casto (2012) present a good overview explaining how these differ and also how each is linked to mental skills.

A useful line of theory around optimal performance states is the concept of 'flow' developed by Csikszentmihalyi in the 1970s. He interviewed people working in a range of creative arts and sports. He found that often when they are at their most creative or most successful they enter a mental state of full immersion, when their normal everyday experience of time and effort is altered – hours pass as seconds and what is normally hard work seems easy. He described this state as one of 'flow'. It is perhaps not surprising that sport psychology became interested in 'flow' as a way of explaining the type of sensation that runners and other exercisers experience, engaging in self-paced repetitive activities. However, performers in other sports, such as tennis, golf and football, have described the state as well.

The flow state is a difficult one to research. Csikszentmihalyi developed a technique called experience sampling as a method of recording flow in real time using a pager or text cue, but this is flawed methodology as the prompting of individuals to reflect on their current state leads to inevitable bias. Psychometric tests were developed but relied on retrospective accounts of flow rather than experimental studies. Jackson and Kimiecik (2008) identified the dimensions of flow to be:

- ◆ challenge–skills balance
- ◆ merging of action and awareness
- ◆ clear goals and feedback
- ◆ concentration on the task at hand
- ◆ transformation of time
- ◆ sense of control
- ◆ loss of self-consciousness
- ◆ autotelic (self-chosen) experience.

This framework is useful but fails to address the key question: Is the 'flow' state/zone controllable, and if it is, how can it be achieved?

Russell (2001) and Jackson (1995) have presented evidence that most athletes report being able to control the experience of flow. This has led researchers to examine whether personal characteristics or skills or elements of the environment could act as triggers. An example of this is the work done by Pates et al. (2002) indicating that performance was enhanced and the perception of flow increased when performers were exposed to self-selected music.

Some research has aimed to examine the relationship between the zone/flow experience and neurochemical events, in particular the relationship between the reported state and endorphin production. This is a difficult area of research as endorphins do not cross the blood–brain barrier.

Bibliography

Boccker, H., Springer, T., Spliker, M.E., Henricksen, G., Koppenhoefer, M., Wagner, K.J., Valet, M., Berthele, A., & Toller, R. (2008). The runner's high: opioid mechanisms in the human brain. *Cerebral Cortex 18* (11): 2523–2531.

Csikszentmihalyi. M. (1975). *Beyond Boredom and Anxiety*. Jossey-Bass.

Harmison, R., & Casto, K. (2012). Optimal performance: elite level performance in 'the zone.' In S. Murphy (Ed.), *The Handbook on Sport and Performance Psychology*. Oxford University Press.

Jackson, S. (1995). Factors influencing the occurrence of flow state in elite athletes. *Journal of Applied Sport Psychology 7*: 138–166.

Jackson, S., & Kimiecik, J. (2008). Optimal experience in sport and exercise. In T. Horn (Ed.), *Advances in Sport Psychology*, 3rd edn. (pp. 377–399). Human Kinetics.

Pates, J., Karageorghis, C.L., Fryer, R., & Maynard, I. (2003). Effects of asynchronous music on flow states and shooting performance among netball players. *Psychology of Sport and Exercise 4*: 415–427.

Russell, W.D. (2001). An examination of flow state occurrence in college athletes. *Journal of Sport Behaviour 24*: 83–107.

Q9

I've heard a lot recently about how important it is to control my 'chimp'. What does this mean and is it something I should do?

What you have heard about is the approach to performance developed by a psychiatrist, Professor Steve Peters. He has worked extensively in elite sport for the past 15 years. Many performers, from a range of sports, endorse his approach. In particular he worked with Sir Dave Brailsford at British Cycling and Team Sky. Brailsford has credited Peters as being responsible for developing a robust and effective approach to performance psychology. Peters' book is called *The Chimp Paradox* and is endorsed by multiple Olympic gold medallists Victoria Pendleton and Sir Chris Hoy.

Peters describes himself as a technician of the mind. In his model he simplifies the complex workings of the central nervous system down into three components – the chimp, the human and the computer. The chimp is a metaphor for the emotional, threat detection system involving the limbic system and autonomic nervous system. When the chimp detects a threat, such as that experienced under the stress of competition, it responds by activating the 'fight, flight, fright or flee' response. This explains the unpleasant symptoms experienced. However, there are positives of this state. Under conditions of threat, the body responds by producing hormones which ready the body for high-energy output. These are useful if your performance requires a powerful whole-body movement, but less so if it requires a precise movement involving fine control. Whilst the chimp tends to engage emotion, the human part of the model aims to process information in order to understand rationally the situation it finds itself in. In Peters' model the chimp is much stronger than the human; the emotion will always overwhelm the thought. The final aspect of the model is the computer. This part of the model refers to the automatic responses associated with well-learned skills, of both thought and movement. Peters' model suggests that one of the ways of preventing the emotional thinking of the chimp dominating your behaviours is to program the computer to react automatically to a threat, before the chimp is engaged. In Peters' model there are structures within the computer which form the basis of this programming. These relate to the habitual thinking the individual engages in.

Peters argues that sometimes it feels like there are two opposing forces operating in your psyche. He advises people to recognize that they are responsible for the management of the chimp. You cannot dismiss a loss of control as 'that wasn't me – that was my chimp'. He states that, just like a pet dog that is difficult to control, we have to take responsibility and offers a range of methods for achieving this.

To determine whether you need to engage this model, Peters challenges you to ask one question before performance: Are you feeling what you'd like to feel? If the answer is 'no' then it is probably the case that your chimp has woken up and is perceiving a threat.

Going deeper into the theory

Peters has provoked considerable debate among the applied sport and performance psychology community. My view is that his work is useful but there are some significant problems.

As a package, Peters has promoted the chimp model without empirical support – reinforcing the issue of evidence-based practice versus practice-based evidence I made in the opening chapter.

That Peters has been extremely successful is not in doubt. He has received endorsements from many high-profile performers. He appears to have had more success in individual sports, such as cycling and snooker, than in co-acting or interacting environments. Peters claims his model is ground breaking: my view is that this is rather overstating the case. He has not presented any new insight into the neurobiology of performance. The genius of the approach is to package the material in such an accessible way that his clients and people engaging with his book have an understanding of what they are experiencing. However, the chimp management part of his book, where the tools for programming the computer are presented, are, in fact, a good example of cognitive-behavioural interventions aimed at challenging and restructuring faulty thinking.

Bibliography

Peters, S. (2012). *The Chimp Paradox*. Vermillion.

Q10

I have heard a great deal about the growth mindset. What is this and how can I get it?

Researchers have identified two distinct types of motivational mindset: fixed and growth. A person displaying a fixed mindset tends to believe that performance levels are fixed by stable and unchanging factors such as ability or talent; in a fixed mindset people tend to focus on the immediate value of an outcome – either good, if the performance is up to standard, or bad, if it is not. Performance provides feedback telling you about your ability and reinforcing the outcome of your performance. In a fixed mindset if you win, it's because you have talent and ability; if you lose it's because you have neither.

In contrast, the growth mindset is focused on performance as an indicator of effort and strategy, not simply talent. Those with a growth mindset see performance as an opportunity to receive feedback, not a statement of unchanging ability. A good performance tells you that you have worked hard and done the right things at the right time; a relatively poorer performance gives you feedback about how much harder you need to work or the skills you need to develop.

The contrast between these two mindsets is important when placed in the context of developing young sport performers. A youngster with a fixed mindset may see low levels of performance or progress as a reinforcement of low ability and withdraw effort and perhaps ultimately drop out of the sport. In contrast, the youngster with a growth mindset is likely to continue, engage more effort and develop skills and strategy firm in the belief that the key phrase is: I can do this, just not yet.

Given that performance often requires long periods of hard training the growth mindset is required to cope with the periods of slow progress, setbacks and road blocks.

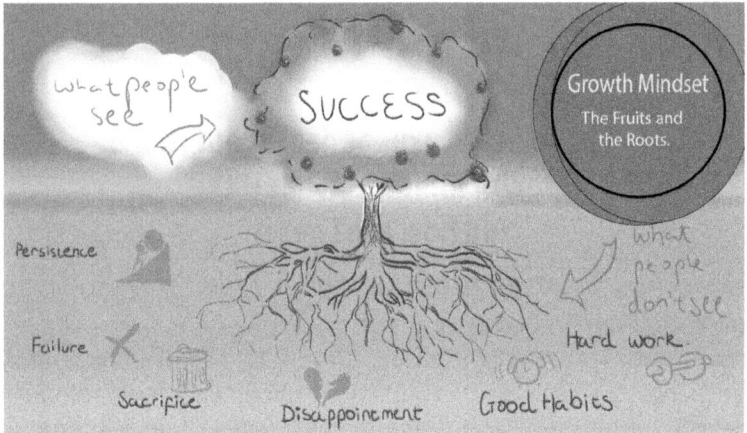

FIGURE 2.1 Fruits and roots.

To develop a growth mindset performers need to clarify their thinking around what leads to successful outcomes – effort comes before achievement. The growth mindset is characterized by performers benchmarking themselves only against themselves: if they are performing better than they did yesterday or last week and that reflects a consistent improvement in performance, they will maintain high levels of motivation. On the other hand, the fixed mindset is characterized by external benchmarking, against other people and external criteria. If the individual is already high-achieving there may be a tendency to avoid further evaluation in order to protect existing status, whilst if there is low achievement, an attribution of low ability may lead to avoidance of future evaluation for fear of being publicly 'shown up'.

Going deeper into the theory

Growth mindset is an idea which has been developed from the work of Carol Dweck, an American psychologist who has been researching motivation for many years. Dweck's work has been applied in educational settings for a number of years and has now been developed in the context of sport performance. Table 2.2 summarizes the key features of the two mindsets.

TABLE 2.2 Summary of the differences between fixed and growth mindsets

	Fixed mindset	Growth mindset
Attitude	Deterministic – intelligence / talent is predetermined or genetically programmed	Sense of autonomy over development
Motivational orientation	Frequently told that you have talent, leading to a desire to look competent to others	Loves the activity and has inherent desire to learn rather than demonstrate competence or superiority over others
Challenges	Tends to avoid challenges where there is a possibility of demonstrating low levels of skill or competence	Embraces challenges as testing existing skills and developing new ones
Obstacles	Tends to give up easily if success isn't immediate	Persists following setbacks
Effort	Effort is viewed as either fruitless or demonstrating low level of talent or competence	Sees effort as the path to mastery
Criticism	Ignores feedback which could be used to develop skills further	Seeks feedback despite it not always being positive. Without feedback there is no development
Success of others	Feels threatened by the success of others	Finds lessons and gains motivation from the success of others
Results	Tends to improve rapidly but plateaus early and achieves much less than full potential	Develops a balanced view of the role of effort in achievement

This article https://www.ted.com/talks/carol_dweck_the_power_of_believing_that_you_can_improve?language=en captures the essence of mindsets and some of the research behind it very well.

Bibliography

Dweck, C. (2012). *Mindset: How You Can Fulfil Your Potential*. Robinson.

Pulling the threads together

The simplest questions are the hardest to answer

In this chapter I have aimed to open the door to the rest of the book; to inform the reader about the nature of sport, and show how the physical, technical and tactical challenges in performance interact with the psychology. Human beings do not come with a users' manual; we quite often have to find things out for ourselves through a painful process of trial and error. In sport we often see performers making the same mental errors time after time, suggesting that they don't reflect on their psychology, or if they do they don't know how to change. Sport psychology offers a way in to the full development of skills, the aim being to enable performers to fulfil their potential and gain as much enjoyment and satisfaction from their sport.

The questions posed in this chapter are general, about what sport psychology is and, importantly, what it is not. They are disarmingly simple questions; to answer them fully requires a great deal of thought and depth. My intention has been to show that sport psychology is a part of the comprehensive preparation to perform for any performer, at any performance level. There are no tricks or gimmicks; like other parts of performance preparation, effort is required to develop skills and apply them.

From its beginning on the periphery, sport psychology has entered the thinking of many performers, those wanting to explore their potential and their limits along with those who use sport as recreational activity. Sport psychology has always embraced the joint aims of performance enhancement and psychological well-being. In many ways it really was the first 'positive psychology'.

III

Motivation – making sense of the will to win

An iconic image of the Barcelona Olympic Games in 1992 was that of the British men's coxed pair receiving their gold medal: two brothers, Jonny and Greg Searle towering over Garry Herbert, their cox, Herbert crying with joy and relief. Interviews after the Games powerfully illustrated the commitment needed to reach that level of performance. Herbert told reporters that in training he pushed the brothers so hard that he felt they would be willing to die in pursuit of their goal. In the race, one of the closest in Olympic history, their boat was level with the Italian Abbagnale brothers. With 150 m to go of the 2-km course, Herbert posed his crew the simple question – 'How much do you want it?' They won the race by about the length of the page you are reading now.

We see the top of the performance iceberg. The bulk of the performers' work is the often dull and repetitive but physically exhausting process of preparation. On competition day we see the pay-off as they push themselves to the limit of their physical, technical and mental ability in pursuit of a goal. There has to be both a will to prepare and a will to win.

A sense of purpose makes pain easier to bear

People who play sport 'get it': they understand why others would want to strive for their personal Everest. The only explanation that is needed is a highly personal *because*: because it's there, because I can, because I want to be the best, even because someone once said I couldn't. People who don't 'get it' often cannot fathom why one would make such commitments: why would someone want to exchange a warm and comfortable bed for a cold swimming pool at 5.30 a.m., every day for years and years, or lift weights to the point of exhaustion, or chase a ball around a field? There is a blank incomprehension. Incomprehension can also be found between sports: games players look at runners and think 'why?', golfers may do the same to gymnasts, and so it goes on. Everyone who plays sport has a personal set of motives, reasons – this is why I do it. It doesn't need to make sense to anyone else, but it drives our behaviour in a profound way.

In this chapter I aim to develop your understanding of motivation in sport and look at healthy and positive ways in which you can develop your own motivation and that of the performers you work with, lead or parent.

Most of us are not preparing for an Olympic Games. We have lower aspirations but they can be just as powerful. The desire to beat an opponent, a team mate or a personal best can be extremely powerful and drive us to train hard and make huge sacrifices. Where does that motivation come from and why do some people have it but not others?

Why we do what we do is a central theme in psychology

Motivation is the most fundamental area of psychology. Many view it as the cornerstone of other aspects of our thinking, feeling and behaving. But there are many paradoxes and hidden motivational traps – even in the story above, asking someone how much they want something can lead to profound anxiety as it becomes closer. Garry Herbert's 'How much do you want it?' question could have backfired: the Searle brothers could have 'tried to row harder' and lost their smooth, efficient form: it didn't, they continued to execute their skills calmly and perfectly – it turned out to be exactly the right thing to say. This is why we need to understand motivation, how it can be developed and exactly the right 'motivational buttons' to press. One motivational technique does not fit all!

If psychologists can't agree on what motivation is and where it comes from, what chance do I have?

Motivation is a broad concept: it almost defies definition. Textbooks identify two characteristics: first, the direction of our behaviour – what we *choose* to do; and second, the *effort* invested in that choice. This is a deceptively simple definition which fails to capture the complexity of what we are speaking about; it encompasses our aspirations, our persistence and our willingness to endure, in short is the essential mental energy that give behaviour purpose and drives us to act.

But where does this drive come from? Why are some people willing to push themselves to the point of physical harm and beyond striving for an Olympic medal, whilst others, perhaps with greater physical and technical ability, appear to be less willing to endure?

Psychologists cannot give a simple explanation as to where motivation comes from

The challenge is that a number of theories or models have been proposed. Each one is really good at explaining some facets of motivation, but none explains everything. The techniques to build motivation are based in each approach, but again no single technique is effective in all cases. The list below provides a summary of the different theories and how the mental energy to act is generated.

◆ Psychodynamic (e.g. Freud):
  ✓ the role of unconscious drives in determining behaviour, emphasis on the role of childhood experience in determining adult behaviour
◆ Behaviourism (e.g. Skinner, 1976):
  ✓ the role of rewards and punishments in determining behaviour
◆ Humanistic (e.g. Rogers, 1961):
  ✓ the drive to grow as a person and achieve a self-actualized state
◆ Cognitive (e.g. Nicholls, 1978):
  ✓ the role of goals and thinking processes in determining behaviour
◆ Biological (e.g. LeDoux, 1996):
  ✓ the role of biological processes in determining behaviour.

I encourage students I work with to contextualize motivation by applying each approach to a specific example. I've never met or worked with the swimmer Michael Phelps. He has won more Olympic medals than any other performer in history.

He has competed at five summer games and innumerable world, regional and national championships. These are his 'Everest summit' achievements. What we don't see is the day-to-day training, the physical pain, the dietary restrictions, all the things he goes through to have these moments of recognition and glory. Why does he keep coming back? Why did he return after retirement in 2012? Will he be back again in Tokyo in 2020? Each theoretical approach will explain why he does what he does in a different way; we can't say definitely that one is 'right' and another 'wrong' – there is considerable overlap.

It isn't my intention to present a comprehensive model of each theory in this text. There are excellent texts on this (e.g. Hill, 2000). The fact that after over a hundred years of research there are still differentiated models of motivation informing our discipline shows that we are dealing with something complex and challenging.

The majority of sport psychology practitioners adopt an eclectic view of motivation which combines some elements of cognitive, behaviourist and humanistic models of motivation. Few work within an exclusively psychodynamic tradition.

What is the best way to make sense of motivation in the context of sport?

The modern sport psychology literature is dominated by two theoretical models of motivation: achievement goal theory and self-determination theory. Both emphasize the role of our thinking about choices and goals to explain behaviour.

Achievement goals – the will to win – but what does winning mean to you?

Achievement goal theory was first developed in educational psychology and applied sport psychology. It is called achievement goal theory because it focuses on our personal criteria for success, the types of goals we set ourselves and how we determine whether we are successful. It divides success criteria into two broad categories. The first is success because the goal of mastering a task has been achieved – this is called task or *mastery orientation*. The other criterion for success emphasizes demonstrating dominance over other people – this is called outcome or *ego orientation*.

People who are mainly task- or mastery-oriented are driven to learn new skills: they tend to be more interested in personal development than the outcome of their performance. These individuals tend to set goals for themselves which reflect enhanced performance referenced against their own performance. If they are able to perform better today than they did yesterday, the goal has been achieved.

Those who are more outcome- or ego-oriented are more concerned with the outcome of performance and are motivated by demonstrating superiority over others in competition. These individuals tend to set goals which benchmark performance against the performance of other people. Winning a match, race or contest is the clearest demonstration of superiority over others.

People are complex in their motivations. They can be simultaneously driven by both task and ego types of achievement goals. Having ego goals alone can be problematic, as the outcome is related to the unstable performance of others. It can lead people to seek relatively easier challenges which can guarantee a winning outcome, winning an easier contest rather than testing oneself at a more challenging level. The optimal balance is to blend both outcome goals and mastery goals. The outcomes are often highly energizing – the prospect of winning an event or being selected for a team, whilst the mastery goals highlight the developments required to make the desired outcome more likely, indicating more of a willingness to prepare to win rather than a will to win. This is a recurrent theme in several questions posed later in the text.

Self-determination: the will to win – but would you still compete if there were no audiences and no prizes?

Self-determination theory addresses the 'why' question: why do I do this sport? Is it because of the intrinsic pleasure and satisfaction from participation and performance? Motives that would still be present if there were no rewards or incentives offered. On the other hand, does the mental energy to begin and continue the sport come from the possibility of gaining some reward or recognition from participating, or possibly that continued involvement helps avoid an unpleasant outcome such as gaining weight or losing fitness?

Self-determination theory is based on the extent to which we are making free choices about what we do and how we do it. The theory proposes that there are many behaviours which are intrinsically motivated – that is, they would be carried out without any tangible (e.g. financial) or intangible (e.g. recognition or encouragement) rewards offered. Most children begin their sporting careers intrinsically motivated: they play for fun. As they become more involved a reward-oriented environment develops. They may receive recognition and rewards which shape their behaviour, until ultimately they may no longer intrinsically enjoy what they are doing in sport, but continue to play either to receive further rewards and reinforcement or to avoid the negative consequences which would come from dropping out.

Self-determination theory identifies three main basic psychological needs which are considered for optimal functioning and growth: autonomy, the need for choice; competence, the need to express skills; and finally, relatedness, the need to feel a social bond with others. These are the conditions in which intrinsic motivation is most likely to develop.

In an ideal world, sports performers would be intrinsically motivated and have an optimal blend of mastery and ego goals.

Parents, coaches and teachers develop a motivational climate around performers

A line of theory developed to clarify achievement goals is the idea of motivational climate. This idea has been particularly developed and applied in the context of youth sport. What coaches, teachers and parents do and say establishes a motivational environment around the young performer – goals are established, some behaviours are rewarded and others punished. This may not be explicit or deliberate but, through subtle use of language and actions it becomes clear what types of behaviour are reinforced and what are not.

Often the motivational climate developed around most performers is skewed in favour of ego goals (interpersonal competition) and extrinsic motivation (striving for rewards, recognition and avoidance of punishments). Understanding how to create an optimal motivational climate is a vital but neglected part of both parenting and coaching.

Can you give other people motivation? The myth of the 'Gipper'

There are many legends around the role of motivational speeches in sporting locker rooms, perhaps most famously the 'Win one for the Gipper' speech, now part of American Football folklore, driving players on to performance they could not have achieved without the inspiring words.

An industry has grown up around the idea of motivational speaking. Commercial organizations often invite high-profile or inspirational figures to address their staff teams: the aim is to reinforce the corporate ethos or team mission – the motivational climate. When these are effective it is often due to the speaker helping people reconnect with their personal sense of purpose and recommit, with increased intensity, to achieving personal and organizational goals. Unfortunately these speeches often miss the target. They become window dressing because they are so far removed from the motivational challenges faced in the organization.

A speech will not provide any benefit if the day-to-day motivational climate in the team or organization is weak or inappropriate. A key quality of effective leadership is the ability to develop an optimal motivational climate around players, in training and in performance. This determines the players' daily commitment to excellence, especially in those dark moments when everything seems to be going against them. This climate reinforces a player's motivation and fans a fire all players set and ignite for themselves – through their sense of purpose, their own personal motives. The coach, parent and peers can influence this but ultimately all players are responsible for their own motivation, their own sense of purpose, their personal 'because'.

So where does the will to win come from?

Different models of motivation explain the striving for achievement differently. Some emphasize the importance of unconscious desires, others suggest that the possibility of rewards or the avoidance of punishments drives us on, still others highlight the role of the goals that we set ourselves. It is unlikely that psychology will ever agree on a single explanation of what drives our desire to strive for achievement. It is frustrating but we can work with it. What sport psychology can do is to find ways to help performers reconnect with their sense of purpose on a regular basis – to renew their intrinsic motives and keep the extrinsic ones in perspective. And ultimately to help performers arrive at the most critical days in their sporting careers with their motivations clear and their stores of mental energy fully charged.

Bibliography

Freud, S., Wilson, S., & Griffiths, T. (2012). *A General Introduction to Psychoanalysis (Classics of World Literature).* Wordsworth Editions.

Hill, K.L. (2000). *Frameworks for Sport Psychologists.* Human Kinetics.

LeDoux, J. (1996). *The Emotional Brain: The Mysterious Underpinnings of Emotional Life.* Touchstone.

Nicholls, J.G. (1978). The development of the concepts of effort and ability, perception of own attainment, and the understanding that difficult tasks require more ability. *Child Development* 49: 800–814.

Rogers, C.R. (1961). *On Becoming a Person. A Therapist's View of Psychotherapy.* Houghton Mifflin.

Skinner, B.F. (1976). *About Behaviorism.* Random House.

Q11

I set SMART goals each season but struggle to achieve them – how do I do right?

Goal setting is one of the most common techniques for increasing motivation to enhance performance. However, goals are not magic – simply setting goals, especially outcome goals, without supporting performance and process goals is a common mistake and can lead to disappointment with the technique.

Many people have come across the idea of setting SMART (specific, measurable, achievable, realistic and time-lined) or SMARTER (plus exciting and recorded) goals in a variety of occupational and sporting contexts. Goal setting of this type is designed to enhance motivation by focusing attention on an outcome or task, increasing effort, persistence and seeking new strategies.

Goal setting is certainly better than just relying on 'do your best' as a motivational approach. However, SMART(ER) goals can encourage you to focus on the wrong types of goal. This is probably why you are not getting the results you'd like.

Many people set themselves outcome goals – such as winning an event, or being selected for a specific team. These goals are very important because they energize and encourage you to train hard. However, there are two other types of goals which I consider to be of equal or greater importance – performance and process goals.

When I speak to performers about their goals I ask a blunt question: Do you want to win? 'Yes, of course', is the deafening reply. My follow-up is the real challenge: 'How are you going to win?' This is really what goal setting is about.

These are the performance goals which make winning more likely and critically the processes which support them.

When you set goals you need to look also at what performance you are aiming towards – for example, what time, distance or score is likely to give you the outcome you're driving towards – these are performance goals and are key benchmarks. Supporting these are an even more important type of goal – process goals – the critical *how* goals. These are the day-to-day behaviours which make the outcome you have established more likely to happen. I encourage performers to put together a mission statement which identifies these day-to-day process goals – this is your goal achievement plan. Things that must become habits if you want to be successful.

Set goals for every session you do, and make sure that you are focusing on behaviours you want to do, not things you don't want to do.

You can set goals about physical, technical, tactical and mental aspects of your game. Look beyond the SMART(ER) goals at the processes which make the outcomes happen. These are your building blocks of success.

If looking at your 100-day, 30-day, 10-day and 1-day goals doesn't excite and energize you, then you've done it wrong!

Going deeper into the theory

Goal setting is a common, and commonly misunderstood, process. As a technique, it doesn't make sense without a good understanding of motivational theory. Effective goal setting taps into a performer's sense of purpose. Written goals are a way of regularly renewing and reconnecting with that sense of mission. It recognizes that for most people motivations are complex and sometime contradictory. Research indicates that there are features of effective goal setting; Burton and Weiss (2008) present a comprehensive overview of the goal-setting research in sport. In particular they highlight the fact that challenging and specific goals are associated with better performance than no goals or simply 'do your best' goals. But the research can be difficult to do. Not least because in empirical studies there is often spontaneous goal setting in the control group.

I have highlighted the differentiation between outcome, performance and process goals. Of these, clarifying outcomes is critical as these are the 'top-line' reasons why performers are competing: they must understand that goal setting is about much more than these. Process goals are of at least equal importance. I encourage goal setting on a timeline – 100-day, 30-day, 10-day and 1-day goals – outcome, performance and process. There is considerable debate about what constitutes a challenging goal. My view of this is that you need to work with an individual client's motivations. For one individual setting a goal to be the best in the world will energize and focus: for another that is too far away and abstract, and a goal closer to existing performance levels will be more effective in mobilizing energy.

Goal-setting research indicates that setting goals can be an effective technique for building or maintaining motivation. But there are specific issues in sport performance which mean that goals set in sport performance do not yield the often dramatic enhancements found in other areas, such as the commercial world (Locke et al., 1981).

Bibliography

Burton, D., & Weiss, C.L. (2008). The fundamental goal concept: the path to process and performance success. In T. Horn (Ed.), *Advances in Sport Psychology* (3rd edn., pp. 339–375). Human Kinetics.

Locke, E.A., Shaw, K.N., Saari, L.M., & Latham, G.P. (1981). Goal setting and task performance: 1969–1980. *Psychological Bulletin*, *90*: 125–152.

Q12

Which do you recommend for building motivation: carrot or stick?

Neither will do the job you want, in the way you want it.

I suggest that you use rewards or punishments very carefully. I have many examples of where offering incentives or threatening punishments produced unintended negative results. Making players run punishment laps for making errors may make them avoid trying new skills: the football team that fined players for yellow cards found that players were inhibited in 50-50 challenges, and teams that fined players for shooting over the bar found that players stopped shooting. Equally I've seen examples of rugby players rewarded for increasing their tackle count, ignoring the team defensive organization just to up their personal tally.

Before you think about offering rewards or threatening punishments to increase motivation, make sure that you have thought through how it will impact on a player's behaviour. For example, if you offer rewards for attending training, make sure that players are not just turning up to gain the 'tick' and are just going through the motions, rather than doing the high-quality training you want them to.

Also bear in mind that rewards and punishments can be very subtle. Personal attention from a coach can be a highly valued reward, which reinforces behaviour when it's given and is perceived as a punishment when it is removed.

In my view it is much more important to build intrinsic motivation through skilful use of choice (autonomy), competence (a culture of high intensity and excellence) and relatedness (social interaction with team mates) than the use of rewards and punishments.

Going deeper into the theory

The idea of using rewards and punishments to shape behaviour is one of the central features of the behaviourist approach to motivation. Many textbooks have given the impression that behaviourist approaches to explaining human behaviour have been completely superseded by the cognitive 'juggernaut'. Yet behaviourist principles remain in evidence everywhere – in schools, in the workplace, in social environments and in sport. This all-pervasive exposure to environmental rewards and punishments can lead to a narrow view that motivations can be built and shaped by behaviour, without much cognitive involvement. In reality 'old-fashioned' behaviourism, with an emphasis on strengthening through reinforcement or weakening through punishment, the link between stimulus and response, has itself been given a new and important context in radical behaviourism and behaviour analysis. All behaviourists aim to explain behaviour in terms of learning and learning occurs when a behaviour fits into an adaptive framework. Such a behaviour is more likely to be repeated. However, this is not simply as a consequence of the presence of a reward or threat of punishment. Each individual builds a context around the environment and it is this which ultimately shapes motivations to act and the act itself. A small financial reward has little leverage in shaping the motives of a millionaire, who has no intrinsic desire to change.

In my view modern behaviourism, which builds on Skinner's radical philosophy, has got a currency in developing sport behaviour. It provides a framework for integrating more extrinsic elements of other motivational models into an approach to motivation which reflects real life.

Bibliography

Moore, J. (2008). *Conceptual Foundations of Radical Behaviorism.* Sloan Publishing.

Q13

The problem I have is that some of the best runners aren't very competitive and don't seem to want to win as much as some of those with less talent. How can I make the talented runners want to win more?

The talent identification and development literature does highlight that competitiveness is an important psychological characteristic for performers aiming for high-level performance.

However, I think your first step will be to clarify the target of the competitiveness. Is it competitiveness focused on an outcome – demonstrating that your athletes are better than others by winning a race? Or is it focused on mastery – improving a time? Motivationally these are different and come with different psychological consequences.

Be careful what you wish for! Highly competitive performers, particularly youngsters, who are driven to achieving outcomes often experience high levels of performance anxiety. They want to win, they expect to win, they project themselves into an uncertain future and worry about whether they will be good enough to achieve their goal. This can lead to perfectionist thinking, which can drive them on but also lead to negative self-evaluations – perfectionism is an issue I develop in several other questions. In a sport as physically demanding as athletics, perfectionism can lead the performer to overtrain and/or underrecover. The constant competitive striving to win may result in lower performance, lower levels of enjoyment and higher risk of injury. On the other hand, the less competitive, more mastery-oriented performers focus more on the process and will only benchmark their performances against their own previous performance. This may not directly lead to linear improvements in running times, you are working with many physical processes around adaptation to the training stimulus, but it will take a great deal of the psychological intensity out of competition. In reality, these two types of motivational orientation are not mutually exclusive either/ors. Most performers have a balance of these – with a generalized gender bias towards mastery in girls and outcome in boys – but beware, there are *many* highly outcome-oriented girls and mastery-oriented boys.

My suggestion is that you speak on a one-to-one basis with each of the runners, find out why they like running and get a clear idea of the goals they have set themselves in the next few months. You might be surprised to hear that the good runners, as you have labelled them, just like running and enjoy being part of a training group. They may appear unconcerned about running times and placing at events. This is *not* a flaw in their character or a barrier to ultimate success. If they are to fulfil their potential as athletes in 5 or 10 years' time it is that enjoyment of running and the social aspect of running which will keep them in the sport and bouncing back from the inevitable setbacks they will experience.

You will get a sense whether runners will accept the next step. If they resist, back off!

Introduce the runners to more structured goal setting, but focus more on process and performance goals than outcomes. This means not going straight to setting goals around winning a particular event or getting to a final. This type of goal focuses on performance relative to others – a factor outside the athlete's control. Focus more on the processes of training and racing and bring it back to individual sessions. For example, when you last ran 6 × 400s you averaged 64 seconds; can we average 63 tonight, with none slower than 64 and none faster than 62?

Going deeper into the theory

The motivational orientation and climate are at the heart of this question. Coaches and parents often bring a narrow zero-sum view of achievement motivation to their interactions with children. In their view the only type of competitiveness worth examining is around outcomes, usually winning. You will hear this regularly with parents and coaches asking young performers if they won after an event. In athletics this is not a great question – in a large cross-country event, there might be 200 runners. Is everyone who was behind the winner a loser? Forget clichés – this is nonsense! Many will have had their *best ever* performance: this must be acknowledged and reinforced. For continued involvement shifting to a mastery orientation is essential.

Goal setting and motivational orientation are inextricably linked. In my experience coaches often place an emphasis on outcome goals over process goals. This often results in high levels of anxiety in performers who focus on the outcome rather than the behavioural steps which make the achievement of the outcome more likely.

In advising the coach to develop a clearer sense of motivation in each runner, using a performance profile may help this purpose further. This technique helps clarify the key aspects of performance, seen through the eyes of the performer. It also opens up important avenues of communication between the athlete and coach.

Bibliography

Butler, R.J., & Hardy, L. (1992). The performance profile: theory and application. *The Sport Psychologist 6*: 253–264.
Gucciardi, D.F., & Gordon, S. (2009). Revisiting the performance profile technique: theoretical underpinnings and application. *The Sport Psychologist 23:* 93–117.

Q14

We have a real problem with girls dropping out of competitive sport in their teenage years. Is there anything I can do to keep them motivated?

I am always cautious about offering advice in areas where I am not the expert. I am not a physical education (PE) teacher and it would be wrong of me to claim to understand fully the practical and pedagogic pressures under which teachers work. However I can offer my insight around the motivation question you have posed. Highschool PE is a psychological minefield. Sport and physical activity quite often start to fall down the priority list as young people, particularly girls, arrive at puberty. There are many other competing pressures which vie for attention and, seemingly very abruptly, even the most committed and talented performers no longer see training or playing sport as important.

I would advise two things as defining the way forward. Firstly, knowledge: you need to understand what the 'push and pull' factors are for the girls you are working with – you might be surprised! Ask open questions about what activities you could offer that would keep them engaged, and also ask about what are the real barriers. The second thing is an open mind. Teachers sometimes feel very constrained by the traditional 'games' ethos in PE.

It is good to see more freedom about how the curriculum is framed and delivered. If these girls remain active into adulthood they are forming habits around physical activity and fitness which will yield benefits in 20, 30, even 50 years' time. Give the girls the opportunity to make choices about what they do and how they do it – this is good psychology as it builds intrinsic motivation, as does the opportunity to work in strong social groups. Above all you must dispel the mindset that many take from PE, that they're not 'sporty' – you don't need to be sporty to be active and gain both joy and health benefits from physical activity.

There is no need always to push interpersonal competition. Traditionally the PE curriculum has served the needs of the few, not the many. I hope this is changing. Intrinsic motivation is the key. If you help the girls to find an activity they love, you have done your job and they will be more likely to remain active throughout their lives.

Going deeper into the theory

This question links to the self-determination theory outlined in the introduction to this chapter. Building intrinsic motivation to engage in physical activity in young people, especially girls, is a very significant public health issue. The PE teacher is in prime position to develop a positive motivational climate. Intrinsic motivation is developed through choice, being able to develop skills and work within socially cohesive and integrated groups. This question also relates back to the mindset issue outlined in Chapter II.

The other theoretical issue which I'd like to highlight here is the issue of self-presentational concerns – particularly around self-esteem. PE can be a powerful means for the development of a positive physical self-image. The motivational climate developed by the teacher can either have a positive or negative impact on how people perceive their physical competence, movement skills or physical self-perceptions. Given the heightened sensitivities around these concerns in teenage girls it is understandable why some girls choose to remove themselves from what they perceive as a negative and evaluating environment. The work of Fox (1997, 2000) and Hagger et al. (2005) is worth following up in relation to this issue. Self-presentational concerns have become magnified in the era of social media and this is also a topic that I suggest practitioners working with young people should follow up.

Bibliography

Fardouly, J., Diedrichs, P.C., Vartainan, L.R., & Halliwell, E. (2015). Social comparisons on social media: the impact of Facebook on young women's body image concerns and mood. *Body Image 13*: 38–45.

Fox, K.R. (1997). The physical self and processes in self-esteem development. In K.R. Fox (Ed.), *The Physical Self From Motivation to Well-being* (pp. 111–140). Human Kinetics.

Fox, K.R. (2000). Self-esteem, self-perceptions and exercise. *International Journal of Sport Psychology 31*: 228–240.

Hagger, M., Biddle, S., & Wang, C.K. (2005). Physical self-concept in adolescence: generalizability of a multidimensional, hierarchical model across gender and grade. *Educational and Psychology Measurement 65* (2): 297–322.

Q15

In my training group there two athletes who are perfectionists – they train very hard but are prone to overtraining, particularly ahead of big events. What can I do to help them?

Let's start by clarifying what perfectionism means. It is habitual thoughts, emotions and behaviours around striving for flawlessly high standards combined with excessive and critical evaluations of performance.

The traditional view of perfectionism is that it is a bad thing, indicating psychological maladjustment or disorder. However there are many walks of life where perfectionism isn't viewed negatively. In academic and work settings, striving for very high standards is reinforced. This is often also the case in sport. What is often unclear is where the line between striving for high standards crosses into unrealistic obsession.

Going back to the definition, the modern view of perfectionism is to divide the positive striving for high standards from the negative and critical evaluations that often come with them. The striving behaviour can be managed by having very clear goals – outcome, performance and process – which give the athlete a view of what is 'good enough'. More challenging is helping athletes to manage their critical inner voice, often a very powerful one which is telling them that 'good enough is not good enough'.

Coming back to your specific question. For many performers training feels like an act of faith. We believe that a 'dose' of training will prompt the body to adapt and grow, to develop characteristics which make us better performers. But there are many unknowns. Often we don't know what the optimal level of intensity is for each individual, we don't know whether one type of training is better than another, and, critically, we don't know exactly how long to rest between sessions in order to maximize the benefit.

In the face of this uncertainty many performers take a very simple decision – more must be better than less – I'll train more, I'll train harder and recover less. If this type of thinking is habitual over a long period of time, then it is inevitable that athletes will develop a chronically fatigued state where they stop adapting to training and underperform. Some call this overtraining. I prefer the term chronic underrecovery.

Modern training theory is highlighting that, of the three factors – volume, intensity and recovery – lower volume, higher intensity and longer recovery are probably the way to optimizing the benefits of training. However, I'm getting away from the psychology – training theory is a whole other book!

In your role you can create a motivational climate which reinforces high-quality training coupled with high-quality recovery. Encourage goals which direct their focus towards realistic evaluations – in particular, focusing on the mastery aspects of their performance.

Going deeper into the theory

There is some evidence to suggest that perfectionism is more common in sports performers than in the general population (Dunn et al., 2005). As a practitioner it is inevitable that you will meet perfectionists and you need to be aware that there may be elements of the motivational climate around the performer which are contributing factors.

Stroeber (2012) presents a very useful theoretical summary of the modern, multidimensional model of perfectionism, dividing the 'healthy' strivings from the 'unhealthy' concerns. However, what can often happen is that the individual presents with a blend of both, and the negative evaluations dominate, causing emotional distress. This distress may ultimately lead performers to avoid high-level competition because they cannot manage the fear of failure which comes with it.

In applied work, I have adapted the cognitive-behavioural intervention exercises of Shafran et al. (2010) with good effect. In this approach the psychologist challenges the very fixed and unhelpful thinking around personal expectations and those of others, the fear of making a mistake and concerns about not being good enough. This is a very useful source and one I recommend.

Bibliography

Dunn, J.G.H., Gotwals, J., & Causgrove Dunn, J. (2005). An examination of the domain specificity of perfectionism among intercollegiate student-athletes. *Personality and Individual Differences 38* (6): 1439–1448.

Shafran, R., Egan, S., & Wade, T. (2010). *Overcoming Perfectionism.* Robinson.

Stroeber, J. (2012). Perfectionism and performance. In S. Murphy (Ed), *The Oxford Handbook of Sport and Performance Psychology* (pp. 294–306). Oxford University Press.

Q16

I'm a runner. I've been racing for 40 years but now I'm really slowing down and find it difficult to motivate myself

What do you want to happen in your running career for the next 5 years? I suspect that you might harbour ambitions to run as fast as you did when you were 23 years old – your age and the fact that there are other responsibilities in your life may mean that you can't train as often or as hard as you used to.

Do you want to improve a time or win an event or simply to fall back in love with running? Or perhaps all three? Motivationally, these types of outcomes overlap, but there are some important nuances which can impact profoundly on your thinking.

If winning or placing well in races was one of your competitive aims when you were younger it can be difficult to come to terms with being further down the field as you get into the veteran or masters competitions. Be aware of the race within the race to be the first in your age category and focus on that rather than the over-all position. However, be aware that focusing on outcome alone is fraught with motivational pitfalls. Your place in the race is deter-mined not by your performance, but by the performances of others.

My suggestion is to look beyond race position and focus on times. Race time is much more under your control. Reboot your running career by looking at each 5-year age category as a new career – where you can set personal bests (PBs) all over again. In masters competition the past really is a foreign country – looking back to PBs set in your 20s and 30s will probably not help in the here and now. Approach training as systematically as you did when you were younger, but be very aware that the old adage about recovery being the most important part of training is accentuated as you mature. Recovery will take longer and therefore improve-ments will be slower.

Let's look at the final issue of rediscovering the joy of running. Try taking a month off running and trying some new activities. If you crave the trails and tarmac at the end of it, you are probably in shape to fall back in love with running. You might seek new challenges, racing new events, taking in more travelling, new training groups, running on different surfaces or doing multievents. Runners can become very tied to old habits of training and racing. Breaking out of these can reignite the pure intrinsic joy of moving over the ground unaided and unrestrained.

Going deeper into the theory

My answer has been informed by goal orientation theory. The danger of the mastery–ego goal dichotomy is that it leads you to believe that people are motivationally binary – either all outcome-oriented or all process-oriented. This is rare. Performers are often a blend of both orientations and may flip between them in different contexts. The ego/outcome goals can be extremely energizing in getting people to engage in thorough preparation over long periods of time – to give them a chance of winning a race or being selected for a team. However, integrating these types of goals with more master/process-type goals which benchmark today's performance against yesterdays are the stepping stones to getting the desired outcome.

On the final point about re-engaging the love of running – intrinsic motivation. It is worth suggesting a period away from running to see whether offering permission not to be a runner any more is really what the questioner is seeking. If it is, then supporting transition out of the sport is clearly within your remit. It usually happens that the sabbatical alone rekindles the intrinsic motivation to be active and restart running, but suggesting different challenges can add to this.

Bibliography

Duda, J. (2005). Motivation in sport: the relevance of competence and achievement goals. In A.J. Elliot, & C.S. Dweck (Eds.), *The Handbook of Competence and Motivation* (pp. 318–335). Guilford Press.

Harwood, C., Hardy, L., & Swain, A. (2000). Achievement goals in sport: a critique of conceptual and measurement issues. *Journal of Sport and Exercise Psychology 22* (3): 235–255.

Q17

I am really good at writing training plans, but I really struggle to stick to them. Any advice?

You and many thousands of others.

The writing of training programmes, the formulation of new year's resolutions, diet plans, revision plans, work schedules – writing them is the easy part. People tend to be resistant to change. Don't admonish yourself for being weak. Developing new, positive habits is challenging. Recall the times when you have not managed to adhere to a training plan. What have been the barriers?

It is highly likely that time was a significant one: you were too optimistic about how much time you would have. Other things cropped up and took your time away from the training. There are 168 hours in the week. It often helps to audit your time and see where gaps exist. Time budgets often give hints about what you are prioritizing. Under pressure of time, people tend to prioritize the things they are most motivated to do. Look at the reasons for training that were powerful when you wrote the programme: have they become less so in time? With motivation comes energy; when you write the programme the motivation brought energy and enthusiasm which may wane in time.

Have you become bored with the training? The combination of repetition with a perceived lack of purpose and physical discomfort is what the military use to test potential recruits – it breaks the motivation of most people! It is very important, where possible, to keep training fresh with variety and different types of challenge.

I recommend performers fit their training into their normal day. If you have long tiring days ahead of you, the prospect of training last thing in the evening is unrealistic – aim to schedule it in earlier in the day when you have some energy. Aim to be flexible in your thinking. If you have 30 minutes, do a hard, condensed workout in the time you have rather than agonize over not having a full hour. Have a balance between thinking in terms of training blocks or weeks and the here and now. What can I do today to make my ultimate goal more likely?

Recruit support. Have a training buddy or buddies, someone whose company you enjoy and who can give you honest feed-back. Make a deal with your partner – no 'soft' back-outs. Give your friend a list of things you can use to miss a session and a list of reasons which are 'soft' – this can be great fun but does have a purpose. Yes, there will be times when you cannot train, but there will be others which are 'soft' and you want your buddy to act as your training conscience.

Remember training is a choice, not a compulsion or addiction. Equally, no one will give you a medal for not missing a day of train-ing: You can miss a day, it's not a disaster. Don't judge yourself as a failure. Restart where you left off. Don't see missing a day as the end of the world or as evidence that you have failed again. Everyone lapses – just don't let lapses last weeks or months!

Going deeper into the theory

Adherence is a major issue in behavioural change. People often get very excited by a training programme, like a new year's reso-lution. But once that initial enthusiasm has dissipated, there is a realization that to get the outcome they want, long-term com-mitment and a high degree of effort are required. A good deal of research has been published looking at adherence in a range of lifestyle-related areas. The review by Dalle Grave et al. (2011) is not specifically about adherence to sports training but is a useful 'way in' to understanding the complexity of maintaining adherence. Their approach adopts a cognitive-behavioural framework which examines the decisions to train or not to train in terms of incentives and barriers. Practitioners are encouraged to work with clients to review the patterns of behaviour around adherence, identifying what the main barriers are; for example, time, price, facilities, lack of knowledge, lack of social support and more psychological issues, such as a reduction in motivation. The role of the practitioner is to work collaboratively, with the performer and perhaps the coach, to make it as easy to adhere as possible.

Bibliography

Bull, S.J. (Ed.) (2001). *Adherence Issues in Sport and Exercise*. Wiley.
Dalle Grave, R., Calugi, S., Centis, E., Ghoch, M.E.L., & Marchesini, G. (2011). Strategies to increase the adherence to exercise in the management of obesity. *Journal of Obesity 2011*: article ID 348293.

Q18

I seem to have lost my motivation to win. I was the leading woman in my age group in a recent 10k race, going well, but at about 8k another competitor came up to my shoulder and passed me. I didn't really mind; I was pleased for her. Have I lost my competitive mojo?

I view running as a very simple decision-making process – at any point in a run, you have one of three (possibly four) decisions to make and act upon: speed up, stay the same, slow down (the fourth is stop!). What complicates the decision is your willingness to push yourself beyond what feels comfortable.

Is this the first time this has happened or is it something which has evolved over the season? Has anything else changed? Are you training with a new group? Are you returning from injury? The reason for all the questions is that it sounds like your motivational orientation has shifted from being focused on the outcome to other motives, such as seeing competition as something to be enjoyed in a different way.

Many performers are driven by a motive to be the best and to be recognized as such. This sounds like how you used to be. You were driven to be the first across the line. This was the reason you trained and raced hard. So what has changed?

Some runners find that, as they get older in the sport and have achieved some success, their motives change from being ruthlessly competitive to enjoying the social aspects of the sport or competing only against themselves.

This feels like mellowing, but actually it is a very useful way of staying in the sport. You are becoming aware that competition with others is always a relative process – outcomes depend on who you are racing. You can benchmark yourself against the opposition but it is competition against yourself which will enable you to improve your times and perhaps place or win. Which is more important to you – a win in a slow time or a season's best out of the medals?

If you want your racing mojo back, we need to design some new strategies which address your current patterns of thinking. The racer only needs to be 1mm ahead at the finish to accomplish her goal – to bear the pain willingly for 1 second longer than her opponent. Can you do this? As a rival comes to your shoulder can you respond? As you catch a rival in a race, can you go by with 'race face' set? All this needs to be practised. You can practise this when you do interval training with club mates – attack them and respond as they attack you. You can also mentally rehearse this. Replay and re-edit the image you have of your rival passing you recently – how do you want to respond? How will that feel? Practise this. How does it feel?

Going deeper into the theory

I think this question again highlights the inextricable link between the goals that people set and motivational theory. For this performer winning has lost some its power to reinforce. The prospect of winning is no longer enough to encourage her to maintain her intensity and effort and respond to the challenge of an opponent. Winning has become a nice possibility, not something to fight for.

To regain its power to reinforce, the runner needs to reconnect with more ego-oriented motives and gain control with thoughts around not that I 'must win' but more that if someone is going to beat me then she will have to work very hard.

Bibliography

Deaner, R.O. (2013). Distance running as an ideal domain for showing a sex difference in competitiveness. *Archive of Sexual Behaviour 42*: 413–428.

Gilbertson, E. (2016). Vicious competitiveness and the desire to win. *Journal of the Philsophy of Sport 77*: 1–15.

Q19

My son has just started competing in downhill mountain bike races. I am very concerned that he will crash and seriously hurt himself. I don't want to discourage him because he has never shown as much interest in any sport but equally I want to make sure that he is not doing anything reckless

A quick reality check: downhill mountain bike racing does present objective risks. The injury data show you are more likely to sustain injury in downhilling than in any other type of riding. However, it should be noted that downhilling presents roughly the same level of exposure to injury as equestrian sport and downhill ski racing. You don't indicate the age of your son, but I suspect that there will be a hint of teenager's brain in the mix here. It is a generalization, but there is some evidence to indicate that a characteristic of the young adult brain is an inability to process fully the consequences of behaviour. His apparent fearlessness may be the result.

I think it's good that you have acknowledged the positive side of his riding – it is a great sport and a great way to be active in the natural environment. The downside is that he probably will crash and some of those crashes will be nasty! But I suspect that the harder you push him to stop, the harder he will push back.

Resist also the temptation of a motivational battle around resources. Downhilling can be an expensive sport: saying that you support his decision to race and then using financial barriers to control his involvement will probably backfire, making him more determined to participate.

My first suggestion is to consider carefully what *you* want to happen. His decision to race downhill may be the first inkling you have received that the relationship you have with your son is changing. He wants to push boundaries, he wants to show he is big enough to look after himself. As any parent would, your first instinct is to protect him, perhaps even to protect him from his own bravado. Aim to put your fears to one side, but if you are unable then you do need to speak to your son about it.

Secondly, if he is really determined to continue with down-hilling, look at the control measures you can put in place. Find a good, well-qualified coach who can build his skill level and expose him in a graded way to competition. Let him mix with more experienced riders. There will be bravado, but he will also get a first-hand appreciation of the risks he is exposing himself to. Look also at the protective equipment he is using, his helmet and armour: this will be his first line of defence should he and his bike part company.

Going deeper into the theory

This is a tricky question!

I have included it here as it highlights a difference in motivations between a young performer and a parent. I could have included it in the later section on young performers and focused exclusively on the motivational aspects of downhill riding. However I have covered the theoretical background of high-risk sporting activities in an earlier question. I will look in more detail at how to resolve this mismatch between the motives of the young rider and those of the parent.

Downhill mountain bike racing is a sport with an objectively elevated risk of physical injury. The motives for participation are often around the thrill and excitement coupled with the technical challenge. However as a parent your instinctive motivations are to protect and avoid risk. This can be a very difficult situation to accept.

I have used materials from the www.raisingchildren.net.au website to help parents get a more positive view of risk-taking behaviour in their children. They take a pragmatic approach to helping parents and their children develop a more balanced and healthy view of the natural tendency among teenagers to be attracted to risky activities. The recommendations are based around maintaining good communication between parent and child, another reason for not getting into a motivational battle.

Where the consequences of actions are discussed, an open discussion can take place around how best to prepare and prevent the more negative ones. Some ground rules for risk management are established around not riding alone and not taking on unrealistic routes through bravado.

You might also encourage parents to 'buddy up' so that they can support each other and discuss their approaches to coping with the anxiety of watching their children compete.

Bibliography

Sercombe, H. (2014). Risk, adaptation and the functional teenage brain. *Brain and Cognition 89*: 61–69.

Pulling the threads together

Motivation – it's complicated!

One of the most useful metaphors for human consciousness is that of an unruly committee, made up of many members with their own individual agenda. Like any real committee, clarity of purpose and a strong convener can create a very effective working group, on task and getting the job done. I view motivation as that strong convenor – aligning and coordinating members and driving them forward towards their goals.

Despite helpful metaphors we must recognize that motivation in sport is a vast and complex topic. There are many lines of theory aimed at explaining why we do what we do. There are also many applied techniques which have been developed from the theory which have been used to build and sustain the mental energy to act. What are the clear 'take-away' messages from all this knowledge and application?

Motivation is a highly personal, even unique, set of thoughts which direct our behaviour. Many of us go through life not reviewing these – not asking some basic questions about what we want to happen, how much we are willing to invest in that choice – we become habit-bound. Reviewing and reconnecting with motives can be a powerful psychological 'declutter' which leads to growth.

The goals we set ourselves are a complex of mastery and outcomes, some determined by the environment and some determined by the drive for intrinsic satisfaction. Some are immediate, some are longer-term – some goals clash with the goals of others and some goals we set for ourselves are incompatible. The key to maintaining motivation is the daily reconnection and recommitment to the processes which determine our self-defined success.

Other people can help or hinder, but motivation is ultimately a fire you start for yourself.

IV

Can sport psychology stop me being sick with nerves before I perform?

You can practise the sport – it's more difficult to practise the emotion.

There are few areas of life where the control of emotion can have such a profound effect on whether you achieve your goals as sport. At the highest level of performance, where individuals and teams are well matched for fitness and skill, the ability to harness positive emotions and regulate negative ones often becomes the deciding factor.

Tuesday 7 July 2014, Belo Horizonte.

Brazil's footballers are playing in the semi-final of the World Cup. Expectations are high. The proud soccer nation demands success. The euphoria and pride of being the World Cup host quickly turned to shock, guilt and shame as the German team systematically dismantled them, scoring five unanswered goals in the first half-hour. Germany eventually won the game 7–1. The team were humiliated and as a country Brazil entered a state of national despair. What had gone wrong? How could this collection of the world's finest players, playing in their home country, have failed so dismally?

They also had on their staff a sport psychologist, Regina Brandão, a professor from the São Judas Tadeu University in São Paulo. Her role was to help the players relax and remain focused in the highly pressured environment of the world's highest-profile football competition. However, even in the lead-up to the semi-final, there were signs that emotional cracks were appearing. In the quarter-final penalty shoot-out three players were seen in tears even before any spot kicks were taken. The team captain Thiago Silva declined to take one of the penalty kicks. This lack of emotional control was noted in the Brazilian press. Antero Greco wrote: 'I see a team that is visibly nervous, I see a team that is tense, I see a team that is a bit desperate'. Another Brazilian sport psychologist, John Ricardo Cozac, was quoted that in the build-up to the semi-final that the team had 'demonstrated a dangerous lack of emotional control'.

That's sport. It has happened countless times before and will happen countless times in the future. The psychological skill of regulating emotion, of thriving under pressure, becomes the deciding factor in competition.

This story looks like a failure for sport psychology. The Brazilian team psychologist was employed to help players manage their emotions: did she fail or did the team fail? Or is it just more evidence that emotional control is perhaps the biggest challenge in sport performance?

People playing sport, at every level, experience a degree of emotional engagement it is difficult to reproduce in any other context. It is certainly extremely difficult to create such levels of engagement in laboratory settings, where psychologists do their research. However, because we are unable to produce the levels of emotional engagement in the 'clean and controlled' environment of the laboratory, it makes it very difficult to determine exactly how heightened emotion impacts on our thinking and ultimately on our behaviour.

The majority of this book so far has placed a great emphasis on the role that our thinking has on performance. In this chapter I will turn the focus on to feelings and emotions, positive and negative, and look at how what we feel can change our behaviour. The nature of emotion has been a key question for psychologists for over a century, and just like the problems we encountered in defining motivation in the previous chapter, despite all this attention there is no real consensus as to what emotion is and how it should be defined.

Pragmatically it is useful to view emotion in the following way:

- ◆ Emotions:
    - ✓ are feelings which sometimes are difficult to describe verbally
    - ✓ are in reaction to some event or situation
    - ✓ are subjectively experienced – two people experiencing the same event may experience different emotions
    - ✓ alter physiological functioning
    - ✓ can alter behaviour, i.e. make us play better or worse.

This summary gives us some clues as to why the study of emotion in sport is so important. Challenging situations may be viewed differently by different people. One player in a big event may experience positive emotions such as excitement, whilst another on the same team experiences negative ones, such as fear. Coupled with the fact that emotion has the potential to help us play better or completely undermine us, this shows us that we should not overlook the impact that emotion can have on both our experience of sport and our readiness to perform to our potential.

How do thoughts and feelings fit together?

Psychologists are often prone to separate the three facets of their discipline – thinking, feeling and behaving. It is usually done in order to simplify the question they are looking at, but there is a danger of looking at them in isolation and consequently offering overly simplistic explanations. A line of theory which aimed to show how thinking and feeling fit together was developed by Richard Lazarus (1991) in his cognitive-motivational-relational theory (CMRT).

In his approach Lazarus identified 15 core emotions (Table 4.1).

It is important to recognize that humans are very complex emotionally. It is unlikely that one emotion is experienced at a time. We weave complex patterns of emotions, some of which may contradict each other. However, at any point in time, there is a dominant emotion. On to this canvas more transient moods may be projected.

What causes me to feel a negative emotion rather than a positive one?

There is considerable debate about the ordering of what causes what in terms of thinking, feeling and behaviour. Some theorists argue that it is the emotion that prompts the thought. Lazarus directly opposes this in identifying the thought processes which generate emotion. He has skilfully integrated existing knowledge on two

TABLE 4.1 Themes in core emotions and their application to sport

Core emotion	Theme	Example of provoking situation
Anger	A physical or psychological offence against me or those close to me	An incorrect decision by a match official
Anxiety	Facing an uncertain threat	Nervousness in anticipation of performance
Fear	Facing an immediate danger	Standing at the top of an icy Black run
Guilt	Having broken a moral rule	Retaliated to foul play by an opponent
Shame	Having failed to live up to an ideal	Having failed when expected to succeed
Sadness	Having experienced a significant personal loss	Losing place in starting team ahead of key game
Envy	Wanting what someone else has	Looking at resources another club has to support players
Jealousy	Resenting another person for loss or threat	Losing players to a rival club that can offer greater incentives
Disgust	Taking in or being close to an unacceptable or unpleasant idea	Reaction to discovery of illegal performance-enhancing drug use
Happiness	Making progress towards the achievement of a goal	Satisfaction at block of high-quality training completed
Pride	Enhancement of one's feeling of self through taking credit for an achievement	Coach approval of consistently high levels of commitment
Relief	Conditions have changed for the better	Discovery than an injury is not as serious as imagined
Hope	Fearing the worst but yearning for the best	Emotions at key moments, such as penalty shoot-out
Love	Desiring or giving unconditional affection	Close trusting and respectful relationship with team mates
Compassion	Being moved by the plight of others	Team mate injured leading up to major competition

Adapted from Lazarus (1991).

thinking processes, cognitive appraisal and coping, to present an explanation as to how emotions are generated and regulated.

Cognitive appraisal is viewed as a two-step process: primary appraisals determine whether a situation or event is viewed to be important in terms of achievement goals. If it is viewed to be important, a secondary appraisal is conducted where individuals assess their ability to cope – do they have the skills, are they able to regulate their emotions and maintain control and also to appraise the costs or benefits of the outcome? Lazarus suggests that the emotional response, positive or negative, is based on this process of thinking. Simplistically, If I believe I can execute the skills and there is a personal benefit to me for doing so, then my emotional response is more likely to be a positive excitement. If on the other hand I am confident that I won't be able to perform to the expectations of myself or others, or will not be able to maintain composure in performance, then the emotional response is more likely to be negative. This of course assumes that the process is a rational and unbiased one – which may not be the case. Some people are prone to filtering out the objective data indicating that they have coped in the past and therefore experience an elevated sense of threat and anxiety – reminding the practitioner that rational thought may not always dominate.

Do I see performance as an opportunity or a threat?

The work of Jones et al. (2009) casts light upon the question of why performance is viewed sometimes as a challenging opportunity and at others as a threat to be avoided if at all possible. Their work has built on two existing lines of theory – the biopsychosocial model of challenge and threat proposed by Blascovich and Tomaka (1996) and the facilitative/debilitative model of stress and performance developed by Graham Jones and Swain (1995). Blascovich and Tomaka had previously shown that threat and challenge produce very different physiological responses – a challenge is viewed as something that can be coped with, whilst a threat is a task which is believed to be overwhelming to one's ability to cope. It is important here to note that we are talking about your perception of your ability to cope, not your actual objective coping resources – these would be very difficult to quantify. People may be biased in their perceptions – they may make biased judgements of their coping resources, either overestimating or underestimating, and therefore tend always to see things negatively as threat or always see things positively as challenge.

Jones and Swain's (1995) model reinforced this idea, indicating that for some people the experience of performance anxiety, although it is negative and unpleasant, can have a positive impact on performance. Graham Jones' directional model of stress and performance shows us that a perception of control is central in determining whether performance is positively or negatively affected by stress. This again is more complex than it seems. Control can mean a number of things: a high level of belief in your ability to execute the necessary skill, or a high level of belief in your personal ability to control emotions. The result of this theoretical development is that some key aspects of thinking are linked to whether you view performance to be a threat and experience negative emotions or a challenge and experience positive ones.

I have adapted a figure from the work of Jones et al. (2009) which identifies the stages in the thought process (Figure 4.1). It should however be noted that linear and blocked diagrams fail to capture the complexity of human thinking. In reality, thoughts don't fit into boxes and the arrows can be double-ended.

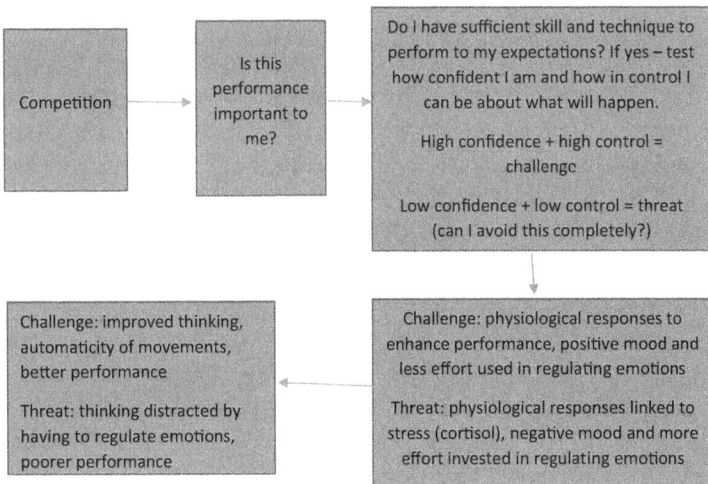

```
Competition → Is this performance important to me? → Do I have sufficient skill and technique to
perform to my expectations? If yes – test
how confident I am and how in control I
can be about what will happen.

High confidence + high control =
challenge

Low confidence + low control = threat
(can I avoid this completely?)

Challenge: improved thinking,          Challenge: physiological responses to
automaticity of movements,             enhance performance, positive mood and
better performance                     less effort used in regulating emotions

Threat: thinking distracted by         Threat: physiological responses linked to
having to regulate emotions,           stress (cortisol), negative mood and more
poorer performance                     effort invested in regulating emotions
```

FIGURE 4.1   Challenge versus threat.

How do emotions have an impact on sport performance?

Figure 4.1 gives a clue about the three ways in which emotions impact on performance in sport. Emotions can influence and be influenced by: (1) motivation; (2) physiology; and (3) the type of thinking processes a person engages in. If a performance is not viewed as important or is motivationally neutral, the emotional engagement is low and the consequences unimportant. However, if a performance is viewed as very important, the performer will invest a great deal of physical and mental effort into getting it right and getting the result strived for. Under these conditions, a good performance or a good execution of a skill in performance will generate pride and happiness and lead to wanting to try to do it again and improve. On the other hand, an error may lead to guilt and shame, which may lead to a more complex behavioural response. If confidence is still high, One might seek opportunities to have another go, to make up for the error; this is a positive response. There is a possible negative consequence to the error: if confidence is low, One might avoid the situation and withdraw, fearing more shame and guilt from making a further error.

Physiologically, emotional responses are closely related to the operation of the autonomic nervous system. It is a very complex integrated series of endocrine (hormone-producing) and nervous structures and I don't intend to go into a great deal of detail in this text. For the purposes of this discussion we need to know that it is the autonomic nervous system which regulates the 'fright, flight, fight, flee' response and that it is this system which is responsible for the production of key performance-related hormones such as adrenaline, testosterone and cortisol. There is evidence that the physiological events linked to emotion are closely related to the experience of emotion, in particular, the way in which increases in physiological arousal are interpreted and impact on the generation of either positive or negative emotions.

We just need to control our arousal levels!

Physiological arousal is a general term to indicate the level of activity in the central nervous system. The concept of arousal is an important one, but one which still provokes some misunderstanding: for example, In the Euro16 soccer competition, Chris Coleman, the Wales manager, was interviewed about an upcoming match against England. He noted that it was important for his players to control their arousal – a comment which resulted in sniggered asides from the journalists. Coleman was using the term accurately, whilst the journalists focused on the link between the term arousal and sex. Sexual arousal is a subsystem within the physiological arousal process: it is linked to the autonomic nervous system but is very specific and, trust me on this, not directly linked to athletic performance.

There is much debate around the definition of arousal, but broadly, the concept is concerned with how awake or alert you feel. In the early days of sport psychology research a number of theories (now thankfully superseded) presented the startling conclusion that the more awake you felt, the better you played. But if you were too awake you started performing worse again. Understanding has developed since then!

Increased arousal has the potential to help us run faster, jump higher and lift or punch more powerfully. However, increased arousal has also been shown to result in a loss in coordination, a reduction in the accuracy of fine movements and a loss of efficiency in movement. Coupled with this, increased arousal presents the thinking part of the brain with a great deal of information to process. High arousal can be interpreted as a whole range of things – excitement, fear, joy or terror. In performance we will often encounter increased physiological arousal – increased heart and breathing rate, increased blood sugar levels, sweaty palms and a desire to go to the bathroom. These potentially are positive signs, especially if your performance involves running, jumping or hitting, but only if these symptoms are viewed positively and generate positive emotions.

Understanding emotion is one thing: understanding what emotion does to your sport performance is quite another. All performers should know their ideal performance 'temperature' – without this knowledge, you are unable to self-regulate. You are limiting your ability to thrive under the inevitable pressure of performance.

Bibliography

Blascovich, J., & Tomaka, J. (1996). The biopsychosocial model of arousal regulation. *Advances in Experimental Social Psychology 28*: 1–51.

Jones, G., & Swain, A. (1995). Predispositions to experience debilitative and facilitative anxiety in elite and non-elite performers. *The Sport Psychologist 9*: 201–211.

Jones, M.V., Meijen, C., McCarthy, P.A., & Sheffield, D. (2009). A theory of challenge and threat states in athletes. *International Review of Sport and Exercise Psychology 2* (2).

Lazarus, R.S. (1991). *Emotion and Adaptation*. Oxford University Press.

Q20

How do you calm the nerves?

This is a great question! One which needs some careful questioning to give additional information before we can make progress.

Firstly, are you usually the type of person who finds performance can make you feel nervous? If you are, then you probably score higher on a trait anxiety questionnaire than others. This means that you tend to see achievement and evaluation situations more threatening than a person who scores lower.

Secondly, are nerves a normal part of your pre-event? Or is this a new experience for you? If nervousness is not a normal part of your experience but something about this event has caused you to feel nervous, then thinking about what is different in this case can be very helpful. For example, I often meet and work with performers who have been selected for a major event. Throughout the selection competitions they have felt excited and challenged but not nervous. Now at the major event they feel nerves, suggesting that they see the event as being really significant and that they *must* prepare differently. If you were selected for the Ryder Cup, it would be the same game as you play in a monthly medal – only it wouldn't be, would it!?

Lastly, are there any specific things, a specific opponent or skill, which you think might be provoking your nerves? The emotions associated with nervousness are often anxiety, which can be quite a generalized feeling anticipating uncertainty, and fear, which is usually focused on to a specific target.

To control anxiety, we would want to understand whether it is the physical symptoms or the negative thinking which are challenging you more. If it is the physical symptoms these can be addressed through general relaxation, focusing on slower, deeper breathing to reduce arousal. You don't want to feel drowsy, but you do want to slow the heart and breathing rate to a point where you feel comfortable and in control.

If it is the thoughts which are more challenging, we need to recognize that the brain can only process limited amounts of information at once. We need to give it a helpful job to do rather than leave it to its own devices. Give it some task-relevant things to think about – things which help rather than hinder, for example, affirmative self-talk or 'swing thoughts'.

Where there are specific fears, these can be addressed using a thought-restructuring technique, so the fearful inner voice, 'I'm no good, I shouldn't be here, I'm not as good as these guys', becomes replaced with 'This is my chance to show how good I am – if they want to beat me, It's going to cost them!'

Going deeper into the theory

Pre-event nervousness is very common. Performers often pro-ject themselves into an uncertain future and engage in irrational, frequently destructive and negative patterns of thinking. Cognitive-behavioural therapy developed from the work of Beck et al. (1979) provides a very helpful framework for identifying the types of thinking which lead to anxiety and the symptoms of nervousness.

These include:

◆ all-or-nothing thinking:
  ✓ where everything is either fantastic or it is awful
◆ overgeneralization:
  ✓ where we always lose against this opposition or on this course
◆ mental filtering:
  ✓ filtering out the positive aspects of preparation and placing emphasis on the parts which haven't been completed
◆ discounting the positives:
  ✓ ignoring all the positive information indicating readiness
◆ jumping to conclusions:
  ✓ making a negative evaluation despite there being no supporting evidence
◆ loss of proportion (catastrophizing or minimizing):
  ✓ if I play badly here, it will be a disaster
◆ emotional reasoning (reifying):
  ✓ thinking my emotions are real and shared by others
◆ labelling or mislabelling:
  ✓ describing a situation in an overstated, emotionally laden way
◆ thinking in absolute terms:
  ✓ should, ought or must – such labelling establishes inflexible parameters – there can be no negotiation around context
◆ personalizing or taking blame:
  ✓ attributing responsibility for failure to oneself – often whilst attributing responsibility for success to others.

Beck described a triad of symptoms: negative thoughts about the self, e.g. that I can't cope; negative thoughts about the environment, e.g. that the world or my immediate version of it is unfair; and negative thoughts about the future, e.g. that I will probably fail in what I'm intending to do. This gives three possible points of intervention. Calming the nerves may require you to address some of the 'faulty' thinking which can generate an experience of threat rather than one of more positive challenge.

Calming the physical aspects of nervousness can be more straightforward. Practising techniques around arousal management through breath control and progressive muscle relaxation has been shown to be highly effective.

Bibliography

Beck, A.T., Rush, A.J., Shaw, B.F., & Emery, G. (1979). *Cognitive Therapy of Depression*. Guilford Press.

Q21

Every soccer game my son plays he feels sick the night before and tells me he doesn't want to play. Most days he is fine when he gets there but occasionally he is sick in the dressing room before he plays. I don't know what to do!

A couple of things before I start. Is your son's reaction the night before a game new, or has he always had that kind of reaction? Is it just football that he responds to in this way, or are there other kinds of performances he feels sick before?

If it's new, what has changed recently that could account for the reaction? If it is just football, would it be possible to speak to your son and find out why football makes him feel that way, but not music performances or school tests?

In general terms children (everyone actually!) can experience nervousness before performances for one or a combination of six reasons:

1. It involves some kind of performance – you have to execute some skills.
2. The performance is public – people will be able to view your performance.
3. The performance may be evaluated by members of the audience.
4. The outcome is uncertain.
5. The outcome is valued – you want certain things to happen but you are not sure if they will.
6. You may have a specific fear about a skill or challenge, an opponent or a role or interactions with team mates/coaches.

Somewhere in there is the reason your son is nervous to the point of feeling or actually being sick before he plays.

Looking at the list there are some things which are more controllable than others. First of all, encourage your son only to think about the things that he can control – execution of skill, his effort levels and his thinking. He needs to work on the thinking habit, 'If I can't control it, I'm not going to worry about it'.

The first three points in the list are around executing skills. It may be that in the hours leading up to performance his thinking becomes preoccupied with the things he thinks he can't do as well as he'd like, or as well as he perceives others to do them. (See the answer to question 20, above.) He may fear negative evaluation from his peers, coach or other important people. No 12-year-old is the 'finished article' in anything, so this thinking should be challenged. 'I can't do it' type of thinking can be restructured into 'I can't do it *yet*' thinking. To achieve this your son should look at what he does in training. Can he spend 15 minutes after training working on the specific skill he is concerned about? This can be difficult as it will stand out with his peers. But if he is comfortable it can help, or the additional skills training can be done away from the club setting. The key thing here is that he only compares himself with himself – not others whom he perceives to be more skilful. If he is better today than he was yesterday he is moving in the right direction.

Addressing the uncertain outcome is problematic. No one has the gift of seeing the future. Your son may well have an expectation that he will be 'man of the match' every week and anything less is a failure. He cannot control this outcome; many other people and events have to be factored into this.

But every week he can work to be the most enthusiastic player on his team, the most positive, the most engaged – he controls those more, and it will probably help. However, he needs to address the way he thinks about and evaluates his own performance. If he expects a 10/10 performance every week, he may become disheartened by the fact that many performances are not perfect, although they are 'good enough'. Strive for perfect, yes, but do not allow it to become a perfect-or-awful dichotomy. Encourage him to reflect on aspects of his performance, take confidence from the things he does well and identify the things he can work on. *Please* remember he is 12 years old. The most important thing is that he continues to love playing football – it is that intrinsic love of the game which will drive his desire to improve.

Lastly, it might not be the football which is making him nervous. It could be that the behaviour of some of his team mates or the coach is provoking his response. You will only find out by asking the right question at the right time.

Going deeper into the theory

There are several strands of theory coming together here.

Anxiety is an emotional response to perceived threat (Spielberger et al., 1983; Spielberger, 1989). It is a complex construct and practitioners should engage with the literature from mainstream psychology to develop a thorough understanding. The sport psychology literature tends to be quite narrow in its scope around anxiety and primarily focuses on the relationship between anxiety and performance. The area is much deeper than this.

This client appears to be highly trait anxious, which is why I have asked the question about whether he experiences nervousness in other contexts. Trait anxiety refers to a negative emotional state that is chronic and pervasive across situations and is not triggered by specific events. Trait anxiety is the basis for a variety of anxiety disorders, including generalized anxiety and social phobia. In contrast, state anxiety refers to anxiety that occurs in response to a specific situation and usually has clear triggers. Not everyone who has high state anxiety has high trait anxiety, but those who have high trait anxiety are likely to experience state anxiety. Trait anxious individuals are predisposed to perceive threat in a variety of objectively low-threat situations and to experience a cognitive and emotional response characterized by worry, apprehension, fear and bodily tension. Trait anxiety should be viewed as a continuum from very low to very high. In my practice I tend not to use pencil-and-paper tests to assess trait anxiety as it can be detected through observation and interview. Also I have found that telling people who are highly trait anxious that they are highly trait anxious usually doesn't help – it's just another thing for them to worry about!

Working with people who are highly trait anxious can be a profound challenge. Literature suggests that highly trait anxious individuals process information differently and are more prone to nervousness interrupting the smooth execution of well-learned skills. At the time of writing this text, I am frustrated by the lack of evidence around the development of interventions for the management of performance anxiety in highly trait anxious individuals. Many highly competent performers fail to fulfil their potential because of their inability to manage the symptoms of anxiety.

Secondly, let's develop the point around interventions. There are two types of intervention typically used to manage nervousness – ones which address the cognitive basis, by stopping or challenging the seemingly overwhelming, automatic negative thinking, and interventions which focus more on the management of the bodily reactions to nerves, through muscular relaxation or breath control. At our current state of knowledge the management of trait anxiety remains a challenge.

Bibliography

Spielberger, C.D. (1989). *State-Trait Anxiety Inventory: Bibliography* (2nd edn.). Consulting Psychologists Press.

Spielberger, C.D., Gorsuch, R.L., Lushene, R., Vagg, P.R., & Jacobs, G.A. (1983). *Manual for the State-Trait Anxiety Inventory*. Consulting Psychologists Press.

Q22

I recently had a horse-riding accident. I wasn't badly hurt but I'm now too scared to get back in the saddle. What can I do?

What do you want to happen?

I'm presuming from your question that you are keen to get back on your horse but something appears to be stopping you. You appear torn – you want to be back on your horse but something you cannot quite identify is stopping you: you are calling this fear.

There is good news, and some bad news.

Once we are able to clarify what the specific fear is, then we can address it and take steps to achieving what you want to happen. The bad news is that it might take a little bit of time.

I suspect that the fear is primarily around the physical injury you suffered as a result of falling. Falling and hurting yourself is an ever-present risk in riding. But let's look at the facts. In your career you haven't fallen very often and when you have, you have had a few bruises, but nothing more serious. This may be part of the issue in itself. When falling is rare and you perceive it as a complete disaster, your thinking is to avoid falling at all costs. All your technical training is aimed at staying on the horse and riding well. Falling may be a prompt to tighten and polish your technique further and even look at stretching to thinking about developing techniques of falling safely. This is the approach taken by jockeys. Look at some of the resources offered at the British Racing School (www.brs.org.uk/courses/fall-train/). They recognize that falling is part of the sport and developing techniques to fall safely are part of thorough preparation.

Don't expect to go from where you are now straight back to where you were directly before the fall. Look at incremental steps back, don't force it and make sure that you feel comfortable at each step before progressing. Some riders respond to a flooding approach, where the sooner they are back on their horse the better. Others prefer a gradual reintroduction. Once the physical injury has fully healed, identify some basic element of riding, for example, posture. For the first week your goal is to achieve relaxed posture at walking pace. I want you to think about that when you ride, not your fall. Gradually you will build up your confidence and return. If the fear begins to build you can calm yourself by taking deep centring breaths and replacing the negative thought with a positive 'I can'-type thought.

If you find you are hitting a block in returning, be kind to yourself. It's not a weakness; there could be something more serious going on. A trauma like this could result in a posttraumatic stress response. If your fears are prolonged and intense, and occur away from riding, I would recommend seeking professional advice via your general practitioner.

Going deeper into the theory

All equine sport has the scope to offer a high degree of risk of physical injury. This is most pronounced in eventing, point to point and national hunt but is apparent everywhere. A fear of falling is rational, but equally rational is to recognize that falling is part of the sport and that there are things than can be done to prepare for falling and mitigate its effect. Helmets and protective gear should be worn and checked regularly.

Risk taking in sport is a relatively poorly developed theoretical area. I have introduced aspects of this in question 19. The understanding of risk-taking behaviour specifically in equestrian sport is not well developed; there are more areas of commonality in active risk perception sports such as rock climbing and mountaineering than more passive ones such as parachuting. What this means is there is a cognitive load placed on riders, as they manage the level of uncertainty they are faced with. For example, in eventing, there are high- and low-risk options on many of the fences and technical challenges. This type of decision making can be part of the risk management preparation for a rider.

I have noted the distinction between gradual (progressive) desensitization and flooding as approaches to returning to riding. These two are the poles of behavioural therapy approaches. Flooding is a technique developed in the 1960s to treat phobias (Stampfl and Levis, 1967). It involves a deep and prolonged exposure to a phobic target. Evidence suggests that it is a weaker and more traumatic approach than progressive desensitization. The more progressive approach aims to reintroduce the phobic or traumatic event gradually, combining it with relaxation and addressing and challenging the negative thoughts associated. This approach is more likely to be effective, but may take longer.

I have also noted the issue of posttraumatic stress disorder (PTSD) here. It is not common but in rare cases a sport injury may present as a very deep-seated anxiety-provoking event. The symptoms of PTSD are hyperarousal, which is a state of increased autonomic nervous activity, flashbacks, avoidance or numbing of memories of the injury event. If this is experienced for a period after the injury, I would recommend that the client is referred to specialized clinical psychology support through the general practitioner. Treatment of PTSD is beyond the competence of most sport and exercise psychologists.

Bibliography

Barlow, M., Woodman, T., & Hardy, L. (2013). Great expectations: different high-risk activities satisfy different motives. *Journal of Personality and Social Psychology 105* (3), 458–475.

Stampfl, T.G., & Levis, D.J. (1967). Essentials of implosive therapy: a learning-theory-based psychodynamic behavioral therapy. *Journal of Abnormal Psychology 72*: 496–503.

Zuckerman, M. (2007). *Sensation Seeking and Risky Behavior*. American Psychological Association.

Q23

Is there a psychological test I could use to identify the players who are most likely to thrive under pressure in a penalty shoot-out?

Personally I am not an advocate of 'pencil-and-paper' approaches to selection for team or specific roles such as the one you have identified. What are my reservations?

Firstly, as a coach you will have either an actual or mental file of how your players cope with different pressures they have been put under in the past. For example, some players will have clearly responded to pressure situations by lifting their performance levels whilst others have struggled to cope. This is likely to be a stronger predictor than any pencil-and-paper test.

Secondly, there is a strong ethical guideline that without complete predictive validity (i.e. the test score predicts performance 100% of the time) psychological tests should not be exclusively used to determine selection.

Finally, players are not stupid. If they know that a score on a pencil-and-paper test is that strong in a coach's thinking they will not answer the test truthfully (incidentally, this is a problem with *all* self-report questionnaires in sport psychology and psychology in general). Quite understandably, they will modify their answers to make themselves more aligned with the coach's thinking.

My advice to you is this: thriving under pressure is a clear indicator for you in your selection processes. This should be communicated to the players. You need good records regarding how players respond. You may well have players who are technically very well developed, but who fail to perform under the highest pressure. You should intervene to prevent this becoming a pattern. Training and preparation should simulate the types of pressure the player will be exposed to. In the short term, you may need to select players of less physical and technical ability who can perform under stress. This is preferable because you can be sure of their performance.

This inevitably leads to the issue of whether you should practise penalties and penalty shoot-outs. Absolutely *yes*. Most skilled players can hit over 90% without any pressure. So let's put the skill under pressure – by adding fatigue and creating, albeit simulated, pressure. Get your team into groups of five and compete – players hate being publicly bested by their team mates. It can get very stressful. Think creatively. See what happens!

Going deeper into the theory

On the issue of using questionnaires in applied settings – there are many questionnaires that could be used but I feel that there are too many 'con' factors to recommend their use: self-reporting, self-presentational biases, practical issues of when they are presented. The majority of these questionnaires and inventories were developed to answer research questions rather than to add depth to assessment in applied settings. This point is developed well in a paper by Hagger and Chatzisarantis (2009). My feeling is that pencil-and-paper tests are relatively weak in comparison to observation and interview as assessments. There is a useful source which summarizes the pro/con debate around psychometric testing (Thomas, 2012).

Ethically, questionnaire and inventory scores are at best correlated with performance, usually weakly. I cannot endorse a predictor; as an applied psychologist I am interested in identifying strong determinants. There are no questionnaires or inventories which achieve this level of predictive validity. Sport psychology research is characterized by self-report measures. Most studies rely on the assumption that participants can accurately access and report the contents of their thinking and emotion, often constrained by the scope and interpretation of the question as it is framed in a questionnaire. This is highly problematic and contentious. Finally, if applied practitioners are to achieve their aspiration of creating interventions that help performers consistently fulfil their technical, tactical and physical potential, it is imperative that we work with coaches to create realistic and performance-like conditions. Despite the players knowing that it's training, not playing, they do need to experience pressure in training before they can be truly confident of their skills holding up when it really matters.

Bibliography

Hagger, M., & Chatzisarantis, N. (2009). Assumptions in research in sport and exercise psychology. *Psychology of Sport and Exercise 10* (5): 511-519.

Thomas, P. (2012) Using psychological tests to enhance skills in sport and performing arts. *InPsych 34*, 6. Retrieved 19 March 2016 from: http://www.psychology.org.au/publications/inpsych/2012#december2012.

Q24

We live in a small rural part of the country. When our team goes to play in the city, the girls are intimidated by the facilities and the support – it's like they are beaten before they begin

It is easy to be intimidated by, and envious of, the facilities and the whole ambience of bigger or better-resourced opponents. It's easy to be beaten by reputations. I would recommend that you talk about it with the team. You might be surprised how 'faulty' some of the thinking is. What sorts of things are the girls saying?

♦ 'They have all the national squad players – they are just so much better than us'.
♦ 'They have much better facilities than us – they must be better'.
♦ 'They have indoor facilities – they can practise when they want – they must be better'.
♦ 'They have much more coached sessions – they must be better'.

All of the first parts of the sentences may be true – they have access to better facilities, more training time and more coaching – but the conclusion that the players are inevitably better is a *faulty* conclusion.

In your questions the faulty conclusion leads to a helpless attitude: no matter what we do, we will not be successful. This is the cycle of thinking that you need to break. Rather than seeing a trip to the city as a threat, it is a fantastic challenge. We will play with the attitude that if they want to beat us it is going to cost them. Every point and every play will be contested, no matter what. We will fight; we will make it as difficult for them as possible. We will support each other noisily and energetically. They might win but they will certainly not take us lightly ever again. We will be good, respectful opponents but we are fearless and we will have a great day out!

Going deeper into the theory

This question centres on how the girls attribute cause. Their style of thinking is characteristically labelled as a *logical fallacy*, where thinking has formed a causal link between facilities, resources and coaching and their opponents' level of performance, i.e. better-resourced players will perform better than poorly resourced ones. This leads to attributional biases – 'if we are successful it is luck rather than ability' – and learned helplessness (Abramson et al., 1978) – a feeling that no matter what we do we cannot overcome this challenge, so therefore it isn't even worth trying.

Self-handicapping is a broad term used to describe a strategic way of thinking by which people reduce or withdraw effort from a task they believe they will not succeed in, in order to preserve their self-esteem (Berglas and Jones, 1978; Baumeister and Bushman, 2008). In this case, the prevalent thoughts about competing against city-based clubs and competitors is that we cannot be successful because the resources are so unequal. What they are ignoring is that it is the same game, requiring the same skills and played under the same laws as anywhere else.

The intervention here is to address openly the faulty thinking leading to self-handicapping, reinforcing the fact that they are performing the same skills as they always do and becoming 'blind' to the playing environment.

Bibliography

Abramson, Y.L., Seligman, M.P., & Teasdale, J.D. (1978). Learned helplessness in humans: critique and reformulation. *Journal of Abnormal Psychology 87* (1): 49–74.

Baumeister, R.F., & Bushman, B.J. (2008) *Social Psychology and Human Nature*. Thomson Wadsworth.

Berglas, S., & Jones, E.E. (1978). Drug choice as a self-handicapping strategy in response to noncontingent success. *Journal of Personality and Social Psychology 36* (4): 405–417.

Q25

After I have made a mistake, like dropped a pass or missed a tackle, I want the ground to swallow me up. I feel awful for the next 10 minutes

The problem here is that you are too good! Your skill level is such that you very rarely make mistakes. When you do, it becomes a very big deal indeed. The error has prompted you to 'go into your head' and become very focused on your thinking. I suspect that you will be future-oriented and 'mind reading' in your thinking – you will worry what your coach or team mates or spectators are going to say, and even if they don't actually say it, you believe that they are thinking it. It would be helpful to break out of this line of thinking. When you make a mistake like this, you need to remember two things. Firstly, the game hasn't stopped whilst you are 'in your head': you still need be engaged; opponents like nothing more than a player switching off for 10 minutes. Secondly, there is nothing you can do to rewind history and remove the error. It is a historical fact; it might be a defining moment in the game, but equally it might not. The critical thing is to ensure that one error doesn't become a second or a third.

How do I achieve this? There are some mind management techniques which can help. First, acknowledge the error and take responsibility for it to your team mates. Certainly don't blame a dropped pass on the passer – it might be that you are both responsible, but acknowledge your part. Allow yourself to get angry for 1 second and then 'park' the error. By 'parking' I mean it is history, so actively consign it to the past by cueing your next job. Remind yourself of the next thing you must execute. Don't make the mistake of immediately trying to make amends for the error. Calmly wait for the next opportunity. If you find yourself habitually dwelling on errors, have a cue word written down on taping or a drinks bottle, just to remind you – play in the here and now!

Going deeper into the theory

It is easy, as observers of sport, particularly high-performance sport, to assume that we are watching automatons executing skills. The precision and efficiency of the movements rarely result in errors and when they do we assume that performers have efficient strategies for 'parking' the error and ensuring that they are in the moment. In my experience, the mental skill of 'parking' errors is one of the most common areas of deficiency in performers at all levels.

As performers ascend the ladder of performance, their skills improve and the consequences of an error, even a small one, become magnified. However, we must always bear in mind that sport is a very messy affair and error is the price of skill, particularly when there is a trade-off between accuracy and speed. Yes, we want skills to be robust under the highest pressure, that is why we train, and in training, we should always aim to recreate as closely as possible the conditions you will compete under.

Of equal importance is the mind management skill of responding positively to an error. Errors can be defining moments in sport, for example, double faulting at a key moment in a tennis match, or missing a penalty in a shoot-out. How to do this is rarely spoken about – but it should be! Why bother giving developing players complex techniques and tactics, but ignoring the skills of management when these break down – as they *inevitably* will.

Psychologically, the key skill here is self-talk. By self-talk, psychologists refer to the inner dialogue in performers' heads as they compete. When all is going well, the voice may be quiet and the content positive. However, an error can turn the voice into an overwhelmingly critical one. Self-talk has several roles: it can be used to prompt the learning of new skills, to address and correct bad habits, to focus attention on task-relevant thinking and to build confidence (Hardy, 2006). In a meta-analysis Hatzigeorgiadis et al. (2011) indicated that self-talk is an effective performance enhancement strategy. There are some nuances to this in terms of the types of task, with self-talk appearing more effective in fine motor skills than gross movement.

The self-talk literature differentiates between types: motivational vs. instructional, positive vs. negative and overt vs. silent. Practically, when designing an intervention this is useful knowledge but the psychologist should bear in mind the individual with whom s/he is working. For example, an error 'parking' strategy for one individual may contain both motivational and instructional elements, aimed at remaining positively engaged and cueing the next skill. Another player may require only the instruction. The psychologist will work with the performer to establish an effective routine.

Bibliography

Hardy, J. (2006). Speaking clearly: a critical review of the self-talk literature. *Psychology of Sport and Exercise 7*: 81–97.

Hatzigeorgiadis, A., Zourbanos, N., Galanis. E., & Theodorkis. Y. (2011). Self-talk and sport performance. A meta-analysis. *Perspectives on Psychological Science 6*: 348–356.

Q26

What is the best way to learn skills to make sure that they don't break down under pressure?

Lovely question – it goes straight to the heart of the matter. If we don't practise skills in a way that recognizes that they will have to be produced under extremes, why are we practising them at all?

Firstly, let's just have a look at how skills are learned. We tend to go through three stages in learning a new skill. At first, we are just trying to make sense of what we are trying to do: this is called the verbal-cognitive stage; I'll call it the 'making sense' stage. The second stage is the 'coming together' stage where skills are more fluent, but still break down when put under any type of time or distraction pressure. As we go through this stage, we become better able to control the skills whilst also being able to do other things; for example, we can become aware of where an opponent is on the court whilst also executing the skill. The final stage is the autonomous stage, where we can execute the skill with minimal conscious thought. This is where the skill maintains its accuracy and efficiency, despite conscious thought going on to other tasks. The goal of practice is to get skills to the autonomous level as quickly as possible.

Now on to the main question. The problem with pressure is that it encourages us to think about the skill, rather than trust the 'feeling' of it. Skills tend to come out the way they went in! When we give people a lot of technical instructions they don't process the 'feeling' of the skill much – they just rely on the verbal coaching. Under pressure this can be a problem. It can lead them to go from executing the skill without really consciously thinking about it to the much earlier thinking-about or coming-together stages where the skill is less smooth and requires more effort.

So what does this mean for learning? Firstly, once the ABCs of the skill have been acquired – these really are the basic building blocks of the skill – coaches need to give less technical instruction and focus more on giving feedback on the tactical – doing the right things at the right moment – aspects of the performance.

They should also look to create drills and practices which aim to recreate the stress of actual competition. In practice, coaches should aim to break skills down, so that they can design interventions to make sure that doesn't occur in actual competition.

I am always pleased to hear performers who say that the training is harder than the competition – it means that the coach has prepared them well!

Going deeper into the theory

The line of theory I have engaged to answer this question is a combination of Masters (1992) and Masters and Maxwell's (2008) work on reinvestment and the cognitive-behavioural intervention around stress inoculation training (Meichenbaum, 1985).

Reinvestment theory is a collection of theories which aim to clarify the role that consciousness, and in particular conscious control of movement, has on performance. In some literature this is also referred to as *conscious processing theory* (e.g. Wilson et al., 2007). This approach suggests that when there is a focus on giving performers explicit instructions or rules when learning the movement, the skills are more prone to breaking down under performance stress. Why is this?

What is proposed reinforces the idea that well-learned skills are performed with as little conscious control as possible. Under performance stress, a performer may try harder to execute these skills and begin to reinvest conscious control of skills which are already established and efficiently controlled at a subconscious level.

The research suggests that a more implicit approach to learning cannot just yield excellent results but also makes the skills more resistant to breaking down under stress. Implicit learning theory acknowledges that many skills are acquired unintentionally and unconsciously. Practically, implicit learning occurs where a secondary task or other strategy is used to prevent explicit rules becoming the mechanism by which skills are learned. This inhibits the process by which conscious control is established for a movement.

Linked to the motor learning element of the question there is also an approach to 'stress proofing' skills by testing them under competition-like conditions ahead of performance. In this way skills can be inoculated and the performer can more confidently enter the competitive arena. Stress inoculation training is a method which can effectively be used in this context, where practices can be designed and worked through which address aspects of the performance that are prone to breaking down. In practice, these can be addressed and specific interventions, both physical, such as relaxation, and mental, such as thought stopping or restructuring, can be worked on.

Bibliography

Masters, R.S.W. (1992). Knowledge, knerves and know-how: the role of explicit versus implicit knowledge in breakdown of complex motor skill under pressure. *British Journal of Psychology 83*: 343–358.

Masters, R.S.W., & Maxwell, J.P. (2008). The theory of reinvestment. *International Review of Sport and Exercise Psychology 1*: 160–183.

Meichenbaum, D. (1985). *Stress Inoculation Training*. Pergamon Press.

Wilson, M., Smith, N.C., & Holmes, P.S. (2007). The role of effort in influencing the effect of anxiety on performance. Testing the conflicting predictions of processing efficiency theory and the conscious processing hypothesis. *British Journal of Psychology 98*: 411–428.

Q27

I'm a pro golfer. How do I manage my emotions when I am playing very well? I feel happy, satisfied and proud, but lurking behind it are fears that it might all start falling apart

This is a good point – positive emotions can be as distracting as negative ones. Supreme confidence can lead to impulsive and risky shot selection. There is also the challenge of managing your thinking in terms of maintaining the good play.

The clear bottom line with all of these possible sources of distraction is this: *Every shot is a discrete and independent skill. This means that every shot is viewed as equally important and every shot is approached in the same way.*

The unhelpful thinking you describe – worry about it all falling apart – is a great example of what I call *stinking thinking*. It is an example of ironic processing – we think about what we don't want to happen. This thought needs to be challenged and replaced by what you do want to happen.

You are playing well. Yes, golf can be a messy game sometimes and you do follow a birdie putt with a wild drive, but that doesn't mean that you are suddenly incapable of getting up and down and getting the par.

This can only happen if you manage your mind. Stinking thinking is unhelpful and serves to undermine.

Going deeper into the theory

The idea of the 'hot hand' or psychological momentum is a very prevalent one in sport. This idea is based on the way the human information-processing system tends to clump aspects of performance together into patterns rather than to view each performance as independent and unrelated. Many spectators, coaches and performers have the impression that when a performer has been successful in executing a skill, the probability of being successful again increases. Some studies have shown that this does occur. For example, a study by Raab et al. (2012) showed this effect in elite volleyball players. However, a larger analysis which pooled data from 22 different studies found very weak evidence supporting the idea of 'hot hand' or psychological momentum. This was the case in both individual and team sports (Avugos et al., 2013).

Research reinforces the idea that performers are best served to approach every play or every phase of play as independent of the last. Developing an effective pre-shot or pre-performance routine will serve them well, and maintain the intensity and effectiveness of play, irrespective of the scoreboard.

Bibliography

Avugos, S., Koppen, J., Czienskowski, U., Raab, M., & Bar-Eli, M. (2013). The 'hot-hand' reconsidered. A meta-analytic approach. *Psychology of Sport and Exercise 14*: 21–27.

Raab, M., Gula, B., & Gigerenzer, G. (2012). The hot-hand exists in volleyball and is used for allocation decisions. *Journal of Experimental Psychology: Applied 18*: 81–94.

Q28

How do you deal with fear in a training environment (particularly looking at gymnastics and trampolining, where learning skills can be scary and athletes experience fear)?

Fear is everywhere in sport. Fear of failure, fear of success, fear of pain, fear of being socially vulnerable – the list goes on. We fear because we don't know what is going to happen: our brains fill in the gaps. (I strongly suggest that you follow this up by reading Steve Peters' book, *The Chimp Paradox* – he presents a very compelling model which explains fear well.) Here you are talking specifically about fear of physical injury, and it is a genuine, objective risk. You are asking trampolinists to do moves which expose them to the risk of injury. Your job is to minimize the risk but you cannot eliminate it. This is why care needs to be exercised. Some performers are sensation seekers – they tend to embrace risk and enjoy the thrill of taking on a risky challenge. Their thinking is, typically, underestimating risk and overestimating their ability. This is potentially dangerous! They may be injury-prone as a result. The teenage brain is particularly poor at grasping the consequences of poorly appraised risk.

You may have performers who appear risk-averse because they overestimate the risk and underestimate their ability. These performers may need help to push on to the harder moves. How do you support them? You cannot force this. They need time and preparation – they will go at their own pace, which sometimes is maddeningly slow. Work through the progressions, recap, work through them again. Ultimately you arrive at a 'parachute moment' – I call it this – it is the moment when you are sitting in the plane doorway and you decide either to jump or not. The question for you to ask the athlete is, 'are you ready?' If yes, then go: if not, *don't push or coerce*: it might work but it might also destroy a trusting coaching relationship. If your performer consistently gets to the 'parachute moment' and says s/he is not ready, ask: 'what do you need to be more ready?' Address the issue and return. If you keep getting there and turning back, you have an interesting challenge. My advice is to back off and wait until the performer realizes s/he has the skills, and just needs to keep calm. Go back to the box breathing exercises, and go for it. A peer model can help. An issue for me is that you are working with the performer's consent at all times: there is no coercion.

Going deeper into the theory

Fear tends to have a specific target or focus, i.e. the person is fearful of something. It is important for the practitioner to get a sense of what specifically the performer is fearful of. In this way the intervention can be worked to address this issue or these issues specifically.

In terms of dealing with fear, a paper published in 1996 offers some good ideas for designing interventions. Magyar and Chase identified the following seven methods of managing fear-related anxieties: (1) thought stopping (a technique to break the automatic negative thoughts which appear to be hijacking the skill – a physical or mental trigger encourages the performer to 'go for it' rather than hesitating); (2) superstition – a superstitious routine or cue, again to replace the negative and fearful thought with a positive or more helpful one; (3) support or advice from the coach; (4) imagery, mentally rehearsing the skill; (5) positive self-talk; (6) relaxation; and (7) developing a skill-related focus. These techniques, which can be used independently or together, appear to act to build self-efficacy, which relates to the material I covered in the section on mental toughness in Chapter 6. Further evidence about the central role of self-efficacy in addressing fear has been presented by De Pero et al. (2013) in a study examining fear in elite-level gymnasts.

As a family of sports, gymnastic events are designed to test complexity and difficulty. All gymnastic sports have a tariff system which provides an index of difficulty. In competition there is a mix of compulsory and voluntary elements. In the voluntary sections, a performer can chose safe or risky elements, recognizing that the risky elements, if executed well, will give a competitive advantage. This can present a decisional dilemma – do I go for easy moves and execute them really well? Although if I do, I will nevertheless probably be beaten. On the other hand if I try moves which have a risk of failing and execute them well then I win.

This type of uncertainty places a great deal of stress on the ability of performers to regulate their emotions. Failure to execute a skill cleanly can, and often does, result in a physical injury. Advances in coaching, the use of foam beds and video techniques are all very useful, but at some point performers have to confront the fear in their minds that causes their heart to beat faster and their legs to feel like jelly. A range of techniques can be useful – self-talk, as discussed above. I would also advocate the use of imagery to rehearse mentally not just the technical elements of the skill but also the emotional components. Mental rehearsal based around the PETTLEP model (Holmes and Collins, 2001, 2002) is a very useful framework in this context, because it specifically addresses the emotional component. An imagery script which specifically addresses the fear of executing a move, by both addressing the accurate execution of the skill and managing the thoughts triggering fear and its emotional result, is addressing all areas.

Finally, there is a key ethical point in this question – the extent to which a coach can coerce the performer to try a skill she doesn't feel ready for. Ethically the dilemma is one of whether the coach believes the ends justifies the means – by pushing the performer to try a move which ultimately leads to her winning a competition – or not. This is a consequentialist view of ethics which is difficult to defend. The non-consequentialist view, where the coach has rules about how to coach all performers – waiting until they are clearly ready – is more defensible.

Bibliography

De Pero, R., Minganti, C., Pesce, C., Capranica, L., & Piacentini, M.F. (2013). The relationships between pre-competition anxiety, self-efficacy and fear of injury in elite TeamGym athletes. *Kinesiology 45* (1): 63–72.

Haselton, M.G., Nettle, D., & Andrews, P.W. (2005). The evolution of cognitive bias. In D.M. Buss (Ed.), *The Handbook of Evolutionary Psychology* (pp. 724–746). John Wiley.

Holmes, P.S., & Collins, D. (2001). The PETTLEP approach to motor imagery: a functional equivalence model for sport psychologists. *Journal of Applied Sport Psychology 13*: 60–83.

Holmes, P.S., & Collins, D. (2002). Functional equivalence solutions for motor imagery. In I. Cockerill (Ed.), *Solutions in Sport Psychology* (pp. 120–140). Thomson.

Magyar, T.M., & Chase, M.R. (1996). Psychological strategies used by competitive gymnasts to overcome the fear of injury. *Technique 16*: 1–5.

Peters, S. (2012). *The Chimp Paradox.* Vermillion.

Weinstein, N.D. (1980). Unrealistic optimism about future life events. *Journal of Personality and Social Psychology 39* (5): 806–820.

Pulling the threads together

This chapter has highlighted the importance of emotion and emotional regulation in sport. For the vast majority of sport performers, at every level, emotions are heightened. They may feel nervous, fearful or anxious, but equally, they may feel excited and hopeful. These feelings are generated from a complex interaction of thoughts which engage our physiological systems to create conditions which can help us play sport better or worse.

The big challenge is to be able to harness the positive effects of emotion, the 'kick' of adrenaline that comes with a challenge, to run faster, jump higher and hit harder, rather than become swamped by the negative effects, often of powerful, intrusive and seemingly automatic negative thinking.

Sport psychologists have adapted techniques from a range of other disciplines which can help performers think better, to experience the emotion as a challenge rather than a threat, whilst also harnessing the positive physiological benefits.

However, what is absolutely clear is that, for most people, regulating emotion is an incomplete and difficult challenge. Our ability to regulate emotion is not given the prominence it deserves as we prepare for performance – and as a consequence the ability to thrive under pressure remains an aspiration that most sport performers don't achieve.

V

Choking, ball watching and 'sledging' – applying the science of attention to staying focused in sport performance

'Keep your eye on the ball' – that often-repeated coaching mantra – is both a literal and metaphorical imperative. In many sports, being able to identify and maintain focus on the key pieces of information is essential to performance. Loss of focus, even for a split second, leads to errors. Unlike many areas of human performance, in sport it is a legitimate tactic to undermine your opponents' concentration by deception, play fakes or by sometimes directing abusive comments to them. Some of this behaviour sits outside of the spirit of sport, but it is common and is intended to disrupt concentration. It is essential that players develop an approach to concentration which allows them to manage and filter distractions and focus on the most important task at hand – the execution of skills at, or as close to, their physical and technical potential as possible.

Concentration and sport performance

Golf is a paradoxical challenge – in a 3-hour, 18-hole round, a player may play fewer than 70 shots, each lasting less than a second. Just over 1 minute of action and more than 2 hours and 58 minutes of thinking: about the last shot, the next shot, thinking about useful things and thinking about things which are about as helpful in the here and now as 'did I lock the front door when I left the house?'.

It is not surprising that most golfers recognize that golf is really a test of concentration.

Winner of golf Majors Paul Azinger said, 'Staying in the present is the key to the golfer's game: once you start thinking about a shot you just messed up. You're lost'.

But it's not just golf where concentration is central. In 1995 England's cricket captain Mike Atherton played one of the finest innings ever seen in test match cricket. Dragging his team back from the brink of almost inevitable defeat, he batted in the heat of Johannesburg against a hostile attack for 643 minutes – almost 11 hours. He faced 543 deliveries and scored 185 undefeated runs. He describes his mental state during that innings in his autobiography.

By the afternoon, and for the only time in my career I was in the zone. It is a state much talked about by sports psychologists and while I can describe my feelings, I couldn't begin to explain how to replicate it ... I was in an almost trance-like state. It was a state of both inertia and intense concentration and *I knew* that I was in total control and they couldn't get me out.

(Atherton, 2002)

In endurance events, performers often develop mental tricks either to distract themselves from the effort or to focus on it. Paula Radcliffe, holder of the marathon world best time, exemplifies this:

When I'm training, everyday things usually go through my mind. If I'm out on a run I might be thinking things like: what shall I have for dinner or what's going to happen in *EastEnders*? – anything really. If I'm running in a marathon race then other mind games come into play to keep my concentration, speed and tempo moving. That's when I start to count to myself. I know that if I count to 100 three times then that's usually about a mile for me at marathon pace.

(Radcliffe, n.d.)

It is interesting and informative that Radcliffe describes a different type of concentration when training – essentially distracting herself from the activity, whereas in competition she tunes into the task and its execution. This is an approach to concentration widely reported in long-duration endurance-type activities, but potentially problematic in game and gymnastic-type sports, where concentration needs to be intense and focused.

In gymnastic sports, technical errors are often attributed to lapses in concentration. A gymnast who misses a catch on the asymmetric bars or a diver who mistimes an entry is painfully reminded that you might be concentrating but you are not necessarily concentrating on the correct thing.

It is difficult to think of a sport where the mental skills of:

♦ identifying the right things to focus on
♦ screening out unhelpful things, like the crowd and the internal voice
♦ rapidly processing a complex, rapidly changing, volatile and often unpredictable environment

are not being tested. These examples, and there are many more I could select, give a powerful indication that maintaining a clear focus under the pressure of competition is an essential aspect of performance. It is one that many performers haven't fully developed and would benefit from working on.

Why do I lose concentration?

Sport psychologists tend to talk more about attention than concentration and focus. There is a reason for this: psychologists define attention as the process by which we direct our mental effort on to the specific features of the environment – the external world – or thoughts or movement – the internal world. The research literature (e.g. Moran, 2012) divides this into three areas:

♦ Concentration:
  ✓ investment of mental effort and resources to what is most important in any given situation
♦ Selection:
  ✓ the ability to zoom in on the most relevant or most task-related information whilst also filtering out what is not relevant or distracting
♦ Dividing attention between tasks:
  ✓ being able to shuttle rapidly between different information as dictated by the demands of the task.

When concentration wavers or becomes distracted it is because one or more of these areas of mental effort has failed or is working below the required or optimal level.

Filters, searchlights and limited capacity – metaphors to help make sense of attention

A number of models have been developed to help understand how these components of attention contribute to the overall picture. Filter theories date back to the 1950s and are primarily concerned with trying to understand what happens to the information that we don't actively attend to. Every minute of your life, you are exposed to a huge volume of information, externally via your sense organs, and internally from your conscious thoughts and your internal senses, giving you information about the position of your limbs and other physiological states. We can only consciously process a fraction of this information. Filter models aim to explain why some information is processed whilst the remainder is discarded.

Another model, using a search light or torch beam metaphor, helps us understand that we can choose where to place the attentional focus. Ideally, we want to point the torch beam of our senses and thoughts towards the information which is task-relevant and allows us to capture the most critical cues. The reason for this relates to the final group of models. Capacity models propose that human attention has a limited size. Where information is complex, conflicting or rapidly shuttling between internal and external focus (as is often the case in sport), it is highly likely that the capacity for processing will be exceeded. When this happens performance is usually negatively affected.

Lapses in concentration come when we turn the search light of our thoughts and senses on to the wrong things, we are unable to control a powerful or intrusive distraction or we become over-whelmed with too many things at once. However, many sports training or coaching manuals provide little in the way of help in guiding us on what to think about or attend to when we are training or playing. This is a vital but neglected aspect of preparation.

Nideffer's model of attentional style

In 1976, Robert Nideffer proposed a model which suggested that people have a predisposition to process information, that is, they

	Broad	
	Focusing on a whole field of play	
Focusing on general thoughts and plans		
Internal		**External**
Focusing on a specific thought or concern	Focusing on one specific aspect of play	
	Narrow	

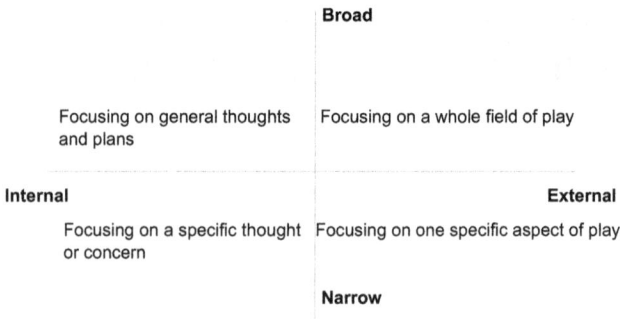

FIGURE 5.1   Nideffer's two-axis model of attentional style – broad–narrow/ internal–external.

tend to turn their 'attentional searchlights' in specific directions. He identified two primary attentional dimensions: internal–external and broad–narrow (Figure 5.1).

This model is particularly useful as it simplifies what often seems like a very complex phenomenon – what am I attending to? And is what I am attending to helpful or not?

When planning or mentally rehearsing, an internal focus, minimizing external focus and possible distraction, is best; when executing a skill, an external focus, being free from distracting internal thoughts, is more likely to be optimal. The broad–narrow distinction is more problematic as some people are better able to filter large amounts of information than others – broad to one player may be relatively narrow to another. Nideffer's model suggested that some people are prone to particular attentional errors, such as becoming overloaded with too much information, either internally, i.e. too much detailed analysis, leading to 'paralysis by analysis' – or externally – too much sensory information or the external field of information changing too rapidly.

Coaches tend to overestimate and overload learners' ability to concentrate

It is vital for teachers and coaches to grasp that when a performer is learning a new skill, overload can be prevented by simplifying and reducing the amount of information to be processed. If a novice or intermediate player has a great deal of information to process it is highly likely that a skill will break down. Frequently coaches make the error of attributing this breakdown of skills to a technical fault. It is more likely to be an attentional overload. Slow the skill down and reduce the attentional load, then build it back up again.

Bear in mind that the skill of adopting an optimal attentional style needs to be taught and developed. Some performers may have a natural ability to do this but most will not – it needs to be taught, practised and coached.

Ultimately, you are coaching to achieve a situation where doing the right thing is automatic – having this as a goal can be useful. Early in learning, keeping things simple, adopting an 'if this – then that' approach, often helps players to think less but do more and execute better.

Which is best: mindfulness or actively managed concentration?

The concept of mindfulness is a theme running through many areas of psychology. Many applied practitioners in health and clinical areas advocate this approach as a method of managing stress and anxiety and achieving optimal psychological health. In its broadest terms mindfulness is a technique aimed at increasing 'here-and-now' awareness of physiological, mental and environmental events without interpreting or imposing judgement on their quality (Kabat-Zinn, 1994). For some people the technique is intuitive and simple, whilst for others it requires time and effort to develop. The key skill is to detach yourself from your perceptions and separate thoughts from responses. In this way thoughts are noted as passing states in the mind that do not necessarily have to be acted upon, enabling a person to respond to situations more objectively.

In sport, there have been relatively few applications of mindfulness in the literature (e.g. Aherne et al., 2011; Mardon et al., 2016); this is partly due to the emphasis in the sport psychology literature on more active concentration management techniques, such as the use of cue words, self-talk and pre-performance routines. All of these techniques are designed to actively create the optimal attentional conditions, in terms of concentration, cue selection and response control under conditions of divided attention.

An example of this type of more active approach to attention is the research on the quiet eye (QE) in aiming skills, such as golf, free-throw shooting in basketball, dead-ball kicking in football, soccer or rugby, dart throwing or pitching. The initial work on the QE technique was conducted by Vickers (1996) and showed that expert performers displayed an optimal timing, i.e. fixated longer on their target, prior to the execution of the critical movement. This knowledge often leads performers to manage their visual fixation actively to ensure longer QE periods directly before executing a skill. There is some evidence also to suggest that performers who actively extend the QE period are less prone to their skills breaking down under pressure.

At this point the jury is still out on the value of a mindfulness approach to enhancing sport performance. In the coming years, as evidence grows, there may be a greater emphasis on this type of 'awareness without judgement' approach to attention in sport and a closer integration between the mindful and QE approaches.

What are the foundation skills of optimal attention?

The preceding text in this chapter has given you some theoretical background about this aspect of human cognition. The challenge for the applied psychologist is to translate the theory into practice: how can I design an intervention to help performers concentrate better and more skilfully filter out the distractions to conscious thought which will inevitably occur at exactly the wrong moment!?

Kremer and Moran (2008) have identified five key principles which can help us translate the theory into practical interventions.

1. *Decide what to concentrate on. Concentration doesn't just happen.*

   Optimal attention is the consequence of a conscious decision to invest mental effort in performance. This means developing a pre-performance routine which enables a performer to eliminate possible distractions. I often describe this to my clients as a mental warm-up. The mental warm-up has much in common with the physical one, in that it is designed to prepare or make the mind ready for what is to come.

The mental warm-up has four distinct steps:

(a) Tuning into the place – is there anything in the imme-diate environment that could distract you?

(b) Tuning into yourself – what could distract you as you prepare for performance? Are you hungry or thirsty? Do you need to go to the bathroom? Do you have something that is so important that it must be done right now? If 'yes' to any of these questions, you need to go and sort them out, so that you have no unfinished business that could distract you during the training session or game.

(c) Tuning into others – are there conversations that you need to have with other people before you begin? Are you carrying unfinished conversations, perhaps about the last game or even about last night's TV programmes, that could distract you? Again, finish the unfinished business – don't allow your unfinished business to become a distraction for someone else.

(d) Tune into the agenda – what are you aiming to do in this session or game? What are our collective goals and my personal goals?

An abbreviated form of this warm-up can be integrated into performance and carried out in natural breaks in the game or event.

2. *One thought at a time.*

Clients frequently complain that they feel overwhelmed by their thoughts or that they think too much. You can only have one thought at a time; being overwhelmed or think-ing too much indicates that you are flipping between many competing thoughts. We have limited capacity to do this and should work in preparation to simplify and clarify. This means only holding the thoughts which are most helpful in supporting the actions we want to execute. It may be helpful to develop cue words or phrases which direct atten-tion and trigger actions – complex instructions are often not helpful, and may cause us to re-engage conscious control of movements which are best executed autonomously.

3. *Do what you are thinking.*

Performers often describe 'having a second thought' as a precursor to an error. It appears that fully committing to executing a skill which is not perfectly correct is preferable to changing halfway through execution. Again this is a feature of attention that needs to be practised.

4. *Focus on features of performance that you can control.*

Attention should remain on aspects of performance which are under the performer's control. For example, a sprinter may become distracted by a rival in the next lane, coming to his shoulder. This is inevitable: it will happen frequently, however it should not disrupt the sprinter's own technique. The sprinter needs to develop a better attentional filter to ensure focus remains optimal.

5. *Under stress, favour an external focus.*

The work of Wulf (2007), particularly looking at the role of attention in closed, self-paced skills such as golf, suggests that under pressure it is best to adopt an external attentional focus, for example, in golf, focusing on movement of the club head, rather than focusing internally on the technical instructions for the swing. An external focus in kicking skills would mean identifying a target, such as a face in the crowd, a strategy used by Jonny Wilkinson, one of the most consistently accurate place kickers in rugby union, or focusing on the base of the off-stump in cricket, a strategy used by Richard Hadlee.

Choking, freezing and yipping – labels are not helpful!

Sport has developed its own vocabulary for when players experience either positive or negative impact on concentration. Choking is a term used to describe what happens to a player whose performance capacities have fallen away, usually in a high-pressure or critical situation: this can also be described as freezing under pressure. This is partly addressed in the answer to question 26 in the chapter on stress and performance. This highlights the overlap between anxiety and concentration – particularly in trying to understand the phenomenon of choking. The 'yips' are a specific variation of this type of experience in self-paced or aiming-type tasks. For example, some golfers are prone to becoming hesitant or tentative midway through the execution of a stroke, almost as if they are analysing the execution whilst it is actually taking place. This type of hypersensitivity to the action is unlikely to help in a skill which is very well learned. Yipping is not restricted to golf – it has also been noted in snooker players, darts players, bowlers in cricket and pitchers in baseball.

Labelling players as chokers, freezers and yippers is not helpful; most players have lapsed in attention at some point. Coaches, teachers and performers should have a simple goal in learning new skills – once the basics are learned, the challenge is to execute consistently with a minimum of conscious attention. In this way concentration can be removed from the technical aspects of the performance and moved on to the tactical – executing the skill at the right moment.

Bibliography

Aherne, C., Moran, A.P., & Lonsdale, C. (2011). The effects of mindfulness training on athletes' flow: an initial investigation. *The Sport Psychologist 25*: 177–189.

Atherton, M.A. (2002). *Opening Up: An Autobiography*. Hodder and Stoughton.

Kabat-Zinn, J. (1994). *Wherever you go, There you are*. Hachette Books.

Kabat-Zinn, J. (2005). *Coming to Our Senses: Healing Ourselves and the World Through Mindfulness*. Hyperion.

Kremer, J., & Moran, A. (2008). *Pure Sport, Practical Sport Psychology*. Routledge.

Mardon, N., Richards, H., & Martindale, A. (2016). The effect of mindfulness training on attention and performance in national-level swimmers: an exploratory investigation. *The Sport Psychologist 30*: 131–140.

Moran, A. (2012). Concentration, attention and performance. In S. Murphy (Ed.), *The Oxford Handbook of Sport and Performance Psychology*. Oxford University Press.

Nideffer, R. (1976). Test of attentional and interpersonal style. *Journal of Personality and Social Psychology 34*: 394–404.

Radcliffe, P. (n.d.). Early memories. *BBC Academy*. Retrieved on 5 May 2017 from: http://news.bbc.co.uk/sportacademy/hi/sa/athletics/features/newsid_3242000/3242528.stm.

Vickers, J.N. (1996). Visual control when aiming at a far target. *Journal of Experimental Psychology. Human Perception and Performance 22* (2): 342–354.

Wulf, G. (2007). Attentional focus and motor learning: a review of 10 years research. *Bewegung and Training 1*: 4–14.

Q29

I play netball. I'm prone to lapses in concentration, particularly when I'm really tired. What should I do to prevent this?

Netball is a multiple sprint-type sport, with frequent short breaks in play. This is similar to other ball games and does give us some scope to manage concentration better. Fatigue is an inevitable aspect of sport performance. It sits at the intersection between your physical, technical, tactical and mental training and is something you can actively work to manage.

Training sessions should be designed to test concentration under conditions of fatigue. Some coaches prefer to work on highly complex skills when performers are fresh. This is perfectly acceptable when the skill is being learned. However I would question the value of this approach later in skill development when there is greater emphasis on tactical training, i.e. doing the right thing at the right time.

In addition to developing concentration, testing the execution of skills under game-like conditions and under heavy fatigue can have a powerful positive impact on players' confidence. Knowing when and how to do this is part of the coach's expertise.

A step in preventing fatigue-related concentration errors is to clarify what type of mistakes you are making. Do you tend to focus on how tired you are feeling or how long there is left to go and miss key moments in the game? Or do you tend to become overwhelmed with all the external information going on around you and can't pick up what is relevant and what isn't: for example, ball watching or juggling a number of different roles?

In my experience most concentration errors in sport are of the first type. I call this 'going into your head' – when you miss information because you have become preoccupied by your thoughts and your thoughts are not helpful.

The best way of addressing this is to develop a routine which cues up your next job. For example, if you ask the official how long is left on the clock and her answer triggers you going into your head, thinking, 'I'm exhausted, I can't go for that long' – there is a tendency to remain in your head and enter a spiral of despair, which effectively takes you out of the game. It is better to chunk the game down into small manageable pieces – the next play. Actively cue your next job. At this set piece, what is my job? Then at the next break in play, recover and refocus on the next job, and so on. Always remember that everyone on the court is tired – if you can go harder than them for 1 second longer than them, you win!

If you are prone to becoming overloaded with external information, for example, watching the ball, rather than shuttling between watching the player you are marking, awareness of your court position and watching the ball, this may be due to nerves causing your attentional field to be narrowed, perhaps due to the game being close and the play being particularly critical. Your strategy for managing this involves a 'first-aid' relaxation exercise – deep, belly breathing to lower your arousal level and then a cue to remember to scan more widely for the important cues and reinforce your response. Simplify this down to: 'If this happens, then I do that'.

Get as much feedback from your coach and the players around you as you can. Video is a very powerful coaching tool for this. Become aware of what happens to your attention as you tire, particularly where and how frequently you scan. Work on eliminating these errors in training.

Going deeper into the theory

This question is an application of the theoretical model developed by Nideffer (1976). The player is working hard physically, but the searchlight of her attention is focusing inward and narrow – 'how fatigued I am' – rather than externally, going from broad scanning of the court to narrow, tracking the ball or the player she is marking.

The player could become much more aware of where her attention is at any one moment. She needs a cue to remind her that the game is being played on the court, not in her head. Having a strategy for 'parking' fatigue and cueing the next task is vital for optimal performance.

There is some evidence (e.g. Royal et al., 2006) that some parts of performance are more affected by fatigue than others. In this case it would be useful to examine in more detail which aspects of the player's performance seem to be most vulnerable to breaking down under conditions of fatigue. The coach can then set up practices to develop these at the end of hard physical training sessions.

Bibliography

Nideffer, R. (1976). Test of attentional and interpersonal style. *Journal of Personality and Social Psychology 34*: 394–404.

Royal, K.A., Farrow, D., Mujika, I., Halson, S.L., Pyne, D., & Abernethy, B. (2006). The effects of fatigue on decision making and shooting skill performance in water polo players. *Journal of Sports Sciences 24* (8): 807–815.

Q30

An athlete I'm coaching is really talented in practice but regularly chokes in actual games. How can I help her/him overcome this?

Choking is when a player's performance suddenly and unexpectedly falls, usually when under the pressure of an important game or a particularly critical phase within a game, for example, an important play which may decide the result.

There are several theories which aim to explain choking: the details are developed in the theoretical commentary below. At this point what we need to know is that the player has choked because his attention is focused inwards rather than externally.

Coaches often view choking as a failure on the part of the athlete. I view it slightly differently. Choking is often the result of a failure on the part of the coach to organize sessions that develop skills and techniques which transfer into match situations. In many sports the difference between practice and competition is so stark that I question the value of practice. Practising the same skill over and over again in perfect conditions and when the performer is fresh can lead to a false sense of security.

The job of a coach is to develop a platform of skills. Drilling skills may be vital in doing this, but it is at the next step that your skill as a coach is really being tested – creating practices which simulate and recreate the pressures faced in actual competition.

Coaches often default to playing large-sided or practice games. This can be appropriate, but creative use of small-sided games and simulated game situations can also be used effectively. Small-sided games are more effective in developing skills in young ball players. They intensively test skills and techniques about first touch, scanning and moving into space which transfer readily into game situations. Critically, they also demand high levels of attention; lapses are easily detected and can be coached.

The coach can also set up simulated game like practices, where four defenders have to prevent six attackers from scoring in a 5-minute period. Or an attacking unit has to retain the ball without errors for a 5-minute period, or create a scoring opportunity. These are all game-like scenarios which recreate what will actually happen in performance.

In other sports, creating game-like scenarios which put skills under pressure are vital for both assessing where performers are in their development and also informing you as the coach what the next practice sessions should include.

Coaches or teachers must be aware of their expectations in designing these match-like drills. Players will make mistakes; initially it will seem like the players' skills levels have declined. This is because they are processing more information under tighter constraints of time. Errors are inevitable, which may dent confidence. Debriefing these fully is important to get the most out of them. High-intensity, game-like drills may also be fatiguing, which is a secondary benefit. Persist – keep challenging yourself and the players. As a coach a fundamental question to ask is: how does this practice transfer to the game situation? If it doesn't, a reasonable question is: 'why are we doing it?'

The last point to consider here is the increased risk of injury in game-like simulations. This is particularly an issue in contact sports. You need to expose players to game-like contact, so that these skills are well learned and robust. The progressions in this are important. Be patient and ensure that players have good basic contact skills before putting these into game-like situations.

Going deeper into the theory

Coaches often assume there is a seamless transition between training and competition. This only happens if coaches actively recreate the pressures of competition in training sessions. There are a range of excellent texts which help coaches to design training drills to develop match-like skills in performers (e.g. ASEP and Anderson, 2009).

The term 'choking' is one that a practitioner should be sensitized to. Coaches, teachers, parents, performers and journalists often appear keen to apply this unhelpful label. It is widely used as a pejorative description of a person rather than of a performance. Baumeister (1984) offers a simple definition of choking as 'performance decrements under pressure' and develops this in later work into 'the occurrence of inferior performance despite striving and incentives for superior performance (Baumeister and Showers, 1986, p. 361). Broadly there are two theoretical models which aim to explain choking. The first is distraction-type models (e.g. Beilock and Carr, 2001) which focus on the high-pressure, anxiety-inducing situation as a trigger for task-irrelevant thinking. The other theoretical approach is more linked to how movement is learned and controlled. In these approaches, e.g. conscious processing or reinvestment theory (Masters and Maxwell, 2008), high-pressure situations cause a regression to an earlier stage in skill learning, where elements of the movement are under conscious control. The aim of practice is to allow skills to become autonomous with little or no conscious involvement. This tends to speed them up and make them more accurate. Clearly regressing back to an earlier stage of learning is not a good thing and leads to skills which were previously automatic now requiring more effort and attention. This is often the case when clients report that they are overthinking or thinking too much about what they are doing.

It is worth noting that choking does have a 'flip side'. Well-coached performers who have skills which have been tried and tested under stressful game-like conditions can produce 'clutch' performances, where skills are enhanced under pressure. This can be linked to either of the two lines of theory – effective attentional control or a recognition that how a skill comes out (is executed) depends on how it has gone in (practised). Interestingly, Wallace and Baumeister (2002) found a link between clutch plays and narcissism. Narcissists, performing in an environment that could lead to self-enhancement, tended to 'clutch'. This may help answer the question about who you select as your penalty takers!

Bibliography

ASEP & Anderson, K. (2009). *Coaching Tennis Technical and Tactical Skills*. Human Kinetics.

Baumeister, R.F. (1984). Choking under pressure: self-conscious and paradoxical effects of incentive in skilful performance. *Journal of Personality and Social Psychology 46*: 610–620.

Baumeister, R.F., & Showers, C.J. (1986). A review of paradoxical performance effects: choking under pressure in sports and mental stress. *European Journal of Social Psychology 16*: 361–383.

Beilock, S.L., & Carr, T.H. (2001). On the fragility of skilled performance. What governs choking under pressure? *Journal of Experimental Psychology: General 130*: 701–725.

Masters, R.S.W., & Maxwell, J.P. (2008). The theory of reinvestment. *International Journal of Sport and Exercise Psychology 1*: 160–183.

Wallace, H.M., & Baumeister, R.F. (2002). The performance of narcissists rises and falls with perceived opportunity for glory. *Journal of Personality and Social Psychology 82*: 819–834.

Q31

If a referee makes a bad decision, I get very angry and tend to lose my concentration. What should I do?

Sport is a messy business. Players and officials make poor decisions and errors all the time. Some of your thinking is 'faulty'. You have an expectation that both you and the official will be perfect in your execution of skills – this is unrealistic. Additionally you expect the referee to be fair, consistent and objective whilst also making decisions that you deem to be in your favour – these are not compatible sets of thoughts. Either you want an official biased in your favour or you have to accept that some decisions will go against you. All of that thinking is going on whilst you are also trying to perform your playing role. My advice is that you should play and let the official officiate.

There will be mistakes, but getting angry is unlikely to make any impact. In fact it may make it more difficult to get a marginal decision in future. In all your experience of playing, on how many occasions has an official said: 'No, you are absolutely correct. I got that wrong. I'll reverse my decision?' Never, or next to never!

All that energy you are directing to anger and frustration needs to be directed towards playing.

Your response to a decision is effectively taking you out of the game for a few minutes. As an opponent I would like to see that. You become at best ineffective, at worst an opponent who is vulnerable and can be attacked.

I would encourage your coach to work on this part of your game in training, setting up practices and drills where you are unfairly penalized. You can work on developing a routine where you immediately recognize this scenario and have a positive response, re-engaging with the game and getting ready for your next job.

Going deeper into the theory

Many players are prone to the type of concentration disruption described. There is a heady mix of 'faulty' thinking and increased arousal, which combines to generate a sense of perceived unfairness pushing players 'into their heads' for a few seconds or longer.

Nideffer's model of attentional style is helpful in explaining what happens. Players whose attention becomes stuck in this sense of perceived injustice tend to be become overly narrow in their attention and internally focused. They need an active nudge back into the external world, where the game is being played.

Coaches and teachers should become sensitized to players who tend to do this and set up drills where they have their concentration challenged. The team needs them back and functioning optimally immediately. This will not happen unless it is practised.

Bibliography

Nideffer, R. (1976). Test of attentional and interpersonal style. *Journal of Personality and Social Psychology 34*: 394–404.

Q32

I have a couple of players who are very talented but tend to drift in and out of games. They are fit enough; they just seem to lose concentration. What can I do to keep them focused?

I think the first thing to do is to clarify exactly what you mean by 'drift in and out'. Do you mean that they do something exceptional in the game and then go back to simply being good? You want them to be exceptional all the time? Is this a realistic expectation?

Or do you mean that they do something well and then appear to switch off and be disengaged from the game for the next few minutes? This is more likely and something that we can work on.

There are several causes for why this happened, so the first thing I would do is to ask the players about those specific moments. Try not to interrogate them in a negative or aggressive manner. Rather, just ask, 'after that great run and cross down the left, what were you thinking about?' You might be surprised at their answers, but it is highly likely that they were spending time in their heads thinking about things – perhaps task-relevant things, such as, how do I get into position to do that again? Or perhaps task-irrelevant things, like writing the headlines for the papers tomorrow. The bottom line for you is that you want them to return to 'bread-and-butter' duty as quickly as possible. Work with them to 'park' the success (as well as the failure) and get back to their main job – working off the ball to give the ball carrier options or marking their opposite number.

It might be a useful strategy to 'buddy' players up on the field. They can give each other cues and remind them to remain focused in a quiet and undemonstrative way. No need for lots of shouting, just a quiet word to refocus.

Going deeper into the theory

In addressing this question it is important to get a sense of what the player feels is happening. There are many reasons why there may be a perception that he is switching off in games.

A well-managed meeting between the player and the coach, facilitated by the psychologist, will get them both on the same page and give some clear actions to be worked on in training and applied in games.

In terms of concentration skills, the player may be aiming to do too much and as a consequence appears not to be doing any of it very well. In that case the coach and player can work to simplify the game plan for this player, thereby reducing the information-processing load on the player and allowing him to focus on doing fewer jobs really well.

Bibliography

Papanikolao, Z. (2011). Attention in young soccer players: the development of an attentional focus training program. *Journal of Life Sciences 3* (1): 1–12.

Q33

My son plays tennis but gets furious if he makes a mistake. He is devastated and inconsolable if he loses. I'm on the point of banning him from playing – I'm embarrassed and I don't think it is healthy for him!

Let me just assure you that are not alone in facing this issue. Many parents are faced with this type of scenario. And if it helps, the parents of one Roger Federer had to manage this, and look how he turned out!

My advice is take a video camera to the next tournament, and if the organizers are comfortable with you videoing the game, capture some of your son's fury on camera. Sit down and watch the film with him. Often, in the heat of competition, players' awareness of what they are doing is altered. He may be shocked to see what he actually does. Once you have watched together, ask about how he feels when he get furious. What is going on in his mind? This conversation can be revealing. He may be so wrapped up in the expectations of other people – you, his coach, other players – that when he makes a mistake, which he inevitably will, his frustration turns to anger and he vents it on court.

Once we have raised his awareness about what he does we need to develop a new way of responding. First of all we need to make it acceptable not to be perfect. Players make mistakes all the time. They don't make them deliberately but to continue to improve we must be willing to push skills and techniques. What we need is a refocus strategy for when these mistakes happen – one that involves reducing the emotional temperature, rather than raising it. The precise nature of this depends on the individual but it would involve the following:

- ◆ Step 1: acknowledge the mistake and take responsibility for it.
- ◆ Step 2: accept that the moment has gone; nothing you do can undo the error.
- ◆ Step 3: review and edit: next time when I go for that shot I need to...
- ◆ Step 4: return to the 'here and now' and use an affirmation, a positive phrase or instruction, to prepare for the next point.

It is also worth pointing out to your son the impact of his behaviour on his opponents. I suspect that they like nothing better than to see him 'lose it'. It probably raises their confidence knowing that for the next few points they are playing a distracted opponent.

Very occasionally, rages on court can have a positive impact on a player's performance. I suspect that this isn't the case with your son, but if it is the case the player is operating on the limit of the spirit of the game. You are unlikely to win many friends with this approach. I suggest that the same type of strategy outlined above is worked on.

Going deeper into the theory

This type of question sits at the overlap between several lines of theory: frustration–aggression models, models of attentional style. The line of theory I have used to answer this question is self-regulation theory, based on the work of Baumeister and Vohl (2007). In this approach regulating behaviour is believed to have four aspects. The first is to understand and internalize the standards of acceptable behaviour, in this case on the tennis court. No matter how much you want to win or be successful, this doesn't legitimize the type of behaviour we see when a mistake is made. The second aspect of the theory is concerns with the motivation to adopt the new behaviour. It might be that sanctions or rewards are offered to shape behaviour. Care has to be applied when using this, because it may be that the new behaviour is not fully internalized: it might only be adopted when the sanctions or rewards are present. The third phase involves the ongoing monitoring of the new behaviour. Are there any circumstances when there is relapse to the old patterns? If so, does this reflect poor impulse control? Or fatigue? The latter is described by Baumeister and Vohs as ego depletion, a state when self-regulation breaks down as a result of the ongoing efforts. This is an interesting idea, which likens self-regulation to a physiological process which can fatigue, which brings us to the last phase of Baumeister and Vohs' model – willpower. This line of theory argues that long-term self-regulation depends on the exertion of mental strength – willpower to change. This is a controversial view. Some applied theorists argue that we should assume that we have no willpower and develop interventions that become automatic. This area is complicated by theoretical arguments around the illusion of control (Langer, 1975), where people tend to overestimate the extent to which they have control over outcomes, and the illusion of introspection (Pronin and Kugler, 2009), where people tend to overvalue their introspective thoughts and feelings over other sources of information. These cognitive biases may serve to reinforce the notion that an error has been caused by something or someone other than the player and therefore the furious response is being controlled by someone other than the player himself.

Bibliography

Baumeister, R.F., & Vohs, K.D. (2007). Self-regulation, ego depletion, and motivation. *Social and Personality Psychology Compass 1*: 115–128.

Langer, E. (1975). The illusion of control. *Journal of Personality and Social Psychology 32* (2): 311–328.

Pronin, E., & Kugler, M.B. (2007). Valuing thoughts, ignoring behavior: the introspection illusion as a source of the bias blind spot. *Journal of Experimental and Social Psychology 43*: 565–578.

Q34

When I play golf, I become preoccupied with the hazards – bunkers, out of bounds and water, so much so that I inevitably hit them!

There is an assumption that this type of mental block only happens with higher-handicap and less-experienced golfers. This isn't the case. I have worked with professional golfers who have developed this type of mindset and have successfully worked through it.

To begin on a lighter note. You have become the course designers' dream! Probably due to a few bad shots you have developed the thinking habit of perceiving all the ways of going wrong, i.e. hitting all the course designers' traps, rather than seeing all the ways you can use your skill to navigate yourself around the hazards.

Using this as a starting point, you can see there are two linked ways to resolve this challenge.

In purely concentration terms, your process of thinking is fine – you are analysing the hole and developing a plan which you then execute. The problem is that you have given much greater weighting to the hazards than your plan to avoid them. This is 'faulty' thinking. Plan what you want to happen, not what you want to avoid!

Firstly let us address the 'faulty' thinking. You have patterns of thoughts where you:

- ◆ see the outcome in all-or-nothing terms – I always hit the water
- ◆ catastrophize the outcome – hitting the hazard will destroy my card
- ◆ reason with your emotions – you tend to give precedence to emotions rather than rational thought.

I strongly advise you to look at the objective data. How frequently do you actually hit the hazards? Are there particular holes which you tend to make errors on?

The second part of the intervention is to look closely at your course management. Course management is another term for how you manage risk on the course. To optimize your scoring you need to look closely at your game, at your club ranges and accuracy. Do you typically take on the high-risk shots? This may be the real issue rather than hitting the hazards.

Going deeper into the theory

In cognitive-behavioural therapy a range of forms of 'faulty' thinking have been identified (see Greenberger & Padesky, 2015). The form I have identified in my answer is a form of thinking called catastrophizing, which is a subgroup of the larger category of minimization/magnification. This type of thinking is usually intrusive, negative and automatic and is characterized by a person giving a greater weight to a perceived failure, weakness or threat, or lesser weight to a perceived success, strength or opportunity, resulting in a difference in weighting from that given to the event or thing by others or the person at a different time or context.

Beck and many other authors have described a range of other types of thinking which can be labelled as 'faulty'. These are outlined in the answer to question 20 on page 90.

There are a range of other types of faulty thinking described in cognitive-behavioural therapy. Because of the pervasiveness of 'faulty' thinking in the applied work of a performance psychologist, I would strongly direct practitioners to good texts such as that by Greenberger and Padesky (2015). The other interesting note about this is that you can see how an understanding of 'faulty' thinking has informed a range of theoretical and applied approaches – for example, self-talk, imagery and goal setting are fundamental aspects of this approach. More broadly, you can see how cognitive-behavioural therapy informs the word on mindset and the 'chimp management' approach outlined elsewhere in this book.

Bibliography

Beck, A.T., Rush, A.J., Shaw, B.F., & Emery, G. (1979). *Cognitive Therapy of Depression*. Guilford Press.

Greenberger, D., & Padesky, C. (2015). *Mind Over Mood*. Guilford Press.

Q35

My enjoyment of golf has been destroyed by the yips. Is there a cure?

I cannot guarantee a cure. I believe there are things that we can work on to manage this blip in your golfing career and move you back to enjoying and developing your game.

The 'yips' is a horrible label for a group of symptoms around the temporary loss or misfiring of movement skills. Even the very first, dramatic recorded instance where a professional player, in a high-profile tournament, took 23 shots at a single hole could be viewed as a blip rather than a catastrophe.

The yips captures the essential challenge of many sport skills – that the physical body knows how to play the game. Undisturbed, the unconscious parts of the brain and nervous system controlling and coordinating movement would do so perfectly adequately, but the conscious brain wants to play too. And often it is the conscious engagement of the brain that is at the root of the problem.

In working with players with the yips, my first thought is to identify the conditions where they are most prone to yipping – commonly, but not exclusively, putting, players may also yip from the tee, fairway or bunker or green. What is the context – a recovery shot, or pressure putt? And then what actually happens, where is the twitch or jerk experienced, if so where, and at what point in the swing?

Once you have information about when, where, what and how the player yips you can start to develop methods of management, if not cure.

I have worked with a player who tended to yip in putting and short game areas in just one hand. This was relatively easy to work around, by developing an alternative grip on the club where the yipping hand was providing minimal support. We got to this by experimentation, starting with removing the yipping hand completely. He could putt one-handed pretty accurately and through practice developed further and we gradually reintroduced the other hand really only as support.

Players who yip off the tee are more of a challenge as two hands and a firm grip on the club are required to generate force. I have had success with players working on a completely new grip, one that appears to engage different muscles than those that have become susceptible to yipping.

Both approaches are put into the context of pre-shot routine designed to relax the player physically and, importantly, to minimize the conscious effort players are investing in a shot – swing thoughts emphasizing the club head rather than the movement of hands or body.

Going deeper into the theory

Research suggests that the yips are experienced by around half of all golfers, and are particularly prevalent in players who have played for more than 25 years. However, it remains unclear whether we should view the yips on a continuum from mild to extreme or whether there is a volume of playing which predisposes a player to experience them.

Our current understanding of the yips is that there are two forms. Type 1 yips is caused by a neurological condition called focal dystonia. The origin of dystonia is unclear: there may be a genetic component. The symptoms include involuntary firing of individual or groups of muscles, resulting in twitches and tremors. This is particularly an issue in fine motor skills such as golf chipping and putting. However, it is also commonly reported in musicians and other sports involving fine motor control. Yips associated with focal dystonias appear to be more difficult to manage, however it should be noted that dystonias are often made worse by voluntary movement, i.e. trying to execute a skill. This reinforces the importance of practising skills to enable them to become autonomous.

The second form of yips is more closely related to performance anxiety and is linked to the theories of reinvestment discussed in question 26. What we don't know at this stage is what proportion of golfers experience type 1 yips and what proportion experience type 2 and, importantly, whether there are links between these. For example, do yips start as type 1 and develop into type 2 as incorrect neuronal firing patterns become established and habitual?

There may not be a cure just yet, but through increased understanding we are better able to manage the yips and work around it.

Bibliography

Clarke, P., Sheffield, D., & Akehurst, A. (2015). The yips in sport: a systematic review. *International Review of Sport and Exercise Psychology 8* (1): 156–184.

Q36

What are the ideal elements of the pre-shot routine?

The pre-shot routine is a sequence of preparatory steps taken before executing any closed skills, such as a golf shot, a dart throw and free throw or penalty. The pre-shot routine is very personal. It is something which most players develop over time. The purpose of the pre-shot routine is to switch on the business of playing the game after a period of switching off. The basic elements are planning, relaxing, visualizing and executing. There may be elements which are repeated, for example, using slow, deep diaphragmatic breathing to slow the heart rate and calm the 'fight or flight' response. This can be used with a relaxing cue word, such as 'calm' or 'loose', to get tension out of the muscles which are going to be used in the shot.

The plan is important because we should not hit a golf shot, throw a dart or deliver a pitch without it having a purpose – deciding on a plan and committing to it is important. You should not be halfway through your execution of the skill and changing your mind.

Visualization is running the shot through your mind's eye – not simply as a video but as if you are experiencing it through your senses. This is called an internal imagery perspective. Use as many sense modalities as possible – what does the shot feel like, look like, even sound like?

Going deeper into the theory

A pre-performance routine has been defined in many different ways. I favour Moran's (1996) 'sequence of task-relevant thoughts and actions which an athlete engages in systematically prior to his or her performance of a specific sport skill'. These are often highly personalized and can appear quirky. I have worked with many performers to develop a routine, but I tend to be very 'hands off'. The reason for this is that players need to develop something which works for them, completely independently of what I say the literature says.

Guiding my thinking is Singer's (2002) five-step approach:

1. Readying – these may be habits or rituals which players go through to bring them to the 'here and now', such as adopting a posture or stance, a cue word or phrase.
2. Imaging – where the player gets a multisensorial picture of the goal of the skill, kicking a goal, driving a ball, bowling an off break.
3. Focusing attention on the key task-relevant cues, visual, auditory and proprioceptive.
4. Executing the skill with a minimum of cognitive involvement. Minimum means handing over control of the movement to the autonomous part of the central nervous system as much as possible. A 'swing thought or phrase' or an energizing verbalization, such as a grunt when serving in tennis, may help.
5. Evaluation – reflection on the difference between the goal and the actual execution is valuable for learning.

As noted above, this is a useful guide, but the specific details are determined by the performer collaborating with the psychologist.

Bibliography

Cotterill, S. (2010). Pre-performance routines in sport: current understanding and future directions. *International Review of Sport and Exercise Psychology 3* (2): 132–153.

Moran, A. (1996). *The Psychology of Concentration in Sport Performers: A Cognitive Analysis.*: Psychology Press.

Singer, R.N. (2002). Pre-performance state, routines, and automaticity: what does it take to realize expertise in self-paced events? *Journal of Sport and Exercise Psychology 24*: 359–375.

Pulling the threads together

Many performers recognize the importance of maintaining optimal attentional focus and would like to be better at controlling this vital aspect of cognition. However, there is often a disconnection between recognizing the importance of developing the skill and what is done in practice and performance. Rarely do coaches and teachers coach or teach concentration – they assume that it will be 'caught' whilst performers are doing physical, technical and tactical preparation. This approach *may* work for some, but unless explicit attention is given to what to attend to, and how to deal with distractions and play fakes, some players will remain very susceptible to losing concentration at key moments.

Can sport psychology make a performer 'choke-proof'?

If I could, I would ban journalists, commentator and coaches from using the term 'choking'. It is an unhelpful label to describe a situation that most performers experience at some point in their career. Once you have been labelled, it can become a self-fulfilling prophesy and follow you throughout your career. Even when you don't 'choke', the momentary lapse becomes the headline story. The type of interventions I have described in this chapter will not make someone immune to lapses in concentration which impact on performance. What they do achieve is to help performers understand what is happening to them and enable them to do something which makes it more likely that they will sustain performance levels under the extreme pressures of competition.

The key theme in this chapter has been the idea that performance can be enhanced by developing the ability:

◆ to select and focus on key information, and
◆ to filter out the irrelevant
◆ whilst coping with a rapidly changing and complex environment.

If we are really committed to performance, we need to acknowledge our attentional errors and use this information to develop practices and training exercises which systematically eliminate them. Equally coaches and teachers should become more comfortable in moving away from simply coaching technique and tactics and recognize that these break down when concentration wavers. Error-free performances are the result of robust physical skills, tactical accuracy and unwavering concentration. If any one element is missing players will underperform.

VI

It's all about having a positive mental attitude – isn't it?

In 1996 in the UK, there was a TV commercial for a brand of washing powder. It featured a young boy preparing for his school sports day. He is advised by his father that 'To perform like Linford [Linford Christie – 1992 Olympic 100m champion], you have to think like Linford – PMA, positive mental attitude'. On the start line, the boy hears the voice of his father in his head – 'PMA'. Of course, the boy is victorious in the sack race and the phrase 'positive mental attitude' entered the national discourse.

The PMA idea goes back much further than 1996. It was first alluded to by author Napoleon Hill in his book *Think and Grow Rich*, published in 1937. He later used the phrase in the title of another book, co-written with W. Clement Stone, called *Success Through Positive Mental Attitude*. In the text, a collection of virtues or 'plus' characteristics were described: faith, integrity, hope, optimism, courage, initiative, generosity, tolerance, tact, kindliness and good common sense. The main idea behind the book is that an optimistic and hopeful disposition is the necessary starting point for positive changes and leads to higher levels of achievement.

Despite the phrase having common currency, many lay people had no real sense of how to 'catch' PMA, or indeed whether it really was a good thing to have. It has an intuitive appeal, but PMA became a rather hollow cliché rather than something that people could work to develop in the belief that it could have a positive impact on sport performance or life in general.

#BELIEVE and the importance of failure

PMA may win you the school sack race, but it will probably not win you an Olympic gold medal – you need some good fortune to have inherited the right blend of physical characteristics, then you need to train to develop the physical, technical and tactical skills necessary to perform consistently at that level. And, perhaps counterintuitively, you need to understand the importance of failure.

Failure is a difficult concept for many people to grasp. There is a widely held assumption that winning *all the time* is essential and that to believe anything different is, in itself, a sign of mental weakness. This is the root of much faulty and unhelpful thinking.

Playing sport means that you 'fail' a lot of the time. This is why failure is such a misleading and misunderstood term. The word covers everything from a tiny insignificant disappointment to major life-changing setbacks, but in essence it is simply a description of not achieving what you set out to achieve. It seems like a very binary idea – you succeed or you fail. Failure is much more complex and important. The seeds of success are often sown in failure as the seeds of failure are sown in success. And it all boils down to *belief*: belief that we have the right people, belief that preparation will develop the performance qualities needed to overcome the most difficult opponents, belief in the systems around the development of talent – the list is endless: with belief comes commitment.

In that general act of belief is the key idea of self-belief: belief before the game that you can outperform others, belief that you can achieve your goals, belief that in this game the magic will return, belief that you can bounce back after a setback, belief that you can refocus after a distraction or error.

Without belief, many would see only the prospect of not achieving our desired outcomes, i.e. failure. Without belief some would see no reason to continue and would walk away. Learning to live with failure, in all its forms, is an important, some would say a defining, attribute for the sport performer. Belief means coming back stronger after each setback.

The problem for the performer, coach or parent is that self-belief takes on so many forms and can often feel like an act rather than an authentic and robust characteristic.

What is self-belief?

Which is better, the extravagant demonstrations of self-belief from someone like Mohammed Ali – 'I'm the greatest' – or the quiet, authoritative, but robust self- belief shown by Katherine Grainger or Jessica Ennis-Hill?

Whether expressed loudly or quietly, self-belief is a statement of your expectation that you can do the jobs that need to be done in order to get the outcome you want. It isn't about constant success: Mohammed Ali was defeated in four world-title fights.

Self-belief is less about confidence and more about competence – and this is where things get interesting and often a bit challenging. In explaining confidence and self-belief, sport psychologists draw heavily on a line of theory developed by Albert Bandura. Rather than calling it self-belief, Bandura (1997) described this set of expectations as 'self-efficacy' and, importantly, expressed the very clear distinction between efficacy expectations and outcome expectations. Efficacy expectations are predictions about our ability to execute very specific skills: these are processes which may or may not lead to the desired outcome. This is critical in sport performance, where we may execute skills at our technical and physical limit, but another competitor may perform the skills 1% better – on that day your opponent wins.

Confidence is overrated: it can be and often is faked. Talk in sport is very cheap. We see this type of theatre played out in sport, from the 'trash talk' before a big boxing event to the glib platitudes of football managers. Competence is the actual doing: the execution of skills, time after time. People are often fooled by a thin veneer of confidence. What we should look for is competence – consistent execution of the skills necessary to achieve outcomes, not necessarily the outcomes themselves.

Confidence that you will win every time you perform is misplaced and potentially dangerous, but confidence that you can execute the skills that make it more likely that you will win is more useful and more likely to stand the real-life tests you will face in performance.

Glenn McGrath, one of Australia's finest bowlers, was quoted as saying that he expected to win a five-match Ashes series 5–0. His logic was simple: he expects to win every game he plays in. If he wins every game, his team wins every series 5–0. Is this arrogance? No, this is a deep-seated belief that he and his team mates have the skills necessary to overcome opponents. It is based in fact. He played in arguably the strongest Australian team of all time. The facts spoke. He also recognized that he personally was not the 'finished article'; he worked hard to continue to develop as a player, to become more competent and more threatening.

The challenge for the sport psychology practitioner is to ensure that performers reconnect with their competence; this is how deep, robust self-belief is built. Many performers I have worked with present with a glass mostly empty perception gap. In the course of a performance they may do 100 things. Ten are outstanding, 80 are good enough and ten are disappointing – and the player tends to dwell on the 10 'failures'.

Building deep, robust self-belief needs to address both extremes – keep working to polish the things you are good at, but more critically, work even harder to eliminate those areas which are less strong. When you walk into a competitive arena with no discernible areas of weakness you are a formidable opponent – you have earned the right to be confident.

Developing a positive psychology in sport

Around the same time as the TV commercial described above, two developments in academic psychology were emerging to put the idea of PMA into a more formal and theoretical context. One was the fundamental redrawing of the parameters of psychology itself, resulting in the development of positive psychology, the other was a revisiting and development of an old idea in sport psychology – mental toughness. Both have links to the idea of PMA, both have been applied to sport performance and both have prompted or framed questions from my clients.

Ever since the Freudian era at the turn of the 20th century, psychology has been characterized as a science which aims to understand and reduce human distress. Despite modern psychology moving a long way from this, there is a common misconception that the focus, particularly of applied psychology, is to understand and treat psychological illnesses. Positive psychology adopted the opposing position. Its aim is to understand the things that make life worth living and use this knowledge to create conditions of psychological growth and optimal human performance.

The positive psychology movement is a recent development, so new that anyone who studied academic psychology before around the year 2000 will probably have missed it. It made a dramatic entry on to the stage. In 1998, Martin Seligman, a very prominent and respected figure in mainstream academic psychology, was nominated as the president of the American Psychological Association, one of the largest and most prestigious professional bodies in the world. In his presidential address, Seligman made the provocative statement that psychology should be as interested in what makes people happy as with what makes people depressed. This put positive psychology on the map.

Seligman and Mihalyi Csikszentmihalyi were the catalysts for research and theory development around four main areas in positive psychology:

1. positive experiences, such as the flow state described earlier
2. positive psychological traits, such as hope, optimism and confidence
3. positive relationships
4. positive institutions, such as healthy functioning families or workplaces.

Seligman remains a key figure in the development of positive psychology as a movement. His theoretical framework identifies five key characteristics of psychological well-being. These are summarized in the acronym PERMA:

◆ Positive emotions
◆ Engagement
◆ Relationships
◆ Meaning
◆ Accomplishments.

The reason we are looking at positive psychology in relation to sport performance is twofold: firstly, sport is something that many people do for enjoyment and psychological growth. It gives many people a means of improving their quality of life, despite sometimes, after a defeat or while experiencing an injury, it feels like the opposite! Secondly, sport is an excellent context for studying optimal human performance, where mental strength can lead to superhuman achievement and overcoming seemingly impossible challenges to achieve goals.

Positive psychology is the theoretical backdrop to much that we do in sport (and exercise) psychology.

Mental toughness

The term 'mental toughness' was first coined by Jim Loehr in his book, first published in 1986, *Mental Toughness Training for Sports*. Loehr believed that being mentally tough was as important in consistent high-level performance as being physically tough. He saw mental toughness as having four components: self-discipline, self-control, self-confidence and self-realization. He also outlined a training system which included relaxation exercises, meditation and emotional control exercises designed to impact positively on performance and enable performers to perform consistently towards the upper range of their talent and skill, regardless of competitive circumstances. Wimbledon champion Arthur Ashe endorsed Loehr's principles in the book's foreword.

In the period following the publication of Loehr's book, the concept of mental toughness became a victim of its own success. Many coaches picked up the idea of mental toughness and 'span' it to emphasize their own views about what constituted mental toughness. It became all things to all people. I recall doing a mental skills workshop for a group of coaches from around ten different sports. Each one had his or her own personal definition of mental toughness and, importantly, whilst some had developed methods they believed could be used to develop mental toughness, others firmly believed that mental toughness was genetically determined and could not be altered.

Because of the lack of general agreement about what mental toughness was, and the extent to which it could be trained, it was not given much attention by the academic research community until 2002, when a group of researchers, led by Graham Jones, published a paper redefining mental toughness. This paper was a watershed event, reigniting interest and debate about mental toughness.

In their research Jones and his co-workers interviewed a sample of international-level performers and then analysed the themes emerging from their definitions of mental toughness. Their research yielded a new definition for mental toughness:

Having the natural or developed psychological edge that enables you to: generally, cope better than your opponents with the many demands (competition, training, lifestyle) that sport places on a performer; specifically, be more consistent and better than your opponents in remaining determined, focused, confident, and in control under pressure.

(Jones et al., 2002, p. 209)

More importantly, the work identified 12 elements underpinning the definition. These are ranked in order of importance to the sample they collected their data from:

1. having an unshakable self-belief in your ability to achieve your competition goals
2. bouncing back from performance setbacks as a result of increased determination
3. having an unshakable self-belief that you possess unique qualities and abilities that make you better than your opponents
4. = having an insatiable desire and internalized motives to succeed
4. = remaining fully focused on the task at hand in the face of competition-specific distractions
6. regaining psychological control following unexpected, uncontrollable events (competition-specific)
7. pushing back the boundaries of physical and emotional pain, while still maintaining technique and effort under distress (in training and competition)
8. accepting that competition anxiety is inevitable and knowing that you can cope with it
9. = thriving on the pressure of competition
9. = not being adversely affected by others' good and bad performances
11. remaining fully focused in the face of personal-life distractions
12. switching a sport focus on and off as required.

In my applied work I often give clients this list to look at as a prompt to explore their views on mental toughness. As an applied psychologist, first and foremost, I am less concerned with the academic detail of defining the construct and more with how it is interpreted by the client and then what can be done to develop aspects through our collaboration.

Jones et al.'s work caused ripples around the world of sport psychology. On the one hand it is very helpful to have a clear definition that we could all agree on. On the other, the 12 themes Jones and his co-workers identified are so broad and generic many psychologists felt that we were back to the 'collection of virtues' problem that we saw with PMA.

Other problems were also highlighted. Many of the characteristics identified could be interpreted differently according to context. For example, is it mentally tougher for a performer carrying an injury to push through pain to complete a game or event, risking a more serious injury, or withdraw in the knowledge that she will recover quicker and be back performing sooner? Critics of Jones' team's conceptualization of mental toughness were concerned that, although it provided a useful 'shorthand' to communicate with coaches and performers, it was really composed of discrete elements.

Another team of researchers, led by Peter Clough, conceptualized mental toughness as being composed of commitment, control, challenge and concentration, an approach described as the '4Cs' model. There were two main plus points of the 4Cs approach: firstly, that the model had developed from a strong theoretical background which could be traced back to work on psychological hardiness which had been done in the 1970s and 1980s by health psychologist Suzanne Kobasa. Her work had examined why some people were able to manage occupational stress better than others. It also indicated that people who were best able to manage stress had developed a psychological hardiness which combined aspects of personality with robust coping skills enabling them to thrive. Another plus point of the 4Cs model was that Clough's team had developed and tested an assessment tool – the MT48, a questionnaire with, unsurprisingly, 48 questions which assessed the four component attributes. This has been very widely used in a range of sporting and business settings.

Researchers led by Daniel Gucciardi proposed an alternative approach to mental toughness. This model views mental toughness as a process, where attitudes, emotions and thoughts influence the way a person approaches or avoids challenges (see Gucciardi and Gordon, 2011).

Mental toughness has had a huge impact on sport psychology since interest was rekindled in 2002. There are many technical and academic debates and disagreements about its nature and its application. The fact remains that mental toughness is a quality that sport performers value and are keen to develop. The applied sport psychologist is tasked with first, clearly understanding what it means to that individual and then putting interventions in place which develop those qualities.

Self-regulation and resilience: are these subsets of mental toughness or is mental toughness a subset of them?

Self-regulation theory was first proposed by Roy Baumeister in the 1980s (Baumeister and Vohs, 2004). It was initially developed as a model explaining how people consciously regulate their thoughts, emotions and behaviours to achieve valued goals. Baumeister's model is applied and developed in question 33 in Chapter V. Some academic researchers argue that mental toughness is best explained through the lens of more general self-regulation theory. I think this is a useful approach – Baumeister's work covers a range of applications where many of the qualities identified in the sport psychology literature are common.

The literature on resilience began to emerge in the mid-2000s with research indicating that resilience is a stronger predictor of academic achievement than IQ. From this literature an application in sport began to develop, with resilience being defined as the ability to respond positively to setbacks, failures and obstacles. This looks a lot like several of the theme items from Jones et al.'s model of mental toughness first described in their 2002 study.

Is resilience the same as mental toughness? It would appear to have elements in common; it would also appear to share elements of Seligman's PERMA framework. In psychology ideas from different sources often converge.

Bibliography

Bandura, A. (1997). *Self-efficacy: The Exercise of Control*. Worth Publishers.

Baumeister, R.F., & Vohs, K.D. (Eds.) (2004). *Handbook of Self-Regulation: Research, Theory, and Applications*. Guilford.

Clough, P.J., Earle, K., & Sewell, D. (2002). Mental toughness: the concept and its measurement. In I.M. Cockerill (Ed.), *Solutions in Sport Psychology* (pp. 32–43). London: Thomson.

Gucciardi, D.F., & Gordon, S. (2011). Mental toughness in sport: past, present, and future. In D.F. Gucciardi & S. Gordon (Eds.), *Mental Toughness in Sport: Developments in Research and Theory* (pp. 233–251). Routledge.

Hill, N. (1937, 2007). *Think and Grow Rich*. Wilder Publications.

Hill, N., & Clement Stone, W. (1960, 2008) *Success Through Positive Mental Attitude*. Simon & Schuster.

Jones, G., Hanton, S., & Connaughton, D. (2002). What is this thing called mental toughness? An investigation of elite sport performers. *Journal of Applied Sport Psychology 14*: 205–218.

Loehr, J. (1986). *Mental Toughness Training for Sports: Achieving Athletic Excellence*. Stephen Green Press.

Seligman, M.E. (2003). *Authentic Happiness: Using the New Positive Psychology to Realise your Potential for Lasting Fulfilment*. Nicholas Brearly Publishing.

Seligman, M.E., & Csikszentmihalyi, M. (2000). Positive psychology: an introduction. *American Psychologist 55* (1): 5–14.

Q37

Is mental toughness something you are born with or is it something that can be taught? If it can be developed, how should we best enhance it?

This is a question that goes to the heart of our understanding of talent identification and development. There is a growing body of evidence to say that genetic factors play a very important part in sport performance, particularly in sports where there is a relatively smaller skill component, such as running and cycling. In these sports, having the right blend of metabolic genes expressed can endow a very significant advantage. However, at the top level of sport, where most competitors share that genetic advantage, other factors will determine success. If mental toughness is genetic and cannot be developed then sport psychologists are effectively redundant – we can have marginal influence in performers who have already had success.

My view is that, in common with almost every personality characteristic ever studied, behaviours associated with mental toughness are determined by a combination of genetic (nature) and environmental (nurture) factors. Without studies on identical twins, where some are raised together and share the developmental environment and others are raised apart, it is extremely difficult to put a figure on exactly how much is nature and how much is nurture. My view is, from a practical perspective, that doesn't matter. If any mental toughness gains can be achieved by creating a rich developmental environment, then we should do it.

This sets up your second question – how do we create an environment which develops mental toughness?

The default that many coaches use is that we have to 'break performers down' in order to make them mentally tough. This is an old-fashioned idea from military training, that you will only get tough competitors who are willing to push themselves to the limits of physical endurance by putting them through unrelenting hardship.

I'm not saying there is no place for that: sport tests people physically and the ability to cope with that should be coached and practised. This should not be the only tool used. Robust self-belief can come from surviving an arduous task, but many performers will have self-belief destroyed by a coach continually telling them how weak and inadequate they are.

Looking at the list of attributes identified in the opening text gives some ideas about how to ensure that mental toughness develops alongside physical and technical toughness.

Here are some ideas.

1. Continual development of skills. Players should be continually challenged to develop skills which make them better than the best opponents they will face, not the average opponent.
2. Graded exposure to the next level of performance. Competition should be as matched as possible – not continually playing against poor or strong opponents.
3. Players should be encouraged to reflect on what they need to do to get better physically, technically, tactically and mentally.
4. A supportive dialogue with coaches on how to cope physically and mentally with the training and competitive environment.
5. A supportive atmosphere among players to develop mutual support.

This looks like a very ambitious agenda – asking players who are competing for starting positions on the same team to support each other. But it can and does help. Equally, old-school coaching demands that players toughen up and 'grow some'. I'd have no issues with these beliefs if they had always yielded results. But they haven't, and it is a complete lack of the softer communication skills of coaches that have meant that many players with physical and technical ability have failed to fulfil their potential.

Going deeper into the theory

This question is an example of the epigenetic complexity of psychology. The Human Genome project was launched in 1990 with the aim of identifying and coding every basepair in every gene in human DNA. The project was formally concluded in 2003, with much greater understanding of the molecular basis of human physiology, but also with more questions than answers.

No one anticipated quite the extent to which the environment influenced whether genes were expressed: this is at the heart of a new science of epigenetics. Over the next decades epigenetics will revolutionize sport, particularly the science of training, where it is absolutely clear that for physical training to yield optimal results it must be tailored to the individual. It is highly likely that mental training will require the same approach.

The research literature gives some general principles as to how best to create an enriching mental toughness environment. A study by Connaughton et al. (2010) identified the development of skills, inherent competitiveness and exposure to high-level competition, along with educational and psychological support. They also suggested a strong framework for reflecting on performance and using both positive and negative experience as the stimulus for developing mental toughness.

However, my personal view is that, as understanding of epigenetics develops, the ability of coaches, teachers and parents to assess the needs of individuals will become more important. Coaching, teaching and parenting have never been easy, but I suspect they are about to become even more challenging. One-size-fits-all coaching will not do.

Bibliography

Connaughton, D., Hanton, S., & Jones, G. (2010) The development and maintenance of mental toughness in the world's best performers. *The Sport Psychologist 24*: 168–193.

Q38

Our coach shouts at us all the time. He says he is toughening us up, but really he is just p*ssing us off. Is there any science behind what he's doing?

This approach to coaching is unfortunately common. It is a throw-back to old-fashioned models of coaching, adapted from military training and very dated physical education practice. In some performers it may be appropriate, but in most cases it is a lazy, inefficient and ineffective way of proceeding.

It's lazy because it indicates that the coach hasn't taken the time to engage with players as individuals and find out what helps them develop and what doesn't.

It's inefficient because the science actually indicates that this type of approach to coaching is one of the major causes of people, particularly youngsters, dropping out of sport. This is talent wasted.

It's ineffective because it's not even a very good way of making people mentally tougher. Mental toughness is better developed by building competence, self-belief and coping skills, related to actual play.

Not surprisingly, the players are getting fed up and switching off. My suggestion is that you speak to the coach and make some suggestions about how he can make positive changes to what he is doing. In the first instance it can be a positive, but assertive, exchange of views. But he needs to understand the players' frustrations and what he is risking in continuing in this way.

Going deeper into the theory

I am answering this question just after the controversy around Shane Sutton's departure from British Cycling. Sutton was the performance director of British Cycling who resigned after a very public breakdown in his relationship with a specific rider and claims from others that the coaching environment was built on a climate of fear and bullying.

This is an extremely difficult and sensitive question. What is perceived as bullying by one person may be perceived in a different way by another. The question goes to the heart of the coach–athlete relationship. Coaching is an important and privileged role. The coach–athlete relationship is a developmental process designed to create optimal conditions for the performer to fulfil his or her physical, technical and tactical potential. With it comes a great deal of responsibility and a recognition of the power imbalance that performers may perceive. Coaches can hold a great deal of influence over the career of their athletes and this can lead to a feeling of powerlessness.

For some performers, there is a need for 'tough love' – setting very difficult goals and then challenging performers to believe they can achieve them. For others, such an approach completely undermines their intrinsic motivation, creates fear and undermines self-belief. But where is the line? The problem is that the line differs for each performer. This is why the first step in any coaching relationship is assessment – the coach must understand what each performer needs and, equally, what will probably switch him or her off.

In some of the discussion that followed the departure of Shane Sutton from British Cycling, a distinction was drawn between coaching practice in elite sport and subelite levels. Some commentators believed that bullying and a climate of fear were acceptable in elite sport. I don't subscribe to this view. Most performers are intrinsically motivated, constantly striving for gains in performance and don't need additional pushing. They need honest and open dialogue, but it does need to be respectful. They are only too conscious that their place on the team is dependent on performance. If they don't deliver, someone else will. Constantly being reminded of their accountability can lead to overtraining, underrecovery and other physical and psychological issues.

Bibliography

Burke, K.L. (2005). But coach doesn't understand: dealing with team communication quagmires. In M.B. Andersen (Ed.), *Sport Psychology in Practice* (pp. 45–59). Human Kinetics.

Rhind, D. (2010). Towards an understanding of the maintenance of unhealthy coach–athlete relationships. In C.H. Brackenridge. and D.J.A .Rhind. (Eds.) *Elite Child Athlete Welfare: International Perspectives*(pp. 101–108). Brunel University Press.

Q39

What is the best way of assessing performers' mental toughness?

I have noted in previous questions about assessment that I'm not keen on 'pencil-and-paper' tests of psychological constructs. They tend to be of more use in research than in applied practice or coaching.

If you are determined to measure mental toughness there are several questionnaires available to use without cost – the Mental Toughness Questionnaire (MTQ) or Psychological Performance Inventory (PPI) can be accessed online. The MT48, developed by Clough et al. (see section on mental toughness, above), is not freely available, but can be accessed at cost from www.aqr.co.uk/.

My preference is for the parent, teacher or coach to invest a little time to: (1) clarify with all players what mental toughness means in their individual context; and then to (2) observe actual behaviour over a period of time; and (3) set goals to develop that specific aspect. For example, a player may find it difficult to 'reboot' in performance after an error. This is a key skill and one that needs to be worked on. Strategies can be agreed in conversation between the performer, coach and perhaps psychologist. These are then tested in actual performance.

This, for me, is a much more valid assessment of mental toughness than a general question on a pencil-and-paper test.

Going deeper into the theory

Some governing bodies require psychologists to collect evidence that their work has been effective. Psychometric testing is a tempting but problematic way to do this. I have been asked to deliver interventions for teams, designed to improve the mental toughness of members. It seems obvious that the best way to demonstrate the effectiveness of my work is to give mental toughness questionnaires to players before the work begins and then retest at the end. If there has been an improvement in scores then the work has been effective. This is flawed and highlights another problem of adopting a purely nomothetic approach. By nomothetic I mean I am assessing people in terms of shared characteristics, i.e. responses to the questions and constructs within a questionnaire. This emphasizes how people are similar. In contrast, assessment of ideographic characteristics identifies how people are unique and different. This is less readily captured in a questionnaire. It is highly likely that the characteristics which make an individual mentally tough and able to outperform others are unique. Using questionnaires to assess the effectiveness of interventions is problematic for a range of statistical reasons as well. For example, do you report a mean change? Or a median? Or a percentage? How do you cope with anomalies in the data, where 50% of the team report a positive change but 50% report a negative one, but the magnitude of the positive change is larger?

Unless you have been trained specifically in the administration and interpretation of a questionnaire, I would strongly advise you not to use it (see Marchant, 2010).

Bibliography

Marchant, D. (2010). Psychological assessment: objective/self-report measures. In S.J. Hanrahan & M.B. Andersen (Eds.), *Routledge Handbook of Applied Sport Psychology* (pp. 111–120). Routledge.

Q40

What is self-belief and where does it come from? What I really mean is, how can I become more confident?

I note that you have used self-belief as a synonym for confidence. I am happy to use it in that way.

Confidence is frequently cited as the single most important psychological factor in sport performance. You know when you have it and you play differently. It leads to all kinds of positive thoughts, emotions and behaviours. But, performers often find it really difficult to conceptualize self-belief, to understand what it is and why it appears to be so fragile.

Everyone has a slightly different personal definition for confidence but when all the differences are boiled away we are left with a definition which is based around the strength of the belief that you can execute a certain skill or set of skills. This is where many people go wrong. Confidence is *not* a belief that you are going to win every game. This type of thought is more to do with optimism than confidence. Optimism in the outcome is fine but ultimately you are not in control of the outcome. You can do everything in your power to win but ultimately it is determined by events outside your control.

From this definition you can see that confidence and competence sit very closely together. Your confidence will go up as you become more competent. In particular, confidence goes up as you see that your competence in the skills you believe to be relative weaknesses improves. Entering competitions with no weaknesses is a goal to strive for.

How can you achieve this?

The first step is to profile your performance to identify areas of your skill set which give you the greatest potential for gains. You can do this using a performance-profiling type of exercise. This is where you benchmark your performance against the characteristic of either an individual or composite of a consistently high-level performer. Identify the performance areas which are perceived to be the areas which will yield the greatest performance improvements. These could be technical, physical, tactical or mental. If you have a coach or a fellow player you trust and feel safe sharing this profile with, do so: it has the potential to add to the value of the process.

The next step is to identify some process-type of goals, i.e. things that you can do on a daily or session basis designed to develop that area of skill. You may be able to develop these process goals into a performance goal or milestone which can give you an indication of the effectiveness of the skill development practice.

The final step in this process is the most important. You should regularly review practices and performances to reflect on the development of the practised skills. The most effective way to do this is to have a review section in your training diary. Identify the goals you have set for each training session or event. Write down the things that have gone well or better than expected. You can break these down into subsections – physical, technical, tactical and mental. Then note down the things which didn't go as well as you'd hoped. The deal here is that you can only have as many in this column as the previous one. I am not having you wallow in all the things you can't do! The final column is the most important if you are really committed to self-development. This is writing clearly what you need to do in the next block of training or next performance to ensure the things that didn't go as well as you'd hoped are either improved or eliminated. Again, working with a coach or colleague can really cement this part of the process.

I've an example of this type of review grid in Table 6.1. Some performers don't like doing this, believing it to be too time consuming. I think this can be done in about 10–15 minutes and its contribution to confidence can be profound.

TABLE 6.1 Review grid

	What was your goal for this session?	*What went better than expected?*	*What didn't go as well as expected?*	*What are my 'work-ons' / what will I do differently?*
Physical	To keep intensity high for full session	Paced myself really well Still engaged in final 10 minutes	Felt I wasn't making big runs early on. Could be missing opportunities to get forward	Speak to coach about this – need to work on 'engine'
Technical	Sharper first touch Accurate passing off left foot	Good scanning – first touch helps Accuracy improving on left	Still tending to look up before getting ball under control Long balls with left were poor	Keep working on this! Work on!
Tactical	Staying closer when marking Finding space when supporting ball carriers	Good – when I remember – need to keep reminding myself Really pleased – kept making runs	Lost focus, the player I was marking got free headers at corners.	Need to stay close and goal side – remind myself
Mental	Keeping head up after an error Staying in the game	Good early on	Got angry after a bad challenge	Staying calm – anger is wasted energy

You can see that this process also acts as a prompt for the development of other mental skills. Firstly, it can help you set goals for yourself. For example, an area of development is cardiovascular fitness – by doing some additional, multiple sprint training, the ability to stay engaged and make 'box-to-box' runs in the later stages can be turned from an area of perceived weakness to an area of strength.

Another area of skill development is the use of self-talk – here to act on an instruction, when defending the set piece. The self-talk acts as an instructional cue, and needs to be practised for it to become a habit.

Going deeper into the theory

Our current understanding of sport confidence has been largely informed by the work of Bandura (1997) and the development of this by Vealey and her co-workers (Vealey and Chase, 2008; Vealey et al., 1998). These theoretical approaches give a good foundation about the sources of confidence but are less helpful in informing practitioners about how to design interventions aimed at building confidence.

Vealey and Vernau (2010) present a useful applied model designed to identify the key features of effective interventions. This model identifies four key areas:

1. *perspiration* – the role of physical (and *tactical*, *technical* and *mental* – I've added these!) training and preparation
2. *regulation* – self-regulation (self-talk, imagery, goal setting/monitoring and review)
3. *inspiration* – inspirational social forces (context: team, coach, family)
4. *validation* – achievement and experience (recognizing and acknowledging that you are good – not in an arrogant way, but that you have worked hard to earn it).

These authors recognize that confidence is embedded in a range of social interactions – the individual, in a particular role, within a particular team, within a larger organization. This is when confidence-building interventions can become very complicated. For example, individuals may have become extremely competent and 'earned the right' to be confident. Within the group, they fear negative evaluation from team mates for being overly confident or arrogant and therefore become unwilling to show how good they are. This can be a barrier to displaying confidence.

Equally challenging are the performers who believe themselves to be better than they really are. Performers with a deep robust belief that they are the 'finished article' are uncoachable. Often this situation develops because they benchmark themselves against the performance of others. To break out of this, a coach needs to challenge them to find new benchmarks, either self-referenced, 'You're good, but let's find ways of making you better', or externally 'You're good, but x does this better than you'.

My final point about confidence and its relationship with competence. The Dunning–Kruger effect is a humbling piece of research which was awarded the IgNobel Prize in 2000. The IgNobels are awarded each year for research which first makes you laugh and then makes you think. What Kruger and Dunning found was that people are often at their *most* confident when they are at their *least* competent. A failure to see the extent and implications of a lack of skill can make a performer very difficult to work with.

Bibliography

Bandura, A. (1977). Self-efficacy: toward a unifying theory of behavioral change. *Psychological Review 84* (2): 191–215.

Bandura, A. (1988). Self-regulation of motivation and action through goal systems. In V. Hamilton, G.H. Bower, & N.H. Frijda (Eds.), *Cognitive Perspectives on Emotion and Motivation* (pp. 37–61). Kluwer Academic Publishers.

Kruger, J., & Dunning, D. (1999). Unskilled and unaware of it: how difficulties in recognizing one's own incompetence lead to inflated self-assessments. *Journal of Personality and Social Psychology 77* (6): 1121–1134.

Vealey, R.S., & Chase, M.A. (2008). Self-confidence in sport: conceptual and research advances. In T.S. Horn (Ed.), *Advances in Sport Psychology* (3rd edn., pp. 65–97). Human Kinetics.

Vealey, R.S., & Vernau, D. (2010) Confidence. In S.J. Hanrahan & M.B. Andersen (Eds.), *Routledge Handbook of Applied Sport Psychology* (pp. 518–527). Routledge.

Vealey, R.S., Hayashi, S.W., Garner-Holman, M., & Giacobbi, P. (1998). Sources of sport-confidence: conceptualization and instrument development. *Journal of Sport and Exercise Psychology 20*: 54–80.

Q41

I am a high-school physical education teacher. How can I help give performers an accurate view of their ability without undermining them? I see high ability performers with no self-belief and those of lower ability with huge self-belief.

Fitness and technique don't always tie up with psychological development. The question centres on the distinction between confidence and competence; in one case we have high competence but low confidence and this is leading to a feeling of inadequacy. Unfortunately this is linked to young people dropping out of sport altogether. In the other case we have low competence coupled with high confidence. This is a dangerous combination which can lead to performers becoming uncoachable or unteachable, because they don't believe they can be better than they currently are. An unwillingness to accept that one can become more competent often leads to a lack of objectivity about why things happen – failure is because someone else made an error.

Let's look at the extreme examples you give in your question: how to develop the confidence of players with good ability who are doing 'mental gymnastics' to avoid recognizing how good they are and seem to maintain their low confidence.

The first question to examine is: what does maintaining low confidence do for them? It might help them fit in with their peers. It can be difficult for a young person to stand up and say 'I'm good at this'.

It attracts negative comments and invites people to be critical if the individual isn't always 'perfect'. It may also be a way of anticipating and avoiding perceived failure – 'See, I told you I was no good'. This is self-handicapping thinking designed to protect self-esteem.

The way to break into this type of faulty thinking is to ensure that the emphasis is always on benchmarking performance against individuals themselves – avoid external benchmarking wherever possible. In this way the outcomes become less important than the processes. The grid outlined in Table 6.1 can be useful in this type of case.

Moving on to the young performer who has less ability but maintains a very high level of confidence, often in the face of contradictory evidence. Potentially the situation is 'stuck' as in the performer doesn't believe he can be better than he currently is and therefore shuts off all avenues for development. Overconfidence often leads to a complacent 'I just need to turn up to win' type of thinking, which may actually be true some of the time. These players may have such a physical and technical advantage at the start of their career that they don't need to work very hard to win. But as they progress in their career, they have to change or risk not fulfilling early potential.

To break out of this type of thinking we must encourage the performer to recognize that being 'a big fish in a small pond' is OK but there is much to be gained by working hard to be the biggest fish in the big pond. Again, don't allow performers to go through the motions in training or in games – set high standards and goals and identify clear process goals for them to hit. Every training session has a purpose and encourage reflection to ensure that the performer doesn't get into the comfort zone – confidence and competence develop together.

Going deeper into the theory

Applied practitioners will, in the course of their career, meet performers who, despite their successes in performance, often over many years, report having no self-belief. They are highly competent but report low confidence. They will also meet the converse: performers who report very high levels of confidence with little to back it up in terms of performance.

The main line of theory which help us to understand how this occurs is attribution theory (Weiner, 1985). Attributions are the reasons people give for why things happen. In the earliest conceptualization of attributions, Weiner proposed that people tended to make attributions around two dimensions – internal and external, stable and unstable. Internal stable attributions were unchanging personal factors like ability, whilst an unstable internal attribution was effort. External stable attributions were task difficulty, whilst external and unstable attributions would be luck.

What happens when individuals are highly competent but not developing self-belief is that they are tending to make external attribution for success – I won because my opponent was poor or I was lucky, not because I have high ability. This is why we need to reconnect them to success and see that the result was a consequence of high effort and good execution of skills, perhaps aided by a poor decision by the opponent. Competence and confidence develop when internal attributions are made.

The converse situation can also be explained in terms of attributions, where performers continually attribute their own lack of success to external factors – I lost because I was unlucky, or because the task was too difficult, *not* because my effort was low or execution poor. It is important to straighten this out because if we don't accept that some part of the performance and outcome is down to personal factors, such as skills or effort, there is no incentive to train and develop.

An understanding of attributions, developing into examining the role of learned helplessness and self-handicapping cognitions, is essential for applied practitioners. In many cases it helps clarify the complex relationship between efficacy beliefs and motivation.

Bibliography

Rees, T., Ingledew, D., & Hardy, L. (2005). Attribution in sport psychology: seeking congruence between theory, research and practice. *Psychology of Sport and Exercise 6* (2): 189–204.

Weiner, B. (1985). An attribution theory of achievement motivation and emotion. *Psychological Review 92*: 548–573.

Q42

What is the most common trait you notice in high-level and very driven athletes?

What is the psychological X factor? I could 'fudge' this and say 'mental toughness' and we will be right back to square one with the bag of 'virtues'. But I'm not going to. I am going to put my money where my mouth is and highlight self-efficacy as the single element which is shared among elite and consistently highly performing athletes.

My working definition for self-efficacy is the strength of your belief that you can organize and execute the skills required to achieve your goals whatever else is going on. For the performer, coach, parent or teacher, the next question is: how do I find out more about self-efficacy and, even more importantly, how do I develop it? This is again linked to the grid in Table 6.1.

- ◆ What are the actions you need to execute to produce the outcomes you want?
- ◆ Build a list of the 'jobs' you have to do, to get the outcome(s) you want.
- ◆ Tell me on a scale of 0–10 (0 = certain I can't do; 10 = certain I can do) how strong the belief is that you can do this job.

This then takes us back to the coaching balance of working on the things you can't do to make sure they improve and working on the things you can do to keep them polished.

Going deeper into the theory

Mental toughness isn't the panacea we all hoped for. In my view it's a headline and below it are the psychological 'nuts and bolts' that really matter. When pushed I'd put self-efficacy as the most important.

Bandura (1997, p. 3) defines self-efficacy as the 'belief in one's capabilities to organise and execute the course of action required to produce given attainment'. However, self-efficacy does cover a range of tasks and skills related to performance. There is an excellent chapter on efficacy by Beauchamp et al. (2012) which gives an overview of the many different forms of efficacy used in sport. I would highlight self-regulatory efficacy as a link between models of self-regulation, confidence and mental toughness. Self-regulatory efficacy, which is an indication of the strength of the belief that individuals have in their ability to self-regulate, covers so many of the bases tested in performance. It is, in my opinion, one of the key 'flags' practitioners should operationalize for themselves and form questions about to pose early in the assessment stage of applied intervention work.

Bibliography

Bandura, A. (1997). *Self-Efficacy: The Exercise of Control*. Freeman.
Beauchamp, M.R., Jackson, B., & Morton, K.L. (2012). Efficacy beliefs and human performance: from independent action to interpersonal functioning. In S. Murphy (Ed.), *The Oxford Handbook of Sport and Performance Psychology* (pp. 273–293). Oxford University Press.

Q43

What's the best way to break out of a slump in performance?

You'll have heard it many times – 'form is temporary, class is permanent'. By common consent it is attributed to Bill Shankly, the legendary manager of Liverpool Football Club between 1950 and 1974.

What Shankly and all those who cited him are saying is that, whilst performances can be inconsistent and unpredictable, what lies beneath – the ability to perform – remains constant.

Many players use this to help manage periods when they are struggling to produce their best and are seemingly not getting the results they feel they should be getting or that they deserve.

So what is form? Good form is when a player or team appears to be consistently performing at or near their potential, over a period of time. Poor form or a slump is the opposite.

But there are also subtleties in this distinction – good form is indicated not just by the outcome but also the processes. When movements feel automatic and spontaneous, and plans are executed smoothly and without conscious effort or fear, players are more likely to describe this as good form. This is the essence of what Shankly was describing as class – the processes underpinning performance.

So how can we use this knowledge to break out of a slump?

♦ Challenge faulty thinking; winning and good performance are not the same thing.
♦ Identify, practice and execute the key processes which make you a difficult and threatening opponent.
♦ Keep intensity and effort high. In your thinking the score board is always nil–nil.
♦ Review performance – reconnect with positives and use negatives to inform the next block of preparation.

If you have lost, look at the defeat in context. What can we learn from it to plan for the next opponent?

Finally, accept that there will be periods in a sporting career when, seemingly for no reason, skills are not as smooth as they usually are, and previously effortless performance feels laboured. Resist the temptation to overanalyse. If you have practised hard and consistently, your central nervous system knows how to do the skill. Relax and trust it to do its work.

Going deeper into the theory

The descriptions of good form appear to have a great deal in common with the flow state I have described earlier in the text (see Chapter II).

Discussions of form and how to break out of periods of indifferent or poor form will be very common ground for sport psychology practitioners and it is important that novice psychologists develop a set of assessment questions which determine whether the client is talking about mental factors linked to performance or whether performance is due to technical, physical or tactical issues. Practitioners should carefully avoid straying into the domain of the coach, or any other sport science practitioner. This is another example of where a multidisciplinary approach to sport performance, involving other sport science and coaching expertise, can benefit the client, if consenting.

An applied self-help approach to 'slumpbusting' was published by Alan Goldberg in 1998. In it he identifies issues around self-control, attentional focus, goal setting, managing expectations and fear, developing confidence and using imagery as being important to break out of a cycle of poor form. I like this book, but it does have the drawback I've highlighted with several other books of this sort. As there is no interaction with a human psychologist, there is no assessment of which strategy is best for this individual client, presenting with this issue. The client may try to do everything, all at once, and find that nothing really sticks.

Bibliography

Goldberg, A. (1998). *Slumpbusting: 10 Steps to Mental Toughness and Peak Performance.* Human Kinetics.

Q44

How can I stay mentally tough? I haven't started a game all season; I usually only get a few minutes on court each week. I train hard and am really committed to the programme but never seem to get a chance to play

Sport can be really difficult sometimes. You probably look around and see players who appear to be favoured in ways you are not. They are selected; you train hard and show great commitment, but do not get selected. It seems unfair. You need to manage this thinking carefully; you can get into a downward spiral of negative thought which means that when your opportunity comes you are so weighed down with anger and resentment that there is no chance for you exploit it. Patience and commitment will probably be rewarded.

There are some key steps to keep you engaged and ready:

- ◆ Challenge your own thinking about fairness. Many things in sport and life in general are unfair; to expect complete fairness is faulty and unhelpful thinking. What you must do is ensure that when decisions are made there is sufficient evidence to support your case rather than someone else's. Evidence is usually based on what you do over a period of time. Staying positive and committed is more likely to get you the result you want.
- ◆ Speak to your coach. Ask very specific questions: what do I need to work on and develop to put me in contention for starting selection?
- ◆ You do need to respect the selection decisions of the coach; there is no need to become frustrated or angry. Coaches often don't like to have this conversation because if you go away and do what they suggest and

they still don't pick you, tension can escalate, causing further damage to the relationship.

♦ Recognize that you might not be the most skilful on the team but you can be the most enthusiastic and committed. This can be tough, working harder than everyone else but it seemingly not being recognized. But it will be worth it.

♦ Recognize that you are one tight hamstring from starting. As a benchwarmer you can switch off, believing that you will never get a chance. Injuries happen all the time – your chance may come at the misfortune of another. But you must be ready – always ready. Expect to start every game.

♦ Know the play book and know what the coach's substitution plans are. Watch how the role you will be filling is developing. If you have a set-piece role, analyse your possible opponents: how are they marking, how will you attack them, how do they threaten you? Know when it is likely that you will get on court or pitch. Make sure you are ready; warm up physically, mentally and technically.

♦ Play every play. Even when you are on the bench, don't switch off mentally. Be ready at 1 minute's notice to be on and playing at 100%.

Going deeper into the theory

One of the first papers published in one of the most prominent sport psychology journals, *The Sport Psychologist,* was entitled The social psychology of the benchwarmer. Rotella and Newberg interviewed three scholarship university-level performers with the aim of understanding the psychological challenges experienced by non-starters. They identified a number of valuable areas: firstly, that a significant amount of players' identity is bound up in their role as an athlete. Not starting was a threat to this and leads to players revising their perceptions of themselves and their commitment to their sport. This can be a profound watershed in players' lives as it is highly likely that they have moved to their current status as a consequence of being one of the highest performers at a lower level. Going from being a high-performer, with the associated status, to being a lower-level performer at a higher level can require significant support.

Secondly, players found the management of their relationship with the coach problematic. They experienced pain and confusion that the coach who had recruited them to play was not selecting them. They felt that 'yardsticks' by which performance could be assessed were not clear and that players were kept in the dark about selection decisions.

Finally, performers may overlook the fact that coaches have responsibility for the whole team. Keeping this in perspective and finding ways to contribute to the team other than playing may be a way of keeping a reserve player engaged and contributing.

Being part of a squad is a fact of life in sport. Most sports now recognize that the bench is an important element of performance. They are tactical options which will probably be used. The psychology of the benchwarmer needs to be revisited to ensure coaches and performers maximize the potential of non-starting players.

Bibliography

Dancey, B., & Hudson, J. (2009). A qualitative exploration of substitutes' experiences in soccer. *The Sport Psychologist 23* (4): 451–469.

Rotella, R.J., & Newburg, D.S. (1989). The social psychology of the benchwarmer. *The Sport Psychologist 3* (1): 48–62.

Pulling the threads together

Non-psychologists quite rightly become frustrated and confused when psychologists use different names for psychological constructs which appear to be the same or very similar. Positive psychology, mental toughness, self-efficacy, self-belief, self-regulation, hardiness and resilience appear to be examples of this. There is considerable debate as to how these fit together and relate to other psychological constructs. This is the kind of question which is of technical interest to the academic but of less importance to the applied practitioner. I would love to be the person who can solve the puzzle, aligning the models presented in this chapter and developing a single simple method of assessing self-belief, mental toughness, hardiness and resilience reliably, with sound validity and objectivity. Such a feat would certainly earn the recognition of my peers.

But pragmatically, as an applied practitioner I am less concerned. It is not essential that we have this consensus – we will still probe and question around our clients' view of mental toughness, whatever we call it. How we proceed in the work with our clients is determined by their understanding, not ours.

VII

Team spirit: accident or design?

Humans are social animals. Our ancestors established, probably through trial and error, that the best way to survive was to cooperate and collaborate, rather than to strive as an individual. Twenty-first-century life is structured around highly organized and complex social processes that operate in our work, social and sporting lives.

The term 'group dynamics' has been coined to capture the way groups of people come together around a common interest or goal and how they interact to achieve it, fulfilling, sometimes, both group aims and individual aspirations. Indeed this is how the first definitions of groups were established. For example, for Lewin (1948) the key was not the size or structure of the group but the interdependence between members. Brown (1988) developed this further: groups are determined by a recognition and awareness of collective identity among members. Group members recognize each other as being part of the group and depend on each other in some mutually meaningful way.

Groups and teams are in constant flux. There are explicit structures, rule and norms of behaviour and conventions of communication, and there are the much more subtle and complex implicit rules governing how the team operates, based on history or custom, things that new members to a group will often only pick up when they make an error or transgress a rule. Groups change over time: personnel changes, roles and norms evolve, but ultimately the purpose remains the same – to establish and achieve collective aims along with the satisfaction of personal aspirations. This is a mechanism by which a group develops into a team. Teams have a more formal structure; they are cohesive and share norms and aspirations (Carron and Eys, 2012). Groups are not necessarily teams, but all teams are groups.

Anyone who has ever reflected on teams they have been part of will appreciate their seemingly incomprehensible complexity. There are some very basic questions to answer:

♦ How is it that teams composed of people who are most technically or physical gifted are often outperformed by teams made up of individuals who are less able but who seem to gel into a better unit?

♦ Do teams made up of people who are friends perform better than teams made up of strangers?

♦ What is the best way to lead a team towards fulfilling its potential?

What these questions are leading to is a question that was posed by the earliest researchers into the social psychology of groups – what factors lead to the greatest levels of group performance?

In very general terms Steiner (1972) answered the question:

Group performance = potential productivity – process losses

where potential productivity is the 'on-paper' resources of the group, its ability, its productivity record and any gains possible from collaboration. Process losses occur when either the internal or external environment intervenes to slow or undermine performance. This could be poor planning, poor communication or external factors intervening. This is a generic model but does help to get a handle on the steps underpinning group performance. It's not just about summing individual performance: it's about how well people can work together.

Team synergy in action

The word 'synergy' comes from a Greek root and means working together. Not many teams are truly synergistic. In fact many sports teams, particularly high-level teams, appear to be the opposite, antisynergistic or anergistic, where the potential of neither the individual nor the team is realized. This is because there are many process losses – conflicting motivations of team members, ineffective leadership, injuries, loss of form, poor planning or the good performance of other teams.

Synergy or synergistic effects occur when the output of a team appears to be greater than the sum of individual parts. For several decades sport psychology researchers and practitioners have been working on the factors characterizing teams that achieve that cohesive and synergistic chemistry.

How do I build a team that is greater than the sum of its parts?

'Talent wins games but teamwork wins championships'. So says Michael Jordan, one of the greatest NBA players of all time.

But what make teams work? This question faces many organizations – corporate, military, public and private sector, and sports teams. Anyone who has played in a team sport will recognize the paradox – you are part of a team of outstanding individuals who, on one-against-one comparisons, are stronger, at least on paper, than the opposition or the competitors. But you are outperformed by seemingly weaker teams.

What is cohesive synergy and how can it be created..?

Carron and Eys (2012) reviewed literature from sports, military and organizational psychology and presented this definition of the sports team:

> a collection of two or more individuals who possess a common identity, have common goals, share a common fate, exhibit structured patterns of interaction and modes of communication, hold common perceptions about group structure, are personally and instrumentally interdependent, reciprocate interpersonal attraction and consider themselves a group.
>
> (Carron and Eys, 2012, p.13)

Carron and his colleague have helped us get a handle on what cohesive synergy is and give some clues about how to build it. Team members share motivation, identity and responsibility and they achieve this by the ways in which they act towards one another and communicate with each other. What this translates into is the culture of the team.

Culture, cohesion and synergy

Rainer Martens, one of the pioneers in applied sport psychology, wrote in 1987 that the essence of coaching is creating a team culture. But, like many other terms, team culture as a concept has been used by many researchers and in so many different ways it has become difficult to define. Personally I prefer the definition of Schroeder (2010), who operationalizes culture as the psychological and social environment that maximizes the team's ability to achieve success.

I am sympathetic to, but less comfortable with, a definition presented by Voight and Carroll (2006, p. 324) that team culture is about the extent to which players 'think alike, speak alike and act alike, so they can support and reinforce the best in each other'. We do not want clones or automatons; we don't want to stifle individual creativity. There will be situations where this type of culture is valuable and correct but others where it is clearly not. In my applied work with teams, I take a more pragmatic view of team culture. It is a combination of our reason for existing, what is the team for? coupled with how we do things – how we think and act to achieve what we are for. Many groups underperform because they don't reflect on these basic aspects of culture. They 'sleepwalk' into routines; individual roles and group norms become habitual and there are patterns of communication without any reflection on the values behind what they do.

Where cultural reflection does take place it is superficial and often doesn't translate into action. There is no thought about the complex jigsaw of factors which turn a shared culture into cohesive team performance.

Teams get stuck because when those who are motivated or capable of initiating change begin their work, all they see is seemingly intractable complexity and difficulty – where do I start?

I want to build a cohesive and synergistic team – where do I start?

Because team dynamics are so complex, there appear to be so many factors impacting on cohesion and productivity and there are many

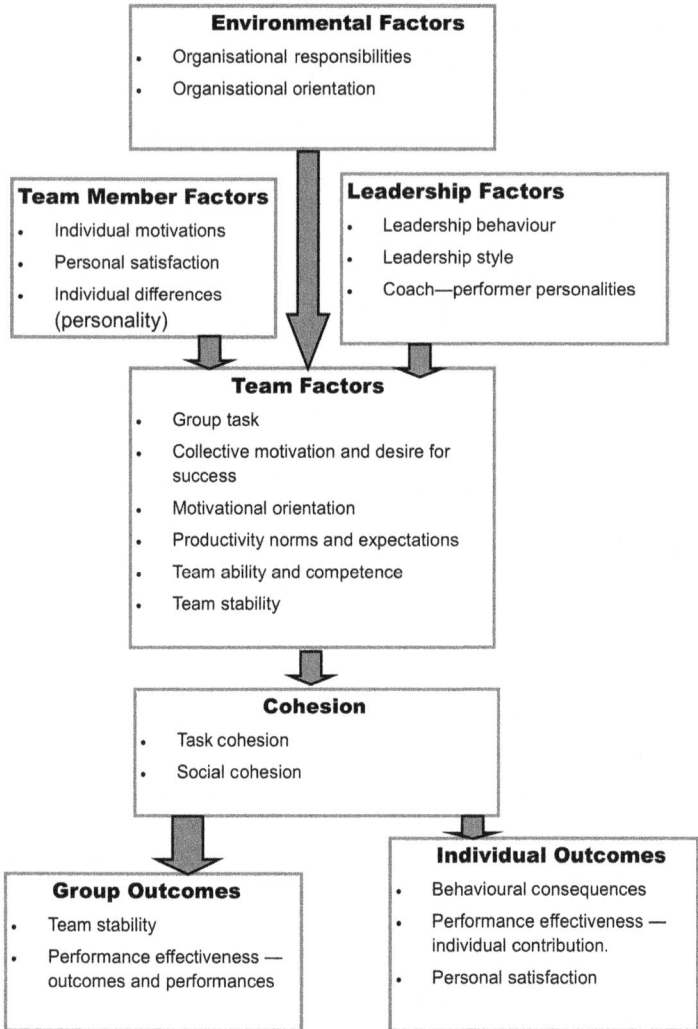

FIGURE 7.1 Adaptation of Carron's (1980) cohesion model of team cohesion in sport.

different places where you can intervene. This is the good news – the bad news is that it can be very difficult to determine the best place to start and which factors are likely to yield the greatest benefit. Ideally what we need is a relatively simple model which gives some straightforward guidance about clusters of factors which can be manipulated or managed to change how a group develops towards fulfilling its potential.

The basic framework for team performance intervention work I do is the model of cohesion first developed by Bert Carron in 1982 (Figure 7.1).

Carron's model identifies four categories of factor which appear to be linked to the development of synergy. It should be noted that I'm not prescribing a recipe for interventions here. Every team environment is different. What I am aiming to achieve is a greater level of understanding of how the groups you are working with function and how aspects of both individual and group behaviour can have an impact on the twin outcomes – group and individual.

Be aware of the limitations of Carron's conceptual model

This type of model, like many others in sport psychology, is descriptive and hypothetical. It is a list of all the factors which could be predictors of cohesion and outcomes. It is easy to look at the arrows and make inferences about what causes what. It looks linear, but in reality groups are dynamic and constantly changing. My view of this model is that it helps me to organize my thoughts about what factors *could* be impacting on the group, either increasing or decreasing the likelihood of cohesion and synergy. It doesn't give me a recipe such as: step 1, fix x; step 2, fix y etc . . . .

What kind of team do you want to be?

♦ Do you want to be a team which is oriented towards the achievement of goals? Is the most important thing to get the job done to the best of our ability, and it doesn't matter if we have interpersonal conflict? This I'd label as a task-oriented team. If it performs well it experiences a *task-cohesive synergy*.

or

◆ Do you want to be a team where it is more important to maintain good interpersonal relationships between team members? Is it more important that everyone maintains positive relationships rather than complete the task to a high level? This is more of a socially oriented team. If it performs well it experiences a *socially cohesive synergy*.

Can teams be both socially and task-cohesive?

This is an important point. It is very difficult for a group or team to be both highly socially cohesive and highly task-cohesive. It's not impossible but it requires some fairly uncommon behaviours among members.

Most groups and teams underperform because they never address this issue – assumptions are made, relationships established and members become rigidly fixed into patterns of behaving and communicating. It is particularly challenging to change a socially cohesive group or team into being more task-cohesive. The reason for this is that it means dramatically re-evaluating and changing the nature of many of the relationships between team members. This has great potential for interpersonal conflict. Often leaders and those facilitating the performance of the group or team decide that such a change is too much trouble. Thus groups and teams become stuck in their underperforming patterns, neither socially nor task-cohesive, failing to fulfil either group aims or personal aspirations.

Task-cohesive synergy

If you ask the question, and the team decides it wants to work towards task synergy, then it enters the type of marginal gains environment discussed earlier in the text. It requires clarity of purpose and very high levels of motivation and commitment. Progress towards the goal may require sacrificing or renegotiating personal relationships within the group and putting individual motivations to one side. We don't need to be friends, in fact there may be conflict, but we do need to be able to work together to get the job done. Interactions are characterized by questions between members of this form: 'What do you need from me to help you perform better?'

Accountability is a big issue in task-cohesive teams – this may result in passionate debate about different options. If handled well, conflict has the potential to be extremely beneficial. I will examine interpersonal conflict a little later in this chapter, when I look at communication. Trust me, interpersonal conflict is not a bad thing – provided a few rules are established.

Socially cohesive synergy

On the other hand, deciding that a team would prefer to be socially cohesive may require individuals to put personal or team task goals to one side in order to maintain relationships. Socially cohesive groups and teams place social relationships above performance on tasks: 'Good enough will do, as long as we remain on friendly terms with each other'. Tasks may be completed but the superordinate goal is that there is a positive and satisfying social environment.

The importance of one-to-one relationships in building cohesive synergy – both task and social

In a team of five members, there are ten one-to-one relationships; in a team of 11 there are 55; by the time you get to a team of 35, there are 595!

One-to-one relationships are the basic units of a team. For synergies to occur, these units must work – it's not imperative that all one-to-ones are socially cohesive, but they must be able to understand and respect each other's roles and work constructively towards the achievement of the group goals. Frequently the most significant blockage to synergy is a pattern within the group interactions, where one-to-one relationships have broken down. There are many reasons why this can occur; people often label them as 'clashes of personality', but this is too general a description. It is more likely to be breakdowns in mutual respect, distrust of motivations and a lack of honesty in communication which result in team failures at this most basic level. If a large proportion of one-to-one relationships in a team are broken or weak, efforts to build cohesive synergy will almost certainly result in failure.

Unpacking Carron's model: environmental factors

Teams form and remain formed for a reason – their core functions. Many sports teams form specifically to compete; their purpose is to be successful in competition. The reason for the formation of a team needs to be explicit – if it isn't, then significant challenges can arise. This is particularly the case in non-elite and grassroots sport. For example, community teams may form with little thought about their aims – is the purpose to offer children from the community an opportunity to play the sport? Or are we aiming to identify and develop talent? It is difficult to do both, without compromising one or the other. This is an issue I pick up in greater detail in Chapter VIII on youth sport.

Clarifying what we are for

Players, coaches and other support staff are recruited and may have a contractual relationship with the team. Contracts are an excellent way to clarify what they have been hired to do, how they will be remunerated and rewarded and make transparent how they contribute to the achievement of the set aims. But many teams operate without these. A contractual approach to team formation is not the same as its culture.

The culture is more abstract and grows out of the organizational environment. There is a view that the most effective organizational cultures grow from the 'bottom up', rather than being imposed on organizations from the 'top down'. This type of approach gives players, who often view themselves as relatively powerless to control things that happen to them in their playing careers, an opportunity to own the culture they work in. They can be a part of the decision-making process determining how the organization works. Some coaches, teachers and leaders are uneasy about handing over this type of control to players, feeling that it is their job to create and reinforce the organizational environment. In my experience, this tends to reinforce a 'them-versus-us' divide between players and coaching and support staff. If that is what you want to happen that's fine, but it may result in a passive and risk-averse team culture.

In his book *Legacy*, James Kerr (2013) examined the culture around the New Zealand All Blacks. This is a team which, despite having consistently, on paper, the best individual players in world rugby, had failed to win the World Cup in the professional era. In 2007, following another unsuccessful World Cup campaign, a new coach was appointed. Kerr's book describes how the coach initiated and cemented a new approach to team culture. This resulted in the team winning the World Cup in 2011 and became the first nation to retain the title in 2015. The strength in depth of the All Blacks is such that they can afford to reject players who would be easily selected for almost any other rugby nation. This means that they can focus much more on team culture, selecting only players who can positively contribute to developing both the team and the wider organization. The factor responsible for the transformation between 2007 and 2011 and beyond was the leadership – another factor in Carron's model. But it wasn't a traditional hierarchical leadership – leadership was found throughout the squad – it was embedded in the culture.

In my work with high-performing teams, I spend a good deal of time determining the nature of the organizational environment – the purpose of the team. Once this has been established I look carefully at the dynamics around three remaining factors in the model – leadership, personal factors and team factors – and, critically, the 'adhesive' that binds them together – communication.

Unpacking Carron's model: great leaders – born or made?

Of all the factors contributing to effective team performance, leadership is perhaps the most researched and discussed. Unfortunately, despite being widely researched, leadership remains a challenging topic, it is not readily amenable to experimental investigation, which makes determining cause and effect difficult. As a consequence there are fewer areas in team psychology where you are more likely to find opinion masquerading as fact, when working with teams, practitioners are advised to listen very carefully for information which indicates the coach's or players' understanding of the term.

The nature/nurture debate related to leadership is a big, unresolvable issue. It is simply impossible to determine with any confidence whether genetics (leaders are born) or learned skills (leaders are made) contribute more to the effectiveness of a leader – both are important. There are some key qualities which anyone can learn, practise and develop. Some other more genetically determined characteristics may influence the expression of these skills but this is what effective leaders tend to do:

- ◆ Establish and clearly communicate the strategic aims of an organization.
- ◆ Create an autonomous environment, creating leaders among the people they are leading.
- ◆ Empathize with their team members.
- ◆ Effectively communicate.
- ◆ Create a day-to-day environment which enables the achievement of both personal and team aims.

Like any other skills, leadership develops with practice; you need to build confidence in being a leader. These are as important as the actual leadership skills themselves. People with excellent leadership skills don't become leaders because other aspects of their psychological makeup hold them back. A distinction often drawn in the literature is that between being a leader and a manager. In essence managers manage resources whilst leaders establish strategic aims and determine the steps required to achieve this aim. But this is often a false distinction – leaders often manage and managers often lead. Leaders tend to ask questions, whilst managers answer them. Learning to question team members as they prepare and perform is a key leadership skill – one I return to and develop later in the text.

Unpacking Carron's model: the personal factor in the team

'There is no I in team'.

This phrase is the favourite of many coaches. It's meant to reinforce the idea that when people work collectively they can achieve more than if they work alone. The sentiment is understood by most people, but the situation is more complex. There is a big 'I' in team. Teams are composed of Is. A soccer team has 11 Is on the field, another five on the bench and then a whole lot of squad Is and coaching and support Is. All individuals in the organization bring with them personal motivations, their personality and their style of interacting with others. Previous chapters have demonstrated that personality and motivation are complex enough when they are viewed in the individual context – when they are put into a complex social interaction they become even more so.

Very often people are recruited into teams on the basis of physical, tactical or technical ability, not their personal characteristics. This is a mistake. Given that one individual can have such an impact on the way members interact and relate to one another, more consideration should be given to the extent to which they are willing to invest in the team culture – a willingness to put the 'we' before the 'I'.

Personal factors can make or break a team

Personal factors, such as personality, resilience and motivation, have a key part to play in whether individuals fit into a team and whether they can add to a culture or undermine it. The All Blacks culture discussed earlier clearly demonstrated this; the culture didn't just require the best players: it demanded the best men. The leaders were willing to remove from the team players who, despite meriting selection on technical and physical criteria, failed on the personal or psychological level. Players were invited to change their attitude or leave. That is a very bold statement about the importance of culture.

Few coaches have clearcut psychological selection or recruitment criteria. Coaches wishing to build cohesive and synergistic teams should look at individuals' ability to perform under pressure, their ability to contribute to the team, their ability to bounce back after a setback. These are indicators of their readiness and ability to connect with their team mates and contribute positively to a team.

A great deal of work has been done on the social psychology of leadership in sports teams; comparatively little has been done on 'followership', the social psychology of being a team member.

When one individual can undermine a team's cohesion and performance

Recent research has identified three types of personal characteristics which can be found in team members, leaders or followers and which have the potential to undermine or prevent a cohesive synergy being created. These have been labelled the 'dark triad': (1) narcissism; (2) machiavellianism; and (3) psychopathy.

Narcissism
Narcissism is characterized by the desire to promote the self over others, very clear ego orientation, pride and a desire for self-promotion over the team.

The problem with narcissists on a team is that they tend to behave in ways which promote themselves (I) rather than the team (we). Successes tend to be theirs, whilst failures are blamed on others.

Machiavallianism
These people tend to seek power: they are characterized by exploitation of others and a cynical disregard for their feelings or happiness. Machiavellians will bend or break rules to get what they want and, because they act in self-interest, if it goes wrong they will ensure others are viewed as responsible.

The problem with Machiavellis on the team is that they see other team members useful only in terms of helping them get what they personally want – usually it is about enhancing their own status or influence at the expense of others.

Psychopathy

Psychopathy is characterized by risk taking and impulsivity, selfishness, a lack of empathy and antisocial behaviour.

The problem with psychopathic behaviour on teams is that people may be impulsive and manage risk poorly. Psychopathic team members lack empathy with others and find it difficult to interact diplomatically with others on their team.

These terms are more frequently used in clinical psychology to describe groups of symptoms associated with psychological illness. However, recent research has suggested that some of these characteristics can occur at a subclinical level and may be more prevalent than you imagine. There is also some evidence indicating that social trends are making these three aspects of personality more common.

Recent research has suggested expanding the dark triad to a fourth factor – *everyday sadism* (Skeem et al., 2011). Everyday sadists are people who behave in ways that deliberately inflict pain on others either physically or psychologically. This may seem like the core business of a sports coach or trainer. The difference in everyday sadism is that the person on the receiving end has not consented and there is no purpose other than pleasure for the perpetrator. In teams and social settings, everyday sadists are cruel people to work with and for: a complete lack of compassion and empathy means that they seize opportunities to undermine others or cruelly expose their limitations.

The dark triad (or tetrad) – team assets or the seeds of destruction?

There is an issue around the dark triad in sport. There are some aspects of all three (or four) characteristics which may be beneficial to performance in the highly competitive world of sport. I have discussed evidence indicating that narcissists tend to cope with pressure better than non-narcissists (Wallace et al., 2005; Akehurst, 2009). As a practitioner, I am very conscious of the balance between the possible benefits of the dark triad of characteristics and its potential to wreck team synergy and cohesion. I suspect that much of the upheaval experienced around the England cricket team in the Kevin Pietersen era was based in poor management of a number of key people displaying elements of the dark triad.

Unpacking Carron's model – team factors: size, role and norms

Team size

The bigger the group, the more difficult to achieve synergy. This is because of a phenomenon called social loafing. Social loafing is the opposite of synergy: it occurs when a group of people becomes so large that people can hide, knowing that their contribution to the overall effort cannot be determined accurately. Social loafing is common in groups over around the size of half a dozen members.

Team structure

Team structure refers to the way in which hierarchies, either formal or informal, operate in the team. Formal hierarchies may be determined by seniority or rank. These can be problematic because they prevent free communication and exchange of ideas between arms or subgroupings within the team. Ideally what we want is a flat organization where there is a willingness to accept good ideas from wherever they come from. Often more challenging are the informal hierarchies or clusters in groups: these can be cliques around nationality or background. These can be benign or can completely undermine the performance of the team. Cliques within a team should always be examined carefully to ensure that they don't become so inwardly looking and cohesive that they detract from the overall team performance.

Group roles and norms

Roles are the designated jobs that team members have been brought in to do – they can be appointed roles or they can be emergent. The key thing is that people are doing jobs they want to do and they have agreed to fulfil. Teams can be fundamentally knocked off course when people are given jobs they don't want or feel unable to fulfil. Norms refer to the normal ways the team operates. These can be formally established norms or a code of conduct, such as codes of dress or behaviour. Equally they could be codes of attitude or communication. It is important that these are discussed. A collaborative approach to establishing norms is often a good way to begin a new season.

Communication – the glue that binds teams or the wrecking ball that destroys them

The glue that holds high-performing teams together is effective communication. Ineffective communication has the exact opposite effect (Burke, 2010).

Communication is usefully viewed as a four-step process – two on the part of the transmitters, clarifying and then delivering the message, and two on the part of the receiver, hearing and understanding the message.

TABLE 7.1 Main stages in the process of communication

		Transmitter	Receiver
Step 1	**Think**	What message am I trying to convey?	
Step 2	**Act**	Selecting the right words Tone, tempo, loudness Posture	
Step 3	**Hear**		Listen to the message Hear its tone See the body language
Step 4	**Understand**		Understand the message Make sense of what the transmitter wants me to do

Most coaches, teachers and parents focus their attention on steps 1 and 2, i.e. what they are saying and how they are saying it. This is important but *not* as important as steps 3 and 4. You will only know what has been heard and understood if you ask questions and follow up, watching how the receivers change their behaviour.

Communication in high-performing teams is an active process designed at establishing three key interpersonal characteristics – there need to be mutual trust, honesty and respect between players and between coaches. These are the building blocks of team synergy. Helping performers to communicate effectively is an important role of the team psychologist. Without this skill many things which should be said remain unsaid and teams drift into a fixed and underperforming state which can be extremely difficult to change.

Good communication skills are a way of using interpersonal conflict positively to develop new understandings and potentials for synergy. Coaches and performers often shy away from difficult conversations. Accountability is not a dirty word – if players aren't fulfilling their role or contributing to the team culture they need to know and they need to understand the consequences. This isn't an issue of 'throwing weight around'; this is an issue which goes to the heart of the team culture – what are we for, if we are unable to discuss this for fear of hurting someone's feelings? We probably have a team which has become very socially cohesive at the expense of task completion. This reflects back to earlier observations about the outcome driven culture in some sports organisations and teams. To some it may constitute an end justifying a means. A recent high profile example of this type of mismatch is the case of Shane Sutton, a cycling coach in the GB track team. Some riders perceived his communication style as demanding and direct, whilst others viewed him as a 'bully'. The lines between these two views is blurred and problematic.

Most coaches and performers are more comfortable with apathy than conflict. This is a dangerous situation – apathy and compliance indicate low engagement. On the other hand conflict means we have highly energized differences; this energy is something we can use.

The 'million-dollar' question: do cohesive teams actually perform better?

I have spoken to many coaches about cohesion. Some very strongly point out that teams become more cohesive if they are successful, whilst others have it the other way round. Which is right?

This is a challenging question. Because we don't study teams in the laboratory it is difficult to determine where the cause-and-effect lies. The evidence indicates that actually both views are right, but it appears that the causal relationship between cohesion and performance is stronger (Carron et al., 2002). As we have seen, successful outcomes are not within personal control, whilst building cohesion can be. This indicates that coaches and team leaders should actively work to build cohesion, rather than expect success to build it for them.

In the longer term, cohesion is probably what will make a team robust and resilient. Highly cohesive teams will weather the inevitable challenges better than low cohesive teams. If your aim is to keep a team together long enough for it to mature and perform, building cohesion is a good strategy.

Questions about teams

The questions that follow have all been posed by coaches and performers who are working in teams or larger organizations. I have established Carron's model as my guiding heuristic but would stress again that formulaic approaches to building teams are doomed to failure. Teams that work actively to develop a culture, recognize and respect the contributions of all members, trust the motives of members and engage honestly with each other are more likely to be effective. Communication is the key element which holds all this together. But, change one person in a team, and it can be an entirely new dynamic; you think you are recruiting a charismatic leader, but in fact you may have signed a team-wrecking narcissist. Teams really are that complicated!

Bibliography

Akehurst, S. (2009). Self-love: understanding the narcissistic sport performer. *The Sport and Exercise Scientist 21*: 27–29.

Brown, R. (1988). *Group Processes. Dynamics Within and Between Groups.* Blackwell.

Burke, K.L. (2010). Constructive communication. In S.J. Hanrahan & M.B. Andersen (Eds.), *Routledge Handbook of Applied Sport Psychology* (pp. 315–324). Routledge.

Carron, A.V. (1982). Cohesiveness in sport groups: interpretations and considerations. *Journal of Sport Psychology 4*: 123–138.

Carron, A.V., Colman, M.M., Wheeler, J., & Stevens, D. (2002). Cohesion and performance in sport: a meta analysis. *Journal of Sport and Exercise Psychology 24*: 168–188.

Carron, A.V., & Eys, M.A. (2012). *Group Dynamics in Sport* (4th edn.). Fitness Information Technology.

Kerr, J. (2013). *Legacy.* Constable.

Lewin, K. (1948). *Resolving Social Conflicts.* Springer.

Mallett, C.J. (2010). Conflict management. In S.J. Hanrahan & M.B. Andersen (Eds.), *Routledge Handbook of Applied Sport Psychology* (pp. 345–354). Routledge.

Martens, R. (1987). *Successful Coaching.* Human Kinetics.

Schroeder, P.J. (2010). Changing team culture: the perspectives of ten successful head coaches. *Journal of Sport Behavior 33* (1), 63–88.

Skeem, J.L., Polaschek, D. L.., Patrick, C.J., & Lilienfeld, S.O. (2011). Psychopathic personality: bridging the gap between scientific evidence and public policy. *Psychological Science in the Public Interest 12* (3): 95–162.

Steiner, I.D. (1972). *Social Psychology.* Academic Press.

Thomas, K.W., & Kilmann, R.H. (1974). *Thomas–Kilmann Conflict Mode Instrument.* Xicom.

Voight, M., & Carroll, P. (2006). Applying sport psychology philosophies, principles and practices onto the gridiron: USC football coach Pete Carroll. *International Journal of Sports Science and Coaching, 1* (4), 321–331.

Wallace, H.M., Baumeister, R.F., & Vohs, K.D. (2005) Audience support and choking under pressure: a home disadvantage? *Journal of Sports Sciences 23* (4): 429–438.

Q45

I coach a cricket team. I get very worried about the effect of some of the banter my players engage in, at training and in games. Basically, the question is, should we take the 'mick' out of each other?

Banter can be part of the social glue which holds a team together. But, banter is in the ear of the beholder. 'Taking the mick' could be perceived by one player as a mark of inclusion – if we do this to you, we are saying that you are one of us and we are comfortable that you will not feel undermined or disrespected. In contrast, another player may perceive himself to be undermined, disrespected and excluded by barbs and comments. This does need to be managed carefully. If it isn't it can lead to groups within the whole group (cliques) which become very socially cohesive and override the task cohesion of the overall group.

It is important that team members have a safe mechanism to share their worries about banter. Bear in mind, one of the qualities you are aiming to develop in your team is empathy – knowing where the boundaries are around banter is essential.

Young and inexperienced players may be particularly vulnerable, as either the targets of banter as a rite of passage into the group or giving inappropriate banter as a way of demonstrating their growing status. I advise coaches and teachers to be sensitive to this. Have a discussion about the dressing-room etiquette and clarify what is acceptable and where players need to exercise care. Ask the players to devise some guidelines about acceptability. You are not being a killjoy, you are anticipating a challenge to the cohesion of the group and making sure everyone knows where lines are drawn.

Going deeper into the theory

Banter certainly has a role to play in regulating the emotion in social interactions in sport. The tone of the communications is often typified by being 'black and blue' – dark humour and/or profane language. As a sport psychologist you should expect this and recognize its function. It can be a cathartic safety valve. However, I recommend that you note carefully who is giving the banter and who is on the receiving end. Be aware that it is often highly reflective of status-based communication, with the strongest directing the banter to the weakest, where weakest may be related to age, experience, ability or duration on the team (Jacob and Carron, 1996).

Careful observation, coupled with follow-up discreet questioning, helps determine whether the banter is useful in drawing the team together or destructive.

Bibliography

Jacob, C.S., & Carron, A.V. (1996). Sources of status in sports teams. *International Journal of Sport Psychology 27*: 369–382.

Q46

How do I build team cohesion?

What type of cohesion are you aiming to develop – task or social? Culture grows from the answer to this question.

Observers are surprised to hear that in some high-performing teams there is little or no social interaction away from training and performance. It is quite rare to find high-performing teams that are both socially and task-cohesive. In high-performance terms task cohesion is essential but social cohesion merely desirable.

I will highlight four factors causally related to cohesion in high-performance teams and strategies for building towards your 'great team'. These are:

◆ stability
◆ leadership
◆ roles/accountability
◆ communication.

As regards stability, in 99% of cases it take time to build greatness. If you have a team of 20 people contributing to an outcome,changing just two people means that 10% of the relationships in the organization have been disrupted, and you effectively have a new team. This is why decisions about who to recruit into your team should be as focused on their willingness to fit into the culture as their ability to perform on the field.

With regard to leadership, the role of leaders is to create a clear vision for the team. This isn't simply about establishing a destination; the vision should also clarify the culture of the organization – what, on a day-to-day basis, we, the team, should be focusing on. The leader establishes the values and acts as a role model. Leadership is often viewed as 'top-down' hierarchy. In fact, in most high-performing teams leadership is more an issue of who has the requisite skills to maximize the outcomes, so leadership can come from any group member. The more the appointed leaders are able to develop leadership behaviour at every level in the team the better, as everyone then feels they are active contributors to team performance.

Team members perform optimally when they are clear about what their role is, they accept it and have the skills to execute it. And they are accountable. This is predicated on the last point.

Going deeper into the theory

Groups and team questions are often difficult to answer. There are so many lines of theory which can be used to inform an answer. I have used the model of effective teamwork developed in Syer and Connolly's (1996) *How Teamwork Works* to identify the four factors – stability, leadership, roles/accountability and communication – which appear to be the strongest determinants of synergy.

Coaches and teachers often believe that high-performing teams can be developed very rapidly. This is partly because a great deal of the research on team performance has been conducted in the North American context and in college sport. Each season there is a change in team personnel and there is no way of knowing if the team would have performed even better if it had remained unchanged for longer than a season. In high-level professional sport, where other factors, such as injury, determine selection to elite teams, team stability is at a premium.

In addition to Syer and Connolly's work, Lecioni's (2002) classic *Five Dysfunctions of a Team: A Leadership Fable* is valuable in guiding interventions around roles/accountability and communication.

Bibliography

Kerr, J. (2013). *Legacy*. Constable.
Lecioni, P.M. (2002). *Five Dysfunctions of a Team, A Leadership Fable*. John Wiley.
Syer, J.D., & Connolly. C. (1996). *How Teamwork Works: The Dynamics of Effective Team Development*. McGraw-Hill.

Q47

Help – I've got a load of cliques in my team!

Cliques form for a range of reasons. Players from different clubs may tend to group together and players from overseas may stick together through their common language or social customs. Whatever the reason, the impact of cliques can be devastating to overall team cohesion and performance.

Cliques form when the goals of a small group become more important to those individuals than the goals of the team or the overall organization. It is usually the case that the small group is highly socially cohesive and inward-looking. The priority for the clique is to promote its own members and its own identity, often at the expense of the wider group.

The best way to manage cliques is to prevent their formation. Unpicking established cliques can be a challenge requiring re-engineering of the entire group. This may involve interpersonal conflict and skilful diplomacy.

How do we avoid cliques forming? Firstly, as the group is forming, discuss the purpose, identity and culture of the overall team. We have come together to do a job. Everyone will play a part in forming the culture and deciding how we interact with each other. Inevitably certain individuals will tend to gravitate towards each other. Leaders need to be aware of this and ensure that as these teams within teams form, they are not establishing exclusive and socially cohesive cliques.

In your current crisis you have two choices – slowly, slowly or a potentially more confrontational approach. The slowly, slowly approach involves gradually introducing exercises, drills and perhaps ultimately selection which encourages the socially cohesive clique to work more with other team members in contexts, for example, a tour or a training camp, where the day-to-day schedule is under your control. This might be the preferred strategy. The more confrontational approach requires preparation and you need to ensure that you will be supported by members in the wider group.

Either way, you will be entering the 'zone of uncomfortable conversation' – you can speak to individuals in the clique on their own or you can bring the clique together. The agenda is clear – that their behaviour is undermining the cohesion of the overall group and they need to change. It is likely that there will be conflict. You need to stand your ground and provide evidence of how the clique is impacting on the wider group. The clique needs some time to assimilate your views and respond. You are not saying that the social bonds need to be broken; what you want is for the members of the clique to contribute more fully to the overall team and support other team members in the same way that they support each other. There might be difficult decisions about selection and recruitment as a consequence of this type of intervention. Team culture is above any individual. A valuable player may need to be dropped in order to maintain the team culture. This isn't done lightly, but there may be no other way.

Going deeper into the theory

Carron's (1982) model of cohesion is the starting point for this response. When cliques form, it is usually that there are strong attractive forces, usually social, which pull some group members more closely together. This can then undermine the wider social and task cohesion. The goal of the clique then becomes to promote its members over others.

Given that cohesion is positively associated with team performance and satisfaction it is clearly important to get this right from the start. To that end coaches and other leaders may use team-building-type exercises to build a sense of trust, respect and honest communication. However, through this process we should not lose sight of the aim – to establish a sustainable shared vision which reduces the ambiguity of an individual's role and makes each person clearly accountable for his or her contribution. *Nowhere* in that vision should there be wriggle room to form a clique. A very successful team within a team, such as a rugby front row or a netball shooting unit of goal shooter and goal attack – should view itself as contributing to the overall performance of the team. Certainly take pride in that contribution but recognize that if others stop playing for you, you cannot do your job.

Conflicted communication is also an issue in this response. People often find that differences of opinion provoke anxiety and unpleasant emotions. As a consequence such conversations are avoided. In this case, avoiding addressing a clique is tacitly complicit in its continued existence and accepts the impact it has on performance. In the Thomas–Kilmann (Thomas and Kilmann, 1974) model of conflict handling, it is noted that people have a preferred style of reacting to and managing interpersonal conflict. In this case there are competing views – the clique believe they are in the right and the coach believes they are not. There is high concern for self and low concern for others. We need to move to a more collaborative style, where the clique see that their needs are being recognized (they like each other and gain personally from interacting) but they also see the needs of the coach (the clique is undermining the larger group). With skilful management there is scope for either collaboration or compromise.

Bibliography

Carron, A.V. (1982). Cohesiveness in sport groups: interpretations and considerations. *Journal of Sport Psychology 4*: 123–138.

Thomas, K.W., & Kilmann, R.H. (1974). *Thomas–Kilmann Conflict Mode Instrument*. Xicom, Tuxedo.

Q48

I coach a serious amateur men's basketball team. We were really close as a team at the beginning of the season but we've had a run of bad results. This has resulted in a group of the more senior players getting together and blaming the more junior players and undermining the coaching and preparation. There is a lot of conflict – what can I do?

What is developing is a highly toxic situation, which journalists often refer to as 'losing the dressing room'. This means that players are losing each other's trust and respect – two of the three key ingredients I discussed earlier as being at the core of effective teams. You need to act!

By blaming others they are moving away from the 'we' ethos to a more individual one. The reason we are losing isn't because of me – I'm good, it's the rest of you that's the problem. Of course they don't actually say this, but they act it out in training and games. Under pressure, effort and commitment drop: they blame others for mistakes and don't engage with coaches or the rest of the team.

What should you do? You need to speak to the individual players, on their own and away from training or games if possible. Ask what they believe is happening to the team; collect and collate as much information as possible. Once you have this, call a meeting of the senior players and reflect back to them what you have found from the individual meetings.

Your aim is to 'reboot' the team – get them back to the state earlier in the season when they were a collaborative 'we' rather than a collection of frustrated and conflicted 'Is'.

What you want to emerge from the meeting is an acceptance that team performance depends on players taking responsibility for themselves and their preparation to perform. You want them to appreciate that sometimes it is important to give and also receive unpleasant feedback about their contribution, but it is done in the context of advancing the whole team, not simply as an opportunity to criticize and undermine.

As the coach your role is to make the 'reboot' happen. Many coaches avoid this type of meeting, fearing conflict. Conflict is part of the territory for coaches. It has great potential to bring about positive changes – you just need to prepare for it, keep calm and learn to love it!

Going deeper into the theory

I'm going to use this question to develop the theoretical model of conflict management.

I mentioned earlier in the text that many coaches and performers are fearful of conflict. They shouldn't be. They should recognize that it comes as part of the territory and learn to develop it constructively.

What happens when we have conflict is that we have two or more people who care about what is happening. If it is skilfully managed we have an opportunity to discuss really important things around our shared values and principles, around the relationships which carry us forward to those and about how we speak and behave towards one another.

There are some rules however. Effective conflict management should not be personalized. It is not an attack on a person's character, it is focused on what that individual does, and how what the person does contributes or otherwise to the achievement of the agreed aims of the team.

The Thomas–Kilmann model shows that cohesion and conflict are not mutually exclusive (Thomas and Kilmann, 1974). In this model we can agree to differ and find a compromise position, but our idea is to find win–win situations.

In my work with teams, I will explicitly ask this question: in this situation where specifically we are in disagreement, what would have to happen to get a win for both of you? If we can't find or work towards win–win, what would be an acceptable compromise? This type of approach is the essence of much legal mediation.

Bibliography

Burke, K.L. (2010). Constructive communication. In S.J. Hanrahan & M.B. Andersen (Eds.), *Routledge Handbook of Applied Sport Psychology* (pp. 315–324). Routledge.

Thomas, K.W., & Kilmann, R.H. (1974). *Thomas–Kilmann Conflict Mode Instrument*. Xicom, Tuxedo.

Q49

My players are blaming each other for losing a key game. How can I get them to take more responsibility for their own performance?

This is a common question. It partly stems from the informal way we review performance in sport. It is usually the case that if we win, we celebrate, and if we lose, we have a bloody postmortem and then we celebrate! Neither is quite right.

At whatever level you play, after *every* performance teams should conduct a thorough review. In the course of a career there will be a handful of perfect performances, ones that simply cannot be improved. Therefore we can learn something from every game – and we should.

These reviews can be handled in different ways depending on the ages and experience of the members. I encourage coaches to skill the players themselves to conduct reviews. This helps to open up communication and also lets players have a more active role in their own personal and team development.

When to review? I suggest that you don't do it directly after the game. Players and coaches are often too caught up in the emotional reactions to results to be objective. I suggest that the review is done within 48 hours of a performance. Video is a powerful coaching tool and one that can be used in the review process. If you don't have access to video you need to have good notes on individual, unit and team performance which can be used as a starting point. If possible your notes should be combined with those of other coaches ahead of the review in order to ensure objectivity.

How to review? It is easy to become bogged down in the review process, looking at the minutiae of every minute of play. At the highest performance levels this *is* worth doing. But there is also the likelihood that you will be able to employ performance analysists to do the 'leg work' for you. If you don't have access to video, my advice is to focus on a few critical incidents – some positives and some negatives. For example, how goals were scored or conceded, so that we can establish a short list of things we need to keep doing – ball retention, working hard off the ball, winning second balls. And things we need to stop doing – defending too deep, going quiet, getting stretched because players aren't tracking back. The purpose of this is *not* to scapegoat players; we want players to be accountable, but equally we are reviewing performance to inform our next block of practice. For example, if we are defending too deep, we need to practise keeping a higher defensive line. The review meeting need only be 10 or 15 minutes, focusing on a few critical incidents. Write the key outcomes down for the players and show how it is informing practice.

If you do get into a scapegoating-type discussion, exercise authority. You cannot have a division of this type in your dressing room. I have often seen team meetings descend into an 'emperor's new clothes' discussion, where everyone misses the point. It actually doesn't matter who is responsible, last week's result is a historical fact and nothing will alter it. We need to prepare for the next game.

Going deeper into the theory

There are many models of reflection which have been developed in a range of different health, education and occupational contexts. I would encourage coaches, performers, teachers and parents to use a simple reflective cycle to get the most benefit from the preparatory work or training. This approach can be developed into something much more detailed but this is a good starting point.

- ◆ What is my aim in this session?
- ◆ What are my indicators? How am I assessing performance(s)?

- What actually happened – physically, technically, tactically, mentally?
- What are the emerging patterns? What evidence do I have for these observations?
- How do I feel about what happened?
- What do I need to keep doing?
- What do I need to change?
- What do I need to stop doing?
- What is the plan for the next period of training/ preparation?

The process of review and monitoring is systematically designed to eliminate inefficiency, weakness and error in performance. In high-performing teams, this is where the marginal gains are to be found.

The main risk of this type of monitoring and review process is that it can be perceived as a mainly negative process, whereby team members focus only on errors and omissions. This shouldn't be the case. Neither should it be a process which reinforces the imbalance in power between a group of players and coaches. I have worked with coaches who hand responsibility for review to groups of players.

Bibliography

Burke, K.L. (2010). Constructive communication. In S.J. Hanrahan & M.B. Andersen (Eds.), *Routledge Handbook of Applied Sport Psychology* (pp. 315–324). Routledge.

Q50

How do I give a great pre-match team talk?

The team talk has acquired mythical status in sport. Films such as *Any Given Sunday* have depicted the coach's words (Al Pacino) as transforming a dressing room from one of low energy and division to one of high energy and unity. Jim Telfer's talk to his pack of forwards ahead of the British and Irish Lions test match in South Africa in 1997 is one of the most popular views on YouTube. These are different and I recommend coaches not to go down the 'Churchillian' approach to pre-match meetings.

There are some general guidelines I advise coaches to consider when preparing team talks. Remember that most of these players know you and have listened to many pre-match team talks from you: they have heard most of it before. There is a tendency to switch off and disappear into their own thoughts. It's not what is said that matters – it's what the players hear and what they understand. For some, they are so focused they recall nothing of what is said. What are you aiming to achieve? Are you trying to lift players or calm them? Are you trying to develop specific unit or team skills? This has to form the basis of your talk. A pre-match team talk is not the place to bring new or unprepared stuff to the table. Technical and tactical instruction should have been done well ahead of this.

The pre-match team talk has three parts:

1. Speak to players individually, all of them if possible, before the team talk. Positively outline their role, briefly review their key skills and positively energize them to keep intensity high.
2. Speak to key units together – back four, forwards etc. – what are the 'bread-and-butter' unit skills that have to be executed to the highest level? Emphasize their role and sense of 'team within the team'.
3. Get everyone together and reinforce the purpose. For all their drama and emotion, Al Pacino and Jim Telfer were just communicating common *purpose* to their players. Keep it brief and positive – say what you want to happen. Remember the pre-match team talk is not a means for the coach to manage his or her stress: model calmness and purpose.

Going deeper into the theory

There is little research on the role of the pre-match talk on actual performance. A whole range of strategies have been used in the final period before play to motivate players and engage them in the purpose of what they are doing.

I would stress the importance of coaches being able to respond sensitively to the mood of individual players. This is part of the skilled communication process I outlined earlier, judging which players need to be calmed down and engaged with their first job, and others who need to be wound up a little to make sure that they are not too relaxed.

In applied work I encourage coaches to view the game as starting 1 hour before kick-off. They should review their own performance – what do they do in that hour to prepare the team optimally to play from the first whistle?

Bibliography

Vargas-Tonsing, T.M., & Bartholomew, J.B. (2006). An exploratory study of the effects of pre-game speeches on team-efficacy beliefs. *Journal of Applied Sport Psychology 36*: 918–933.

Vargas-Tonsing, T.M., & Guan, J. (2007). Athletes' preferences for informational and emotional pre-game speech content. *International Journal of Sport Science and Coaching 2*: 171–180.

Q51

What should I say at half-time when we are losing and playing poorly? Is it worth throwing tea cups around the dressing room?

I'd certainly not advise throwing cups about – no matter how angry and frustrated you are. I suggest a calm and structured approach to half-time, or any break in play, such as time-outs. By the time you have all the players in the dressing room, you have between 8 and 12 minutes with them. That time has to be productive.

As the players come in, you have some priorities – knocks or injuries need assessing or treating. Players should take on nutrition and hydration, according to their own preferences. Inform players of any changes to personnel on the pitch. This will take a maximum of 3 minutes. You then have 5–9 minutes to get your message across.

I strongly suggest that coaches make notes before speaking. There is good evidence that coaches make the same errors and biases common in other eye-witness testimony – they tend to recall most accurately the first things that happen in the period of play and the things which happened most recently. So a pre-prepared timeline of events can be useful. The basic few sentences you have are:

1. The score is always 0–0 – you play with that intensity, winning or losing, no matter how big the margin.
2. This is what we must *keep* doing – maximum three points – briefly here's how.
3. This is what we must *stop* doing – maximum three points – briefly here's how.
4. Affirmation – to keep intensity high; there is an increased incidence of goals scored/conceded after breaks.

I would then give the captain and other senior players (such as defence leader) a minute each. You may want to hand points 1–4 to the captain, if you think the players respond better. Either way, I think this type of structured approach to half-time helps everyone understand that half-time isn't just a rest – it is a structured period of appraisal and reorientation of efforts.

Going deeper into the theory

Experienced coaches tend to recall accurately only around 50% of key events in a game (Laird and Waters, 2008). Inexperienced coaches recall even less. This means that often what they report to players during breaks in play is biased and subjective. Not all coaches have access to notational or video analysts so keeping good notes on key aspects of offensive and defensive play really helps to prepare an effective half-time talk.

Shouting is great stress relief for the coach but I suspect that the players will stop listening after a few seconds. They know what they did and will probably not respond to invective or sarcasm. Much better for the coach to recognize that they haven't made errors deliberately and to ensure there is a modification to the plans to make sure that they don't happen again. Coaches must appreciate that what is heard and understood is much more important than what is said. This is why I emphasize simplicity – *keep* doing this, it's working. *Stop* doing this – it's risky/not working.

Leave players with affirmations designed to build confidence and intensity – wrap your message in an affirmation. If the players recall nothing else, the instruction to keep working at high intensity keeps them engaged in the game.

Bibliography

Laird, P., & Waters, I. (2008). Eyewitness recollection of sports coaches. *International Journal of Performance Analysis in Sport 8* (1): 76–84.

Q52

Every season I get a new batch of players. What is the best way to get them to gel together?

If you have time and financial resources it can be beneficial to take the group away for a pre-season tour or training camp, which removes them from their normal environment and gives a concentrated period of contact to accelerate the process of team development. In that tour or camp, you can have meetings about team culture.

You don't have a great deal of time to develop the three main qualities linked to fostering synergy – trust, honesty and respect.

These are difficult qualities to teach: they emerge as people work together. So don't push them hard, but find activities which give people an opportunity to spend time with each other, doing activities which have a purpose. These can be sport-related or they can be unrelated – you are looking to develop a sense of 'we-ness' overriding personal motivations and agenda.

Often you don't get time away with a new group of players. They arrive at pre-season in stages after holidays, late transfers and registration, or other commitments.

I'd aim to structure induction around some key activities:

◆ Welcome and reconnect all players, new and old, with the history and heritage.
◆ Present my vision for the team for the season, at least for the first part of it.
◆ Break the team into smaller units, mixing players up randomly to introduce themselves and discuss how they are going to contribute to the vision for the year.

Going deeper into the theory

There has been a great of research into the process by which people come together to form a team and then establish the dynamics through which they perform.

One approach which I have used in a variety of contexts is the team performance model of Drexler et al. (1988). In the same way as I use the Carron model as heuristics to help me understand team cohesion and leadership, this seven-stage model helps me to understand where a group is in the development cycle (Carron and Eys, 2012).

There is a lot to this model so my description here will be a little superficial:

1. Orientation – why am I here?
2. Trust building – who are you?
3. Goal clarification – what are we doing?
4. Commitment – how will we do it?

5. Implementation – who, what, where, how?
6. Performance – wow! Review and analysis?
7. Renewal – why continue?

The reason I like this model is that, for each aspect, there is a second more behavioural tier, identifying the resolved aspects of performance and also the unresolved. It also recognizes that team development is not a linear process – teams can, and frequently do, regress due to changes in personnel, ineffective leadership and changes to the environment.

Bibliography

Carron, A.V., & Eys, M.A. (2012). *Group Dynamics in Sport* (4th edn.). Fitness Information Technology.

Drexler, A., Sibbet, D., & Forrester, R. (1988). The team performance model. In W.B. Reddy & K. Jamieson (Eds.), *Teambuilding: Blueprints for Productivity and Satisfaction* (pp. 45–61). NTL Institute for the Applied Behavioral Sciences; San Diego, CA: University Associates.

Minahan, M., Vogel, L., Butler, J., & Butler Taylor, H. (2007) Facilitation 101: the basics to get you on your feet. *OD Practitioner 39* (3): 53–59.

Pulling the threads together

As I have been writing this chapter the England soccer team has been knocked out of the Euro 2016 competition by Iceland. Iceland is a team ranked 34th in the world, England 11th. All the England squad are playing in the country's highest level of competition, the Premier League; by contrast, Iceland's players are drawn from a wide range of clubs around Europe and a wide diversity of levels. Only two are playing in the English premiership. But Iceland won.

Why did this happen? Not surprisingly there has been a great deal of speculation on causes from pundits, journalists and the football-supporting public. Were technical deficiencies at the root of this underperformance? Did the coach adopt the wrong tactics? Or make errors in player selection? Of course we will never know conclusively; football tournaments are not controlled experiments. Going right back to the start of the chapter, we can attribute the productivity losses to this group to tens, possibly hundreds, of factors, some personal, some environmental and some concerning leadership. This is why this chapter could have been a book in its own right.

Which was the most important? Again, it is speculation. However, if we put this underperformance of this group of players into a historical context, English football at a national level in major competitions does appear to have a cultural problem. Since 1966, it has won a handful of games 'when it really matters'. And then the players return to their clubs and play in what is purported to be the best league in the world. What it clearly is not the best at is producing players who can win games for an England *team* in global or regional competitions.

In summarizing this chapter, I think the case study of the England football team captures very well the complexity of team psychology. It almost seems that cohesive synergy is so difficult to achieve that trying to create it is like a form of alchemy. But it does happen, more regularly than would seem possible. It is done by people who understand the true nature of teams and work to create day-to-day environments that make the achievement of the personal and the collective goals achievable. Rainer Martens' assertion has been borne out – the essence of effective coaching is creating a team culture.

VIII

Children and youth sport: the mind of a child is not a vessel to be filled, it is a fire to be kindled

Childhood is a period of physical and psychological development, built around learning, playing, socializing, exploring and testing out what it's like to be part of the adult world. Biology has a large part to play in this period; the dramatic physical and physiological changes in the body mean that there is a constant dynamic interplay between developing children and their world. Sport psychologists should be aware of the developmental issues associated with working with children. The child's experience of the world is not a miniaturized version of adults' experience – it is completely different.

Across the globe, millions of young people participate in sport, giving it a unique place in their lives and the lives of their families. However, we do have a significant challenge. Participation rates in sport peak at around the age of 10 years, but by the age of 13 around 70% of young people have dropped out and have either stopped playing completely or changed the nature of their involvement. The percentage of girls dropping out of sport far exceeds that of boys. The reasons for dropping out are complex. Other things appear on the child's horizon: public examinations loom large, social relationships, other leisure time activities. The sport which entranced the child at 10 becomes less attractive at 13 and many children simply drop out. A problem with many sports is that they are unable to respond flexibly to these changes. Sports are fixed at a time and venue, requiring many participants and kit. They also implicitly demand a level of competence. It is difficult to play 'just for fun'.

For many sport psychologists of my generation one of the first books which specifically addressed behaviour in sport was Rainer Martens' *Joy and Sadness in Children's Sport*. His view was that, as sport became more formally organized, driven by adult structures and used as a method of formally identifying talent at younger and younger ages, so the children found it less and less intrinsically enjoyable. In my view, Martens was not falling into the trap of nostalgically looking back to the days of neighbourhood games, where open spaces could be used for local children to play safely, unsupervised and in an unstructured way. Rather he was looking at the impact of formal, structured and supervised sport on the psychological development of the children participating. He saw a step change in both the experience of the child and also the perceptions and expectations of adults – parents, teachers and coaches.

The sporting environment has changed dramatically in the almost 40 years since Marten's book. Sports now compete for leisure time with a range of other activities which could not have been dreamt of in 1978. Richard Louv (2005) captured this in his book *Last Child in the Woods*, coining the term 'nature deficit disorder' to describe how children now tend to use their leisure time indoors, preferring online 'friends' and virtual 'sport' to their real equivalents. Louv's view, a controversial and untested one, is that many developmental disorders can be attributed to this change in childhood behaviour. This is debatable, but what is clear is that all sport, but particularly youth sport, has become commodified, with many clubs depending on the income from youth sport sign-ups for their viability.

It is now rare to see children having informal, unstructured 'pick-up' games in public spaces. 'Stranger danger' and the fear of leaving children unsupervised mean that until children are relatively mature they're unlikely to be left to play. The scenario outlined by Matthew Syed in his book *Bounce*, where a hotbed of table-tennis talent developed around a local facility that children were invited to attend and given unlimited access to by a local coach, is much less likely to occur in the present climate. Clubs and more formal sport coaching and games have recognized this and filled a gap – for some parents sports programmes act as child care for a couple of hours on a weekend morning. But it's organized and formal, memberships have to be paid, kit has to be bought and legal forms have to be signed. And behind it are some complex psychological issues. Welcome to the adult world of sport – for children.

We all want the best, but what is best?

All parents want the best for their child. Every coach and teacher is equally well motivated, but from what appears to be common ground emerges a really difficult question – what is best?

This is a deep philosophical question. Scholars have wrestled with the question about right courses of action for centuries and I couldn't do this whole debate justice in the space I have. However, in the context of young people in my view there is a basic hierarchy of bests.

Best is safe: physically and psychologically

At the top of my list of best practice is do everything possible to ensure that the sport environment is safe. Safe doesn't just mean physically safe, it also means that the environment is psychologically safe. These overlap. A timely but extremely challenging example of this is the current emphasis on head trauma and concussion in youth contact sports. Why would any responsible adult consent to a child engaging in an activity which risks long-term brain damage? Parents, coaches and teachers should recognize that the willingness of a young performer to accept and thrive in contact sports reflects complex psychological processing on the part of the child.

There is a current emphasis on head injuries and concussion, but the same applies to bone and muscle development. Sport has a unique place in promoting lifelong health, however equally it has a unique place in risking long-term problems if the nature, load and intensity of the activity are inappropriate or the pace of progression too fast. Child protection also covers questions of whether children are sufficiently trained and experienced in techniques which keep them safe – a salutary point for grassroots coaches of contact sports.

Psychological safety is also concerned with formal child protection and parental codes of conduct. Adult behaviour around children in a sporting context should at all times be unambiguous. There are excellent resources on this developed by the Child Protection in Sport Unit of the National Society for the Prevention of Cruelty to Children (NSPCC) in the UK. I strongly advice coaches, parents, teachers and sport psychologists to read and reflect on this material (NSPCC, 2005).

Best is fun

People, irrespective of age, are drawn to activities they find intrinsically motivating, activities that they would engage in whether incentives or rewards were offered or not. In educational research there is evidence that as children get older their intrinsic motivation tends to drop and they become more motivated by extrinsic rewards and the avoidance of punishment. The trend is well documented in classroom settings from the middle years of elementary school onwards. We think of sport and exercise as being recreational relief from the pressures of education, affording children and young people a way of letting off steam from the pressures of formal education. There is evidence that, by adopting an outcome-oriented motivational climate, that is, one that promotes winning and interpersonal competition, exactly the same trend is found – extrinsic motivation tends to swamp intrinsic motivation. With the range of alternative leisure-time activities on offer, children and young people can readily disengage from sport and find some other activity they enjoy more. This may be at the heart of the 'drop-out' statistic I gave earlier in this chapter.

Best learning something: and learning goes beyond physical, technical and tactical skills

Developmental psychologists have researched extensively the role of sport in aspects of personal and social development. Benson (2006) presents a very comprehensive list of developmental assets associated with sport participation. These are divided into internal assets around personal development, including development of competence and self-esteem, and external assets which extend into family relationships and social support. A condensed version of this approach was presented by Lerner et al. (2005), who identified five main positive youth development goals, the 5Cs – competence, confidence, connection, caring and character. A large volume of research published before and since highlights that sport has the potential to be a potent source of positive developmental experiences, but it doesn't just happen, and this is why the question of how youth sport is delivered is such a critical one.

Skilled and experienced teachers and coaches recognize that learning in sport is big and long.

- ◆ *Big* because there are so many other lessons which sport can teach – about the value of effort and dedication, about trust and loyalty and being part of team, about respect for officials, team mates, opponents and respecting the sport.
- ◆ *Long* because many sport skills are complex and difficult to master; they require effort and dedication. Unless people engage for a long period they are unlikely to gain mastery. Enjoying what they are doing is a vital aspect of staying engaged.

The philosophy I am touching on here is drawn from what I consider to be an excellent resource for coaches at this level, *The Power of Double-Goal Coaching*, authored by Jim Thomson from the Positive Coaching Alliance. In my view, all coaches in all sports working with children and young people would benefit from reading about and applying this approach.

Are children for sport or is sport for children?

This is a complex question: does sport offer a context for broad social experience and learning or is sport a means of identifying and developing talent? Can it be both?

If we endorse the first argument we need to recognize that being a sports coach or teacher is not simply about drilling skills and techniques, it's about developing young people.

If we endorse the latter, we need to understand the process by which talent is developed and be comfortable that most young people will not make the grade and will probably drop out.

It is very difficult to achieve both simultaneously.

And here we hit, what for me, as both parent and psychologist is a really difficult issue. On the one hand I am aware that the majority of coaches who work with children and young people are volunteers. Sport in the UK and in many other countries relies upon these coaches and leaders to function. As a parent I am extremely grateful. As a sport psychologist I have concerns that are they sufficiently trained and experienced to grasp fully the complexity of what they are doing and thereby run sessions which effectively achieve their intended outcomes.

I will offer two case studies to highlight key issues around developmental sport psychology, in the hope that parents, coaches and teachers will both see how complex what they are doing is and how they may need to modify their behaviour in order to maximize the impact of their involvement.

Case 1: The father who aims to create 'two of the greatest female tennis players the planet has ever seen'

Ray Wood has received a great deal of media attention in response to his public statement that he intends to create 'two of the greatest female tennis players the planet has ever seen' (http://www.bbc.co.uk/sport/tennis/36367629).

Few of us would take issue with this statement if Ray was a coach, but he is a parent and is talking about his two daughters, aged 7 and 2 years respectively.

For a moment, reflect on your own personal thoughts and feelings as you read about his plans for his daughters. In my view this story is useful in confronting and 'unpackaging' one of the most unhelpful labels in developmental sport psychology – the 'pushy parent'.

If you had a negative response to Ray Wood's story, why do you think you responded as you did? He is a well-intentioned parent, wanting the very best for his children. He has tasked himself with being an active parent, engaged in their development, aiming to secure a happy, healthy and prosperous future for them. No one could accuse him of neglect. He has researched what he needs to do to develop his children to become high achievers and has developed a clear plan for their future. How is he different from a parent who stands over his child while she practises piano or learns French verbs? Why does 'hot housing' a child in the way Ray is doing seem so much worse?

Rather than use the term 'pushy parent' I would use, and advise others to describe his behaviour as, either positive and helpful or negative and unhelpful. There are some aspects of Ray Wood's behaviour towards his children which are positive and helpful. In contrast there are some aspects of his behaviour which are not. In my opinion Woods' behaviour has crossed a line, where on balance there is more risk in his approach than potential benefit. My concerns about his approach are fundamentally about a style of parenting which is commonly seen in sport, where the parent is doing two potentially damaging things. Firstly the parent is placing his needs at a higher priority than his child's and secondly he appears to be placing conditions of worth on his parental love. The research is clear on the role parents play in many aspects of psychosocial development, particularly in the early and middle years of childhood (Weiss et al., 2012). At this stage, children seek the attention and positive regard of their parents, and acting as both coach and parent means that frequently parents will be providing feedback about competence in a way which compromises their parental role. The child may learn to fear failure, not because it is a failure, more because it causes a negative emotional response from the parent. Parental love has become conditional. You get my love when you do well.

Whilst the parent may be able to maintain a clear divide between 'this is me – Dad' and 'this is me – coach', this can be a difficult distinction to manage for a child, potentially leading to the child having a love–hate relationship with the parent, which is challenging in the 'here and now' and may present problems in the future. The child also has a love–hate relationship with the sport. On a good day, when the child does well, she brings the positive emotion home and loves the sport. On a not so good day, the negative emotion is triggered and reinforced by the parent – literally it comes home and eats dinner with her!

The multiple-role problem for the coach is particularly compounded by the perceived lack of autonomy experienced by the child. What happens when the child decides she doesn't want to continue with the sport? This can be a profound emotional challenge for the child, who may play on, fearing the parent's reaction, motivated only by extrinsic rewards. In this case, play has become work – an outcome Ray Wood wanted to save his children from.

As the child develops beyond the middle years of childhood, the peer group begins to replace the family as the primary social influence. Ray Wood is projecting his children into a future with great uncertainty around the peer group. He has made them very different from their peers and also created an environment where they have little time to connect.

Ray Wood in my opinion is not a pushy parent; he is one for whom the unhelpful outweighs the helpful. It is a highly risky approach. But one that appears to have worked for many high performers, for example, Seb Coe, Tiger Woods and the Williams sisters. However, this is far from confirmation of its effectiveness. How many parents have created similar scenarios and irreparably damaged their relationships with their children and possibly also damaged the children, undermined their love for sport and wasted any potential they may have?

Case 2: Winning is the only thing: the case of the overly competitive coach

Justin Byrne was a volunteer coach at his local youth football club in England. I think he was misguided but I respect him for bringing a particularly difficult 'elephant' out of the corner.

In December 2013, Byrne was sacked as the under-10s soccer coach because he sent an email to parents in which he stated that he was not there so the boys could have fun – he was 'only interested in winning'. He went on: 'I am only interested in winning. I don't care about equal play time or any other communist view of sport'.

He concluded his email by anticipating the parental response. Those parents who disagreed with him were 'weak-minded' and 'think sport is about knitting' and weren't doing their children any favours in this highly competitive world.

I don't think Mr Byrne's approach is correct, but do I respect him for his honesty? He has made us confront one of the biggest challenges in youth sport – what is it for?

Unfortunately there are countless Mr Byrnes in youth sport, not just soccer. Byrne's emphasis on competence as demonstrated by results creates an ego- or outcome-oriented motivational climate which is unsustainable and potentially highly damaging to everyone, even the talent he believes he is developing. Inevitably in this type of environment there is an emphasis on interteam and interpersonal competition. Children quickly perceive who the best players are and equally who are the weakest. Both get stuck in the kind of fixed mindset discussed in Chapter II. Children also quickly 'twig' that if we want the approval of the coach we must win the game, and our best chance of doing that is to give the ball to our best players. The best players don't improve and the weakest drop out. Byrne's premise is that this is excellent training for adult life, a kind of Darwinian 'survival of the fittest' in under-10s football as a lesson in life. Many would argue that there is nothing wrong with this approach. But would they be happy to see the same principles applied in other areas of development, for example, in the classroom, with the foundations of reading and writing?

There are many reasons why emphasis on the outcome of games is so damaging in the early stages of learning. Some of them are due to the nature of the sport. There are some sports where the fundamental skills appear easy to pick up and this can be a big challenge. Football (soccer) is an example of this; the problem is that it is an easy game to play badly. The individual basic technical skills of controlling and kicking a ball are picked up very quickly, but to turn them into mastery and then put them into even more complex team tactics is extremely complex. Grassroots sports coaches tend to move straight into the most complex scenario – the competitive game. This is exactly the error made by Mr Byrne and many other coaches at this level. With more understanding and skill, coaches would appreciate the breadth of their role and also put together coaching sessions which developed technique much more effectively. One ball for a coaching session for under-10s is like having a single pencil in the writing classroom and requiring the children to compete for it! Why is it obvious that every pupil needs a pencil to develop writing skills, but not that all players need the ball at their feet as often as possible in young footballers?

The talent myth

Youth sport coaches frequent report that one of their key roles is to identify and develop talent. But how? Does what makes a child stand out against his or her peers at the age of 10 or 12 predict longer-term achievement? The answer is complicated but probably 'no'.

Early developers have a distinct advantage – . . . until the rest catch up

Youth sport is usually divided up into age categories. This means that within an age band there can be almost a full year's difference in physical and psychological maturity. This might seem trivial, but at the age of 8 or 10 years, or even older, as the physical changes associated with puberty begin, this can lead to very significant differences in physical and psychological characteristics. One of the most robust findings around talent development is the relative age effect (RAE) (Andronikos et al., 2016); at developmental levels performers who develop physically or technically before their peers tend to gain a performance advantage. The 'early bloomers', typically those born at the beginning of the age band, tend to be overrepresented in talent identification processes, more likely to be selected for academies and receive scholarships. However, when the same analysis is applied to the professional ranks, the 'early bloomer' effect is either much reduced or disappears completely. It seems that something happens either to deselect those who develop early or their places are taken by increasing numbers of those developing later.

When performers in talent identification programmes are tracked over long periods of time, some interesting things happen. Most notably, the criteria for progression change. Youngsters selected because of *physical* characteristics (e.g. size, speed, power) in the early stages are deselected because of deficiencies in their *psychological characteristics* (e.g. motivation, mental toughness). When researchers follow-up cohorts of performers identified as above average at younger age groups they typically find that a large proportion of them have left the sport, typically for reasons around emotional burnout caused by parental pressures or bad coaching experiences. Others were no longer playing because of either injury or an interest in another sport. These 'drop outs' tend to be the 'early bloomers'. These are the athletes who had success at their sport early in their development, 7–10 years of age. This group also had a tendency to have their growth spurts earlier than others.

Early developers tend to dominate opponents in the early stages of their careers. They win often and as a result they receive a good deal of extrinsic reward. This leads to a misplaced sense of superiority and causes athletes to believe they are naturally more gifted than others. This may be reinforced by coaches and parents. They are the 'big fish in a relatively small pond' and prime candidates for the fixed mindset outlined earlier. However, as an athlete matures, the competition becomes more concentrated because of 'drop-out' and the discrepancy in physical size and skill because of early development starts to even out. Now the 'early bloomers' don't find it as easy to dominate. They have to work harder to gain the success that once came easily, if they haven't developed intrinsic motivation, they start to burn out and look to others to blame for their lack of enjoyment and success. The early developers still have the fundamental skills to be successful, but they haven't developed the psychological skills and resources required to succeed at the highest levels. Many of my clients at the highest level tell me of team mates from junior teams or competitors they played with or against who were more skilled than they were, but didn't make the transition. Their stories indicate that the elite end of sport is *not* filled with the best players. It's filled with the ones who just didn't burn out, get disillusioned, lose motivation or get injured, the ones mentally able to make the transition to senior performance. Effective and expert coaching at each stage of the journey is required.

Armed with knowledge about the impact of the RAE, and the statistics that a tiny proportion of performers identified as 'talented' make it to the elite level, it is easy to conclude that talent development programmes are constructed for the benefit of the club or franchise, not the young performer. The financial gains from identifying one world-class player will sustain an academy for several years. The vast majority of players selected, perhaps as early as the age of 8, as talented, but discarded at 16 as not good enough, are unfortunate collateral damage.

There have been some innovative programmes which aim to address the RAE through biobanding, a technique which matches players on the basis of the stage of their physical development rather than age. These are in their early stages and have many challenges, not least that young performers with 1 or 2 years' additional technical and tactical development may be physically matched with younger players and vice versa.

Turning potential into expertise

Sport psychology has drawn heavily from a broad range of literature to develop its understanding of what it takes to become an expert. Bruner et al. (2010) summarized the literature in the area. They identified two distinct ways of approaching the development of sporting expertise: talent development models and career transition models.

The talent development models draw together material from the fields of cognitive psychology (the study of how humans think and process information), skills acquisition (how movement is learned and controlled) and expertise in other psychomotor areas, such as music and art. From this approach emerged the message that extensive deliberate practice is the key to developing expertise.

What does extensive mean? Ericsson and his co-workers (1993) cited the figure of 10,000 hours of practice. This is highly contentious. It is very probable that for many skills high levels of performance can be achieved with less, particularly in sports where genetically determined physiological factors are critical. They also coined the term 'deliberate practice' to denote the fact that practice should have the goal of improving performance. Deliberate practice requires effort and may not be enjoyable or have any immediate benefits, it is specifically challenging the processes of adaptation and learning (Ericsson et al., 1993). Motivation is important: 10,000 hours breaks down to around 20 hours a week for 10 years! Doing anything for this long, using deliberate practice, where having fun isn't the main purpose, requires you really to love what you are doing.

The second type of model focuses on career transitions in sport. These types of models tend either to focus on the transitions in sport, such as Cote's developmental models of sport participation (Cote, 2007), or take a broader view of sport in the life of the child – such as Wylleman and Lavellee's developmental lifespan model. Both approaches recognize that children go through a period of sampling different sports before moving on to a deeper commitment and specialization. Wylleman and Lavellee's model places this in the broader context of social, academic and vocational landmarks in a child's development.

Cote produced a useful set of summary conclusions from his work which make interesting reading for coaches, teachers and parents. In these he concludes that early in development the sampling of a wide range of sports is a positive feature. He sees deliberate 'play' at this age, i.e. play with focus on fun rather than purpose, as more important than deliberate practice. His view is that specialization in one sport before the age of around 13 may be counterproductive, in terms of both skill development and intrinsic motivation. He advocates late specialization, after the age of 16. Case studies of high-level performance seem to bear this out.

It should be acknowledged that, in some sports, very early specialization is viewed as necessary. For example, performers in aesthetic sports involving moving the body against gravity, such as gymnastics, gain an advantage from being physically small. This can be a very significant issue, as performers can find themselves in perfect physical condition to compete but their psychological maturity is still some way off. This mismatch between physical and psychological readiness means that performers require very supportive coaching and parental environments.

In summing up, I believe I have challenged some established thinking about motivational climate and parental and coach behaviour. I have set out to give a sense of the deep complexity of youth involvement and commitment to sport. I don't think it is a coincidence that the biggest drop-out from sport comes between the ages of 10 and 13 years, when children and young people tend to move from the sampling to the specialization stages. The clear finding from this material is winning games or competitions is a different challenge to long-term player development. Youth coaches should be clear what they want to achieve as there is only a small degree of overlap. What would happen if children were encouraged to continue to sample until much later, there being no requirement to compete, no parental or coach pressure to compare their performance with that of others? Would we convert more talent into mature expertise? Would there be more joy and less sadness?

Bibliography

Andronikos, G., Elumaro, A.I., Westbury, T., & Martindale, R.J. (2016). Relative age effect: implications for effective practice. *Journal of Sports Sciences, 34* (12), 1124–1131.

Benson, P.L. (2006). *All Are Our Kids. What Communities Must Do to Raise Caring and Responsible Children and Adolescents* (2nd edn.). Jossey Bass.

Bruner, M.W., Erickson, K., Wilson, B., & Cote, J. (2010). An appraisal of athlete development models through citation network analysis. *Psychology of Sport and Exercise 11*: 133–139.

Cote, J. (2007). Opportunities and pathways for beginners to elite to ensure optimum and lifelong involvement in sport. In S. Hooper, D.J. Macdonald, & M. Philips (Eds.), *Junior Sport Matters: Briefing Papers for Australian Junior Sport* (pp. 29–40). Australian Sport Commission.

Ericsson, K.A., Krampe, R.T., & Tesch-Romer, C. (1993). The role of deliberate practice in the acquisition of expert performance. *Psychological Reviews 100* (3): 363–406.

Lerner, R.L., Almerigi, J.B., Theokas, C., & Lerner, J.V. (2005). Positive youth development: a view of the issues. *Journal of Early Adolescence 25*: 10–16.

Louv, R. (2005). *Last Child in the Woods: Saving Our Children From Nature-Deficit Disorder.* Algonquin Books.

Martens, R. (1978). *Joy and Sadness in Children's Sport.* Human Kinetics.

NSPCC. (2005). *Standards for Safeguarding and Protecting Children in Sport.* Retrieved on 28 April 2017 from: https://thecpsu.org.uk/resource-library/2013/standards-for-safeguarding-and-protecting-children-in-sport/.

Syed, M. (2011). *Bounce.* Fourth Estate.

Thomson, J. (2010). *The Power of Double-Goal Coaching: Developing Winners in Sports and Life.* Balance Sport Publishing.

Weiss, M.R., Kipp, L.E., & Bolter, N.D. (2012). Training for life: optimizing positive youth development through physical activity. In S. Murphy (Ed.), *The Oxford Handbook of Sport and Performance Psychology*. Oxford University Press.

Wylleman, P., & Lavellee, D. (2005). A developmental perspective on the transitions faced by athletes. In M. Weiss (Ed.), *Developmental Sport Psychology: A Lifespan Perspective* (pp. 507–527). FIT Publishers.

Q53

My 8-year-old daughter has just started at swimming club. She is faster than a lot of the other girls and has won some local races. I'd like her to compete at regionals and nationals but don't want to push her. How can I avoid being a 'pushy parent'?

Parents have become much more sensitive to the balance between actively and positively supporting children in sport and becoming overinvolved and 'pushy'.

There are some big issues here for me. I'll develop each a little here.

Reflect on your own motivations

Why do you want your daughter to be successful? Why swimming? What is more important, your daughter being successful or having fun? Of course you want them both. But there can also be an issue of parents transferring unfulfilled dreams and ambitions on to their children. To avoid being 'pushy' you should examine this and be prepared to back off if necessary. It's not about you.

Manage your expectations

Be aware that at the age your daughter is, probably her biggest motive is to gain your approval. If you reinforce expectations around winning races and swimming faster, that is what she will want to do, which is fine, whilst she is winning and swimming faster. But this won't always be the case. As she moves into higher levels of competition and as the early gains in performance plateau, the outcomes become less certain and swimming to please parents can lose its gloss and motivational pull.

What do you want to happen? Do you want a successful swimmer this season? Or do you want your daughter to be still enjoying the sport in 5, 10 or 20 years' time? Your expectations and behaviour are a key part in this.

To keep your daughter engaged and loving swimming you need to look more on swimming as fun with a purpose rather than performance training. Be aware that children develop at different rates; the performance advantage your daughter is currently enjoying may be due to relative age effects or her picking technique up faster than her peers. These may dissipate in time, and without an intrinsic love of swimming, drop-out looms.

Avoid early specialization

Let your daughter sample other sports and activities. Swimming is an excellent foundation for many sports skills as it develops many transferable aspects of fitness. It is also technically complex and requires development coordination between limbs, again a useful foundation for other movement skills. Specialization can come later. Recognize you face a significant challenge as your daughter approaches puberty. If you are looking to keep her in the sport, intrinsic love of swimming is vital.

Create mastery motivational climate

Create a mastery climate around your daughter. Emphasize learning and effort, not outcome. How do you do this? After practice ask, what was fun? And what was learned? Not what the times were and whether she was faster than others. Use the time travelling to and from practice and races to talk about anything other than swimming, not, as many parents do, to give masses of instructions before and then conduct a forensic postmortem of the race or practice after. Children quickly come to dread these car journeys.

The motivational climate around children in sport may be complex and conflicted. What you do may contrast and conflict with the coach. You emphasize fun and mastery, whilst the coach emphasizes competition and ego. You may need to speak to the coach about this.

Remember, ultimately it is not what you want or the coach wants: the issue is, what does your daughter want? She wants to have fun and she wants your love and support – whatever the time on the stopwatch or the place on the results sheet.

Going deeper into the theory

There are so many corners to this question. I'm going to pick up one of the themes, but others are developed elsewhere in this chapter.

A study by Brummelman et al. (2013) explored an issue central to the notion of the 'pushy parent', that of parents vicariously fulfilling their ambitions through their children. It is an idea that is pervasive in the popular media and can often be seen in grassroots sport. The psychology literature has acknowledged the question. Unfulfilled ambitions and other missed opportunities are frequently cited as people's biggest regrets in life. There is some parenting literature which suggests that parents see their children as an opportunity to symbolize their success and fulfil their own dreams. This can be a significant issue in developmental sport psychology. Where children's motives are not autonomous and parental love becomes conditional, we have a situation where unhappiness is almost inevitable. This can be an extremely difficult conversation for a sport psychologist to have with a parent.

Bibliography

Brummelman, E., Thomaes, S., Slagt, M.I., Overbeek, G., Orobio de Castro, B., & Bushman, B.J. (2013). My child redeems my broken dreams: on parents transferring their unfulfilled ambitions onto the child. *PLoS One 8* (6): e65360.

Q54

My 10-year-old son has real talent in tennis: how do I develop his mental skills?

How do you know your son has talent? Is your son winning tournaments against other children? Has your son's coach or teacher identified him as being talented? In short, what criteria are you making this judgement on?

Irrespective of the criteria used, there are many pitfalls the parents and coaches of young performers can fall foul of. One important one is the relative age effect (RAE). At the age of 10, up to a full year's advantage can be very telling. Linked to this is the banding of age groups. In most sports, youth competition is age-banded. It varies from sport to sport, but often the age groupings are 2-year spreads. A player may go from being the best player at under-10 level to struggling in the under-12s. Motivationally this can be a huge challenge. A young performer who has received a great deal of attention and praise for being the best in the younger age group may not receive such attention in the next age group. If the attention and praise are really what the child craves, not the sheer enjoyment and satisfaction of playing the sport, there may be a problem of continued involvement.

Now, on to the issue of mental skills. Here again we need to be very specific on what we are talking about. The aim of practice in any sport is to develop a set of physical, technical, tactical and mental skills which support consistent performance under the pressure of competition. Therefore, my suggestion is to ensure that practice sessions strike a balance between the development of the technical and physical aspects of performance, e.g. ground shots, serving and volley, back- and forehand. All of these need to be well developed. Add to these practices some elements of competition, such as simulated game practice, where skills are tested under pressure. These can be fun exercises, where the challenge is to get ten consecutive first services into play. These shouldn't be just ten straight from the same side: mix them up, have some running in between. But the task is to get to ten in play without error. As you get beyond five, the player will be tempted to pat the serve over to ensure it goes in – that's *not* allowed! Hopefully you can see that with some imagination all kinds of scenarios can be simulated and they are *fun*! This is the way – tie the technical development with the mental development and you get the absolute maximum transfer between practice and performance.

Going deeper into the theory

I have used the question as an opportunity to offer the parent an insight to the process of identifying and developing talent. There are now several excellent references on the issues of the RAE (Cobley et al., 2009; Andronikos et al., 2015). The practical problem with the RAE is that it can have the effect of establishing and reinforcing the expectations of parents, coaches, teachers and the young athlete. People around the performer may rush to judgement when a previously outstanding talent suddenly disappears into the pack. The assumption is that the child is not trying or not taking it seriously, when in fact all that has happened is that physically and technically others have caught up. It is for this reason that I aim to put developing talent into a broader context and in particular to apply a subtheory within the umbrella of self-determination theory (Ryan and Deci, 2006) – organismic integration theory – to intrinsic motivation for playing, in this case, tennis.

Bibliography

Andronikos, G., Elumaro, A.I., Westbury, T., & Martindale, R.J. (2015). Relative age effect: implications for effective practice. *Journal of Sports Sciences 34* (12): 1–8.

Cobley, S., Baker, J., Wattie, N., & Mckenna, J. (2009). Annual age-grouping and athlete development: a meta-analytical review of relative age effects in sport. *Sports Medicine 39*: 235–256.

Ryan, R.M., & Deci, E.L. (2006). Self-regulation and the problem of human autonomy: does psychology need choice, self-determination, and will? *Journal of Personality 74* (6): 1557–1587.

Q55

My daughter is a talented golfer. She is 12 years old and has been playing since she was 8. She has a handicap of 12 and has won the girls' under-18 championships at the local club for the past 2 years. In the past year she has started to show what I would describe as 'perfectionistic' characteristics. I don't understand where this has come from as she doesn't show it in any other area of her sport and schoolwork. I want to know how best to help her

My approach to this type of behaviour is to probe around how the perfectionism manifests itself. Is it around what she says or is it around what she does, or is it both? The literature around perfectionism points towards it having two aspects – perfectionist concerns: the thoughts which drive the performer, and perfectionist strivings: the behaviours associated with thorough preparation. Broadly, perfectionist concerns are negative and need to be addressed, whilst perfectionist strivings not associated with the concerns tend to be positive and lead to better performance levels.

Perfectionist concerns tend to be associated with high levels of anxiety and burnout and lower levels of performance. But where do they come from? Perfectionist concerns usually manifest themselves in the form of negative, automatic and intrusive thoughts related to not living up to standards you have set yourself, doubting your own skills and concerns about whether your actions are up to the expectations of others. I would encourage you to listen carefully to the type of language your daughter is using around her golf. Does she have a lot of outcome goals she is working towards? Are these turning into 'musts, shoulds or oughts'? Are these starting to get in the way of her enjoyment of playing? Does she tend to play down or doubt her own ability? Have people around her started to project expectations on to her? All of these are potential sources for perfectionist concerns. Be aware that you may, unintentionally, be planting some of these thoughts into your daughter's thinking. All parents wish the very best for their children and I'm sure that you are no different. However, parents often create expectations around children they perceive to be talented. This can be highly destructive and lead to the child having to make a choice between living up to the parents' expectations and disengaging from the sport in order to have a more 'normal' unconditional relationship.

The best way to address the 'faulty' thinking around perfectionism is to give your daughter two things – firstly, absolute autonomy about what she wants to do, in terms of practice and performance. You want her to 'fall back in love' with the game, in the way she did when she was 8 years old. Secondly, to remind her, that she is your daughter first and a golfer second. You love every three putt and every wayward tee shot, because they're hers. Ultimately you want her still to be playing when she is 20, because by then she will probably be even better than she currently is!

Going deeper into the theory

Perfectionism has been conceptualized in different ways by different researchers. For example, Frost et al. (1990) identified six dimensions obviously focused on young performers: personal standards, organization, concern over mistakes, doubts about actions, parental expectations and parental concerns. Hewitt and Flett (1991) identified more on to the three components – self-oriented perfectionism, socially prescribed perfectionism and other oriented perfectionism.

The consensus in the literature is that there are two broad dimensions – perfectionistic strivings and perfectionistic concerns. In the absence of perfectionistic concerns, strivings appear to be related to positive outcomes. However, the combination of high concerns and high strivings is associated with negative outcomes – performance anxiety, burnout and depression.

Perfectionism is often associated with a focus of outcome over process goals, where the achievement of particularly outcomes is perceived to be valued by key others such as parents and coaches.

The way to address perfectionist thinking is to restructure 'faulty' thinking towards processes and reinforce the agency the performer has, i.e. she is doing this for her own intrinsic satisfaction, not to please or impress others.

Bibliography

Frost, R.O., Marten, P.A., Lahart, C., & Rosenblate, R. (1990). The dimensions of perfectionism. *Cognitive Therapy and Research 14*: 449–468.

Hewitt, P.L., & Flett, G.L. (1991). Perfectionism in the self and social context. Conceptualisation, assessment and associations with psychopathology. *Journal of Personality and Social Psychology 60*: 456–470.

Q56

A young athlete I coach is losing weight rapidly. I'm concerned that she might have an eating disorder: what do I do?

Most sport psychologists are not qualified to address clinical issues such as eating disorders. A minority are, and you need to establish the qualifications and expertise of the psychologist before engaging his or her services and support.

As a first point of contact I advise coaches (or teachers and parents) to examine the excellent document produced by UK Sport (2007). It is an extremely comprehensive document which, in layperson's language, helps to identify whether a performer has an eating disorder or whether she has subclinical or overvalued emphasis on weight, body composition or nutrition.

It should be noted that disordered eating patterns are more common in sport performers than in the general population. But there is a threshold at which the coach should act. For me a key issue is when the weight loss is no longer about performance enhancement; in fact, poor or inadequate nutrition is leading to a fall in performance level, either directly due to failure to recover between sessions or indirectly through changes in emotions. This is where I would recommend that a coach intervene and suggest that the athlete seeks additional support, in the first instance from her family doctor. There may also be an important conversation about selection. I think coaches, teachers and parents should think carefully about removing an at-risk performer from her sport. It seems a very paternalistic decision, but may help the performer regain perspective on her behaviour.

Going deeper into the theory

I strongly advise practising psychologists to gain as much knowledge around this topic as possible. The prevalence of eating disorders appears to be increasing and it is highly likely that you will encounter it in some form or another in your work. The other piece of advice I would offer is that you establish a referral network with an experienced clinical colleague. In this way you can quickly refer clients on and where appropriate speed up the process of returning to performance.

The line of theory which informs my work when I encounter performers at risk of eating disorders is the sociocultural model of disordered eating presented by Petrie and Greenleaf (2007). Research in this area is highly problematic due to the nature of the issue and the lack of controlled experimentation. However, even with these potential limitations the model has good face validity and highlights some key areas for possible intervention.

The model identifies six potential causal elements, considered to be not specifically linked to involvement in sport. These are: sociocultural pressures, the internalization of social body or appearance ideals, body dissatisfaction, negative emotional responses, dietary restraint and weight control behaviours modelled by others.

There is a growing body of literature indicating a difference between males and females around the internalization of societal ideals and body satisfaction. In this literature the drive for muscularity is a prominent feature in males (Cafri et al., 2005), whereas leanness whilst maintaining feminine curves is more prominent in females. Petrie and Greenleaf add sporting pressures to their model to indicate that certain sports, particularly those with aesthetic or endurance requirements, tend to place an implicit pressure on performers to focus on either how they look or their body composition.

One of the key aspects of the model is how social or sporting pressures become internalized and lead to body dissatisfaction. Coaches, parents and peers have a role to play in making sure that focus is placed on what is done with the body, not what it looks like or the numbers on a set of scales. Certain practices, such as public weigh-ins for teenage female performers, are extremely risky and should be discouraged. Sport psychologists can and should address positive eating and weight management behaviours in the work that they do with performers, coaches and parents.

I would like to conclude this section with a warning. In eating disorders there is a risk that a little bit of knowledge is a dangerous thing. I would not be comfortable in designing an intervention for an eating-disordered performer. My advice is always to seek out qualified, skilled and experienced support.

Bibliography

Cafri, G., Thomson, J.K., Ricciardelli, L., McCabe, M., Smolak, L., & Yesalis, C. (2005). Pursuit of the muscular ideal: physical and psychological and putative risk factors. *Clinical Psychology Reviews 25*: 215–239.

Petrie, T.A., & Greenleaf, C. (2007). Eating disorders in sport. From theory to research to intervention. In G. Tenebaum & R. Eklund (Eds.), *Handbook of Sport Psychology* (pp. 352–378). Wiley.

UK Sport. (2007). *Eating Disorders in Sport*. Retrieved on 28 April 2017 from: http://uksport.gov.uk/resources/eating-disorders-in-sport.

Q57

My son has recently been discarded by a professional club academy. He is upset and ashamed. He feels shattered by the experience, and he's not even looked at a ball since. He's 16 years old – is there anything I can do?

To your son this feels like a bereavement. It has probably been his dream for as long as he can remember to make it to the big team. And now it looks like his dream is over.

There is no quick fix for this. It may be the biggest emotional upset he has ever experienced. You need to be patient and work with him. I have found that there is a grieving process which needs to be worked through, similar to that found in other contexts. There is shock and denial; your son probably didn't know he was in danger of being dropped. There may be shame and guilt, a feeling that he has let himself and you down, anger and frustration about the unfairness of it all – the game he loved and the club he was committed to have dealt him this blow. It is not surprising that he is experiencing a whole load of negative emotion.

Talk to him, listen to him. You cannot go back and change the decision but you can grow from it. Ideally we want your son to bounce back stronger and with a greater awareness of the importance of his sport and a determination to enjoy it. This will take time, there is no need to hurry. There is no need to pile on more pressure at this point. I've heard parents in a similar position to yours tell their children that all will be well because they can concentrate on their studies now! This is unlikely to help.

When he is ready, it is an opportunity to re-evaluate. What do you want to do next? You can still play the game, just at a different level and perhaps have more fun. Reconnect with friends who had to take a peripheral role when he was in the academy. Sample other sports. There is a whole world of opportunity for him to explore, he just needs some time and heavy-duty emotional support.

Going deeper into the theory

If you work in talent identification and development in any sport, but particularly in a sport with a well-developed youth and academy system, I strongly advise you to read Chris Green's book, '*Every Boy's Dream*'. It is an account of the youth development system in English soccer and is a thoroughly depressing indictment of a process which makes almost every mistake it is possible to make in the development of young performers. I accept that the book was published in 2009 and things may have changed. It is clear that the system fails on two levels. Firstly, it fails to develop talent efficiently and effectively, and secondly, given that most of the young people are often recruited at a very young age, it pays little or no attention to the psychological welfare of the players.

There is a real paucity of psychological research into the impact of deselection. Brown and Potrac published a study in 2009 which indicated that those young players with a very strong athletic identity (i.e. who define themselves primarily in terms of their sport) were most likely to experience psychological trauma as a result of deselection. And why wouldn't young boys or girls who have played that sport for possibly 10 years, focused all their hopes and aspirations on a career in the game, not have a well-developed athletic identity? The club demands their full commitment but provides little or no support when they are deselected.

A paper by Barker and his colleagues looking at the experiences of psychological support in cricket and football academies covers some useful material on the delivery of mental skills but fails to address the issue of deselection. All youngsters in the academy are probably aware of the statistics and, particularly in soccer, the fact that one other player in the cohort 'makes it' diminishes their own chances.

Bibliography

Barker, J., McCarthy, P., & Harwood, C. (2011). Reflections on consulting in elite youth male English cricket and soccer academies. *Sport and Exercise Psychology Review 7* (2): 58–72.

Brown, G., & Potrac, P. (2009). You've not made the grade, son. De-selection and identity disruption in elite level youth football. *Soccer and Society 10* (2): 143–159.

Green, C. (2009). *Every Boy's Dream*. A & C Black.

Q58

I'm worried a 15-year-old male power athlete I coach is using banned performance-enhancing drugs – what should I do?

My view with suspected drug misuse is to believe that the athlete is *not* using them until you have evidence to the contrary. Given the potential negative impact of raising your concerns with the athlete you need to be sure before you act.

Coaches often become suspicious about drug use when there are significant and seemingly sudden changes to physical appearance, changes in behaviour and a step change in performance levels. Before acting you need to be sure that these changes are not due to maturation and training; as boys develop they can legitimately change quite dramatically in size and stature.

Before acting I would suggest discreetly speaking to training partners and other team members, not just about the athlete's training habits and performance, but also about his general demeanour. Has he become more secretive? Is he more prone to changes in mood? These are relatively weak sources of evidence on their own. Ultimately the only confirmation will come with either the athlete telling you or a positive test.

In parallel to the detective work, develop the general drug education arm of your work. As a coach you need to be aware of anti doping protocols and procedures and ensure that this information is communicated effectively to all your athletes. You may invite an expert speaker to come and talk, not only about the drug and anti doping protocols that operate in the sport, but also more generally about the associated health issues. There are excellent resources online that you can make available to your athletes.

This is a very sensitive topic and one that is frequently not addressed. Prevention is far better than cure.

Going deeper into the theory

This is a particularly challenging research area. No one really knows how widespread drug taking is in sport. Surveying prevalence is fraught with methodological problems. What is interesting is that many studies report that what was once a problem of doping for performance benefits has developed into the problem of both performance and appearance enhancement. Many young men are using, in particular, anabolic agents to enhance their appearance. The youth risk behavior surveillance study (Centers for Disease Control, 2010) estimated that non-prescription steroid use in the United States was around 3.3% of the student population. There is no means of verifying this statistic but it is likely that a large proportion of this usage is not for performance gains but to satisfy a drive for muscularity.

Data from the youth risk behavior surveillance study and studies such as that by Irving et al. (2002) suggest that there are some relatively weak psychological indicators of drug use in sport: impulsivity, aggression, low self-esteem and body image disturbance. There is also a 'gateway' hypothesis that legal nutritional supplementation is a stepping stone to illegal drug use. The evidence around this is flimsy. However it should be noted that Martello et al. (2007) and several other studies have found that a proportion (up to 10–15%) of legal supplements are contaminated with illegal elements.

Bibliography

Centers for Disease Control. (2010). Youth risk behavior surveillance. United States 2009. *Morbidity and Mortality Weekly Reports 59*: 1–146.

Irving, L.M., Wall. M., Neumark-Sztainer, D., & Story, M. (2002). Steroid use among adolescents: findings from project EAT. *Journal of Adolescent Health 30* (4): 243–252.

Martello, S., Felli, M., & Chiarotti, M. (2007). Survey of nutritional supplements for selected illegal anabolic steroids and ephedrine, using LC-MS/MS and GC-MS methods, respectively. *Food Additives and Contaminants 24* (3): 258–263.

Q59

I coach a player who performs well in practice (particularly when working on top-spin backhand – her weakness). As soon as we are in a match situation and she goes for the backhand she loses all confidence. One mistake and she starts just to tap it over the net with no spin or pace. What can I say to her (the player is 10 years old)?

My first point is to put your question into context. What do you want to happen?

Do you want the player to have perfected her top-spin backhand and use it effectively in games next month or do you want her to have perfected it and still be playing the game when she is 12 years old, 18 years old and beyond? Decide whether you are coaching the person or the skill.

My view is that if you coach the person, the skill will develop. If you coach the skill, the person may not.

A couple of things drop out of your question – one that she appears to be 'playing' in practice sessions. She appears relaxed and feels able to 'go for it' because there is no fear of making a mistake. In contrast, she is 'tight' and fearful in games, because she has internalized that this is a game, therefore I *cannot* or *must not* make any mistakes. She has stopped playing. This is not what either you or she want. You want her to keep 'going for it'. At the age she is, it is more important that she plays in an uninhibited and fearless way.

The other point from your question is that there is an emphasis on weaknesses – things that she cannot do. Because of the ways you have emphasized it, I think it is highly likely that the issue with the backhand is already prominent in her thinking. At the age of 10 the word 'yet' is really important. She cannot execute this technically very difficult shot – yet. Patience and playing it long are important.

I would strongly advise you to slow down a bit and focus more on fun. Intrinsic motivation – fun and enjoyment – is what will keep this young tennis player in the game.

Going deeper into the theory

Frequently coaches present with a technical challenge, but in reality it is a challenge which straddles the technical–psychological boundary. The technical skills are there but they are not being expressed due to psychological constraints. This case is an example. In a performer at this stage of development I would not be inclined to probe deeply as to why she is fearful of making an error.

However, later in development, as the performer becomes more specialized in her performance and there is greater emphasis on the systematic elimination of areas of weakness, it will be important to find out what is holding the performer back and rather develop the mindset that every error is part of the learning process. There are mistakes worth making. They help us to understand how to do it better.

In this case it might be useful to use a modelling approach to develop the performer. Expert and peer modelling is frequently used in coaching (Hodges et al., 2007). Less frequently used, but potentially highly effective, is self-modelling. In self-modelling, video is used to capture images of the individual executing a skill. Be aware that there may be self-presentational concerns around this, and ethical ones in capturing images of young performers, but potentially video provides a powerful tool for gaining self-awareness and changing how skills are executed (Ashford et al., 2006).

Bibliography

Ashford, D., Bennet, S.J., & Davids, K. (2006). Observational modeling effects for movement dynamics and movement outcomes measures across different task constraints. A meta-analysis. *Journal of Motor Behaviour 38* (3): 185–205.
Hodges, N.J., Williams, A.M., Hayes, S.J., & Breslin, G. (2007). What is modelled during observational learning? *Journal of Sports Sciences 25* (5): 531–575.

Q60

I coach young tennis players, of very wide levels of ability. I've always been interested in why some learn quicker than others. Is my coaching at fault or is it their ability to learn?

Well done for reflecting on what you have observed. For me the first step in becoming an excellent coach, teacher or mentor in any context is the ability to make the step from being preoccupied with what you are doing, e.g. designing drills and sessions, to becoming preoccupied with what the learner is taking away from your sessions in terms of learning and performance.

My first point is to encourage you to see the difference between learning and performance. If you set up a drill where you focus on a simple forehand drive for 10 minutes, at the end you will have 'grooved' that skill through repetition and performance will be improved and reasonably consistent. If you move on to another skill for 10 minutes and then come back and test the forehand again, some will have retained the skill and their performance level will be maintained, whilst others haven't and it will seem that they have gone back to their baseline level. This is more a test of learning. Performance is relatively easy to develop through repetition. Learning is more difficult because it depends on the skill being rehearsed, elaborated and understood at a deeper level. It is tested by seeing what is retained and what can be transferred to other contexts, for example, from a stationary drill to a moving one.

In your groups you will often find that some performers appear to learn quicker in drills but fail to retain the skills. You will find others are able to retain aspects of other similar skills which they can apply to the one being learned. It is worth highlighting this when you set up drills by drawing attention to things that have already been learned.

Learners go through stages in acquiring new skills. Initially they are in a thinking stage, where they are aiming to see, understand and reproduce the key movements of feet, body and racket. Because they are using so much of their processing capacity on these basic features, any added complexity, like pace on the ball, variable bounce or additional body movement, is likely to cause the skill to break down. At this stage, your job is to simplify the movement and offer many, many opportunities to repeat the skill. Avoid talking too much at this stage – pictures paint thousands of words.

Progress to the next stage depends on how readily existing skills can be applied in the new context. In this stage, the movements become more fluent because the parts are combining to form more coherent wholes or more functionally significant parts such as footwork or whole-body position. At this stage, I advise coaches to look at the single feature which is inhibiting progress, rather than overloading the learner with information. The learner may already feel overwhelmed with too many things to think about: this is a clear sign that the individulal's processing capacity has been reached.

In the final stage of learning, the learner, after long exposure to practice, is able to place the skill on autopilot and turn attention to other parts of the visual or in response to their opponent's movement. When a skill is less automatic, the performer can concentrate on either the shot or the opponent's movement, but not both. The true test of skill is at this end of the spectrum. If a secondary task can be executed it is very well learned.

Going deeper into the theory

Over the past 20 years sport psychology has evolved away from some of its historical links with motor control and skill acquisition. Today it is more commonly found that these principles are taught in specialized coaching or even biomechanics courses rather than sport psychology. I think this is problematic because often the psychological context is lost. For example, in learning new skills, the physical and the mental aspects are often challenged together. On the direct point of whether people learn at different rates, there are several ways to look at this. Firstly, examining the notion that some people are more movement-competent than others. Giles (2011) has developed a method of assessing the basic building blocks of movement. In this work the seven basic movement competencies which form the basis of physical literacy are identified: squat, lunge, push, pull, hinge (ability to bend at the hip joint without loss of lumbar posture), brace (control of the trunk under load) and rotation of the trunk. It may be that the ability to learn is limited by deficiencies in one or more of these.

There may also be an issue of matching the style of learning to the types of sessions you typically deliver. Before I start, it is important to acknowledge that there is a wealth of material on this and also that it is a highly controversial topic. From the work of Piaget onwards there is a consensus that 'learning by doing' is an important aim to make your sessions as active as possible (Piaget and Inhelder, 1962). This might seem obvious – but I see coaches at every age and ability level spending too long explaining and reviewing and performers spending most of a session not engaged in any meaningful practice.

Models of learning style such as Fleming's VARK model (Fleming, 2001) indicate that people have preferences for the way material is presented and organized in teaching/coaching sessions – with some visual, some auditory, some read/write and some kinaesthetic (Fleming and Mills, 1992). Clearly the strength of the preference is important. Like most normally distributed phenomena, most people score average for all three and will respond to material presented in each of the modalities equally. The evidence for differences in learning styles and strategies is equivocal and its practical application can present paradoxes. It is worth being mindful of this when you are designing interventions.

Bibliography

Atherton, J.S. (2013) *Learning and Teaching; Piaget's Developmental Theory*. Retrieved 18 July 2016 from: http://www.learning andteaching.info/learning/piaget.htm.

Fleming, N.D. (2001*). Teaching and Learning Styles: VARK Strategies*. N.D. Fleming.

Fleming, N.D., & Mills, C. (1992) *Not Another Inventory, Rather a Catalyst for Reflection. To Improve the Academy*. Paper 246. Retrieved 17 July 2016 from: http://digitalcommons.unl.edu/podimproveacad/246.

Giles, K.B. (2011). *Physical Competence Assessment Manual*. Movement Dynamics.

Piaget, J., & Inhelder, B. (1962). *The Psychology of the Child*. Basic Books.

Q61

Is it true that in order to be mentally tough children need to be exposed to adversity?

This is called the 'rocky road' hypothesis. A number of sport psychologists working in the area of talent development have presented evidence to suggest that many of the top performers across a range of sports have experienced adversity in their development and that this appears to have given them increased motivation, developed their coping skills and helped them to keep their sport in perspective.

In many cases it appears that this process does facilitate the important transitions into senior-level competition and upward into the higher echelons of performance. However, care must be exercised. I am aware of several coaches contriving setbacks and adversity, such as dropping a performer for seemingly no reason, or acting in a consistently negative way towards a performer to harden him up. This is a risky strategy that can serve to undermine a coaching relationship and may be counterproductive.

Adverse events, such as injury or loss of a place on a representative team or performance setbacks, will naturally occur. It is more important for coaches to support and mentor performers to confront these and come back more motivated and stronger.

Interestingly, the 'rocky road' approach is often the opposite approach to that taken in many talent development processes where performers are identified early and effectively buffered from many of the harsh realities of sport.

Going deeper into the theory

Talent identification and development is a rich and important line of contemporary research. Across the sporting world national governing bodies of sport, professional teams and franchises are investing heavily in trying to distil down the essence of talent and its development in order to streamline and optimize the processes and gain the maximum return. As this work has developed, it has moved from what now looks like the very primitive talent search that took Megan Still, an Australian rower, from never having sat in a boat to winning an Olympic gold medal. At that stage, talent identification was more about physical characteristics. As the process evolved it became clear that psychological characteristics were also very important (MacNamara et al., 2010a, b).

More recent work has served to clarify the nature of the 'rocky road' (Collins et al., 2016). The most recent published work by this team identifies what they called 'superchampions'. These are people who have been identified as talented and made a big impact on their sport at the senior level. It wasn't just trauma that discriminated them from their peers, who may also have been successful, it was the maintenance of commitment and interest despite the trauma and their ability to respond positively to a challenge, trauma or setback. The 'superchampions' also appeared to echo the supportive but 'non-pushy' parenting identified earlier.

Bibliography

Collins, D., & MacNamara, Á. (2012).The rocky road to the top: why talent needs trauma. *Sports Medicine 42*: 907–914.

Collins, D., MacNamara, Á., & McCarthy, N. (2016). Super champions, champions and almosts: important differences and commonalities on the rocky road. *Frontiers in Psychology 6*: 1–11.

MacNamara, Á., Button, A., & Collins, D. (2010a). The role of psychological characteristics in facilitating the pathway to elite performance. Part 1: identifying mental skills and behaviours. *The Sport Psychologist 24*: 52–73.

MacNamara, Á., Button, A., & Collins, D. (2010b). The role of psychological characteristics in facilitating the pathway to elite performance. Part 2: examining environmental and stage related differences in skills and behaviours. *The Sport Psychologist 24*: 74–96.

Pulling the threads together

Of all the chapters in this book, this has been by far the hardest to write. This is for several reasons. Firstly, because there is so much material I could have focused on. I think maybe there is another book, solely focusing on the issues of the psychology of parenting in sport and the psychological basis of double-, triple- or more goal coaching. Secondly, having focused specifically on the issues around 'pushy/unhelpful parenting', talent and expertise and the mastery achievement orientation, I am conscious of a small voice from the 'real world' reminding me that coaching children is often like herding cats. In the real world coaching, teaching and parenting is frequently a pragmatic process of trying to get children and young people who are, in varying degrees, unmotivated, disengaged and unfocused to do things that they will benefit from at an unspecified point in the future.

I think this is an unnecessarily pessimistic view. At the outset children are intrinsically motivated. Give a group of children a ball and a game of something will almost inevitably break out. It is the efforts that adults make to organize sport that often begin to cause the difficulties. Without knowing, adults impose conditions, constraints and structures on sport which make it difficult for most children to enjoy what they are doing. Early specialization is a particular challenge, children's psychology is a fragile and volatile thing and the potential for burnout is ever present. Which brings me back to Plutarch, the source for the title of the chapter. Some fires burn brightly for a short while and then naturally burn out. If we want children to realize their potential fully, the adults around them need to understand that what fuels the fire at the start, beginning and end is fun and enjoyment. More joy!

IX

The psychology of sport injury: there are two types of performer – those who are currently injured and those who will become injured

Injury is an occupational hazard

> Athletes are stronger, quicker and presumably sturdier than the rest of us. They seem blessed. We so rarely see them at their most vulnerable – in pain, and out of commission. And we almost never hear, from their perspective about those injuries that disrupt their existence and play havoc with their futures.
>
> (Stein, 1984, p. 62)

At whatever level you participate in sport there is an ever-present threat of injury. Despite their best efforts almost all performers will experience periods when participation is either not possible or strongly discouraged due to an injury. These may be minor, requiring only a few days of down time, or severe, leading to extended periods away from training and performance. Injury can end a performer's career. Sports medicine practitioners tend to focus on three areas: the physical causes of injury, the assessment of these physical signs or symptoms of the damage to soft tissue or the skeletal system and the process of healing and rehabilitation. The psychological aspects of injury and rehabilitation are often neglected.

Put yourself in the shoes of an Olympic-level performer. Three weeks before your event you have a new and distinct pain during training. It could be minor, it could be nothing, but equally it could jeopardize your participation in the Games. Psychologically this is a 'landmine' in your hopes and dreams. It is distracting, it drains your confidence and provokes anxiety, the opposite of what you want in the last few days before the Games. It's not just Olympics performers – exactly the same process operates at all levels of sport.

The psychological effects of injury are profound and poorly appreciated. In my work with elite-level performers, the title of the chapter could not be more appropriate. In certain sports, particularly contact sports, I have spent between a quarter and half of my work with performers providing support through a period of injury. Most performers have a long history of injuries, some of which have been caused by incomplete healing and rehabilitation from the previous one, such is the pressure on them to return to play. Pressure from both external forces, such as coaches, but also internal pressures, their own motivation to return to play quickly and an expectation of no change in performance level.

The psychology of sports injury is complex. In this chapter I intend to set the scene for the coach's and performer's questions by addressing three main areas: the question of injury proneness in sport, emotional responses to injury and their impact on healing and finally the role of mental skills in the rehabilitation process.

Sports injuries are pretty infrequent, aren't they?

One of the reasons people play sport is to keep fit and healthy; however the sports injury data suggest quite the opposite. Prevalence of sporting injury is extremely high. Finch et al. (1998) presented evidence that around 20% of accident and emergency consultations in hospitals were sport-related. In the UK data from a 1995 study indicated that there were around 30 million sport-related injuries each year (Nicholl et al., 1995).

If we accept that Brown's (2005) assertion, part of this chapter's title, that there are two types of performer is accurate, it does beg some important questions. What is causing these injuries? Is it poor technique? Inadequate conditioning? Or are there some psychological factors at work? What happens after an injury, how do people respond to injury and does this response influence the process of rehabilitation and return to play?

Are some sport performers more prone to injury than others?

In the 1970s and 1980s there were some ground-breaking studies examining the links between the stress a performer was experiencing and the incidence of injury (Bramwell et al.,1975; Passer

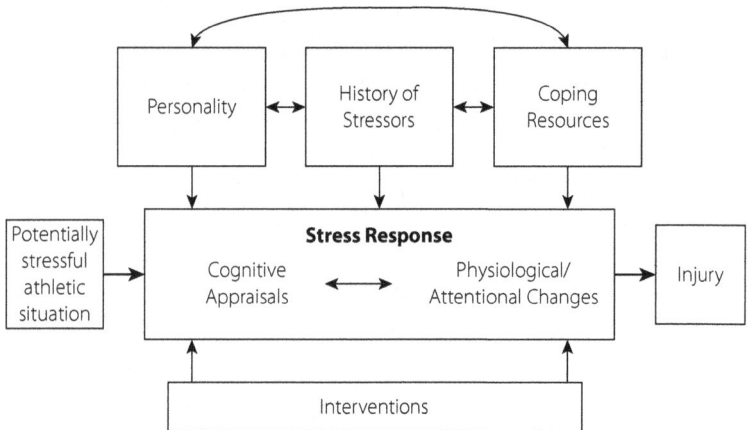

FIGURE 9.1 The stress–injury model (Andersen and Williams, 1998).

and Seese, 1983). These studies showed that not just perceived stress in sport, from the pressures of competition, but life stress in general, could make a performer more liable to injury. In response to these findings Mark Andersen and Jean Williams developed a model which sought to put the psychological factors which precede and possibly predict injury into a more theoretical context (Williams and Andersen, 1988; Andersen and Williams, 1998) (Figure 9.1).

This model shared some of the problems discussed earlier surrounding psychological models. The arrows can be misleading; they are not designed to infer the direction of causality or the precise sequence of a chain of events. However this model is particularly important in highlighting some key psychological factors behind the incidence of injuries:

◆ personality
◆ history of stressors and daily hassles
◆ coping resources
◆ psychological interventions, particularly cognitive-behavioural stress management techniques
◆ stress response.

Is there an injury-prone personality type?

To the psychologist, personality refers to stable and enduring individual characteristics. It is a controversial topic and there are many
models of personality which aim to explain behaviour. The existing research indicates that there are some traits – stable aspects of
personality – which predispose people to injury.

People who score highly on the trait anxiety scale seem to be
more prone to injury. Trait anxiety is a predisposition to view situations as threatening. These people see possible threat and adverse
outcomes in situations their team mates, who are lower on the trait
anxiety scales, see as challenging or neutral.

Highly scoring sensation seekers tend to be impulsive and are
attracted to activities with high levels of risk. This can make them
vulnerable in situations where there is the possibility of injury.
Another aspect of personality linked to injury is trait perfectionism –
these performers tend to present with perfectionist behaviours in
training such as failing to recover adequately between training sessions. Often these performers appear highly committed and 'push
through' pain and fatigue. This may be counterproductive in the
longer term.

Stress: a complex process with a part to play in many sports injuries

In this context stress should be viewed as an imbalance between
the perceived demands of a situation and the perceived ability to
cope. Some of the earliest work on the psychology of injury indicated that players who reported higher levels of stress reported
higher incidence of injury. In the more general health psychology literature, at around the same time, researchers were finding
a similar set of findings – high levels of life stress were linked with
disease, particularly cardiovascular disease (Holmes and Rahe,
1967). The researchers rank-ordered stressful life events indicating
their relative impact on health. At the top of the list was bereavement

of a spouse or partner, further down the list were financial difficulties and towards the lower end are events such as family holidays and seasonal celebrations like Christmas. This type of list is useful in highlighting life events but because these happen relatively infrequently there has been a move in the research away from looking at these and towards examining the influence of daily hassles. Research indicates that there is a close correlation between the incidence of high levels of hassles over weeks or months and the incidence of injury (Fawkner et al., 1999).

Coping – the buffer between stress and injury

Performers with well-developed and effective methods of coping with both life stresses and daily hassles appear to be less vulnerable to injury. I have used the word 'appear' because the research evidence is mixed. Some studies have shown that coping is pivotal, whilst others have not found evidence to confirm this point.

Coping takes on many forms, from personal and general factors around self-care, making sure that you are recovering between sessions, through adequate rest, sleep, nutrition and hydration. Coping may extend into the development of mental skills which can further foster recovery, such as management of self-talk, physical relaxation and the use of imagery. More broadly, coping can extend into the development of supporting social relationships. All of these strategies of coping appear to be useful in providing a buffer between the physical and mental response and the often unavoidable and accepted stress of training and competition.

So how does stress actually cause injury?

Within the Williams and Andersen (1998) model it is proposed that stress is the causal factor because of two responses – one physiological and one psychological. Physiologically, stress makes movements less relaxed and less efficient. Movements which are normally smooth and effortless become inefficient and effortful. This negative impact on movement control exposes the musculoskeletal system to risk. A good example of this is a pitcher in baseball or bowler in cricket, who has become aware that his place in the starting line-up is under threat. The stress impacts on him to force the movement, to try harder, rather than to relax and 'allow the skill out'.

The proposed psychological mechanism is linked; under stress attentional focus tends to narrow and you become less aware of what's going on around you. You may also tend to point the attentional focus inwards at your thoughts rather on what is happening around you, exposing you to risk of injury.

What makes someone injury-prone?

I have pointed out that 'labelling' individuals is not a helpful strategy. If a player is presenting with patterns of injury which appear to be more frequent than in others, I would explore underlying factors. Does the player tend to manage risk situations in ways which increase the risk of injury? Does she tend to be impulsive, where others are more considered? Does she have a problem differentiating the pain and fatigue associated with heavy training from the pain and fatigue which is flagging that she is not recovered? Is the player managing the pressure of a limelight role? Is the player experiencing stress from outside the sporting environment?

All of these could be important, but you can do little to make training and competing less stressful, therefore you must address the other side of the equation, developing psychological skills which help make the stressor load manageable.

It can be helpful for the psychologist to work with strength and conditioning staff, medical staff and the coach to establish strategies which foster both the physical and mental sides of injury prevention. Psychological factors which lead to increased stress have the potential to impact on decision making, alter movement mechanics and slow the recovery process. Being fit to train and play is the single biggest factor in performance enhancement, therefore everything that can be done should be done to ensure it.

How do performers respond to injury?

One of the earliest explanations of how sport performers respond to injury was an extension of a model originally developed to describe how people adjust and cope with the news that they have a terminal illness (Kubler-Ross, 1969). This grief/loss stage model suggested that individuals moved through a series of stages – disbelief, denial, isolation, anger, bargaining and depression before finally acceptance and resignation. Sport psychology researchers observed similar stages with injured performers. However, whilst the model was appealing to sport psychologists, it was not a perfect fit; very few performers were having to cope with a terminal diagnosis, most would return to performance. When tested, researchers found that the progression of the emotional reaction was not linear, or stage-like. Performers moved forwards and backwards through various emotional states depending on how their rehabilitation was going and in response to other events in their lives.

A useful development of the grief/loss model was the work of McDonald and Hardy (1990), who identified two distinct phases of response to an injury. The first one is the reactive phase, immediately after the injury or confirmed diagnosis. In this phase, performers experience shock, panic and helplessness. This is often magnified by two things: firstly the performer is often experiencing pain or discomfort and secondly, because the individual is unable to train or play, he has a great deal of time to think about what's happened. The second phase is viewed as a more positive and adaptive phase, where the performer has acknowledged that he is injured and that he needs to receive treatment and rehabilitate the injury.

What do performers do when they're injured?

Performers tend to be action-oriented, and this is one of the challenges of injury. Therefore they should have an injury plan – just like their training plan. In their injury plan there are a few essentials.

Assessment and diagnosis

Uncertainty often causes a great deal of anxiety for the injured performer. An undiagnosed or inconclusively diagnosed injury can be a very significant challenge to the performer, who doesn't know what to do and will often operate on the 'optimistic bias' I noted earlier in the text. In the real world, performers will often 'shop around' between clinicians and therapists for a diagnosis. I have worked with performers who have been to the same clinic with a new injury, but seen three or four different practitioners, all of whom have given a different diagnosis and different treatment plans and prognosis. This is confusing for the performer. I always advise performers to find a medic or therapist they trust and who understands them and their sport. I'm aware that this isn't always possible but the aim is always to see that one practitioner.

Perceptions of seriousness

In one of the first published studies on responses to injury, Crossman and Jamieson (1985) found that there is frequently a disconnect between the perception of seriousness by the performer and the trainer or therapist. Players who overestimated the seriousness of their injury tended to experience greater anxiety and a range of negative feelings, such as apathy, anger and isolation. There may be a number of heuristic biases operating here, where players optimistically believe injuries are less serious than they actually are, and believe that they will rehabilitate quicker than the judgement of medical staff, who have greater experience and objectivity.

Stress and rehabilitation

There have been ground-breaking advances in the science of psychoneuroimmunology. Many of these advances are around the impact of stress on the healing process. There is considerable evidence to show that the healing process is slowed down by the release of cortisol associated with stress (Glaser, 1995). It is often difficult to remind performers that stressing about a return to play date, or that they are nearing the end of their contract period and are not playing, could actually be slowing down their recovery.

In my view this is another reason why stress management strategies should be taught early in a player's career. These skills transfer readily from performance to rehabilitation.

95% of your body is fine . . .

A strong indicator of poor adjustment to injury is a feeling of apathy and lack of interest. Where possible, I encourage injured performers to work with their rehabilitation staff to find aspects of training that they can do, which will not risk progress in the site of injury. Players like training, they like to be active, so working to develop other aspects of their fitness can be a useful distraction – but it must not risk reinjury to the original site. In addition to the physical training performers can do a good deal of mental rehearsal during injury rehab. This keeps the technical and tactical parts of their game sharp and can speed up the process of returning to play.

Beware the 'macho' culture

In many teams there is a mindset that injury is a sign of weakness or a flaw in your character. In these teams a culture of 'pushing through' pain and injury often leads players to underreport injury and not seek treatment. Where injuries are reported they are often downplayed and there is an implicit pressure to return to action. There is a clear long-term danger in this (Messner, 1992).

Putting it all together

In an effort to draw together comprehensively a wide range of factors which appear linked to the emotional response of performers to injury, Wiese-Bjornstal et al. (1998) proposed an integrated psychosocial model (Figure 9.2).

This model highlights many of the concerns that the injured performer may present with, but is weak in terms of actually predicting the emotional or behavioural response.

It is useful in that it cements two things in the practitioner's thinking; firstly, that it is imperative to tune into the athlete as

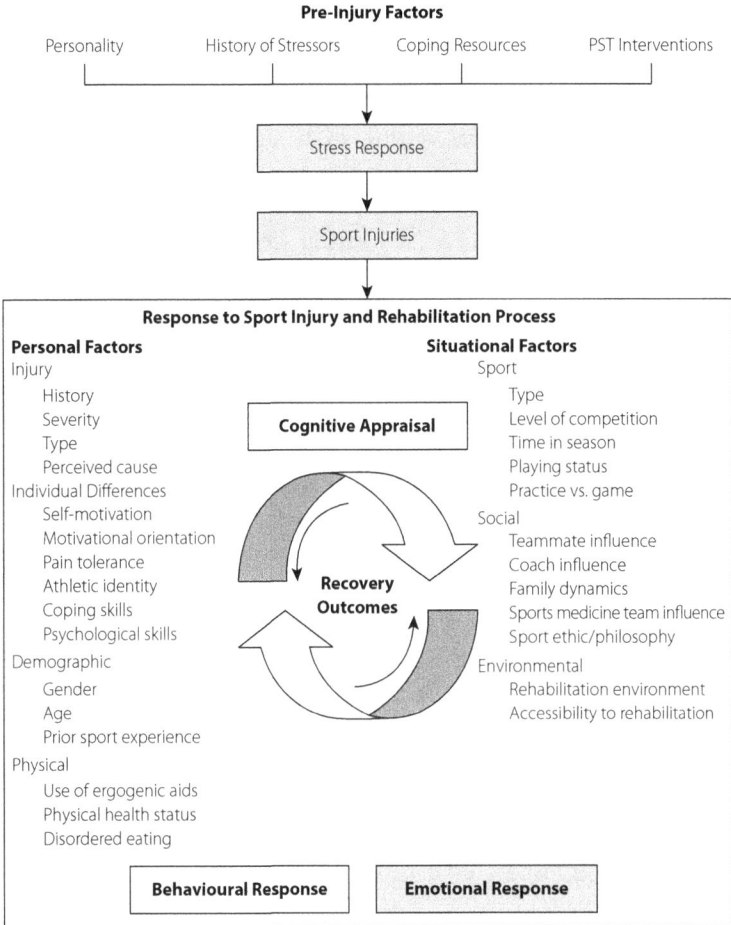

FIGURE 9.2 An integrated model of response to sport injury: psychological and sociological dynamics (Wiese-Bjornstal et al., 1998). PST, psychological skills training.

an individual. Two performers with exactly the same injury at exactly the same point in the season may respond completely differently. The other point is that the practitioner should be aware that a change in a single factor can act as the catalyst that changes the whole appraisal.

Mental skills and rehabilitation

Goal setting

We have examined goal setting in a range of other contexts. However there is evidence that this is one of the most widely used psychological interventions in sports injury rehabilitation. Performers are often used to setting goals and will often be attracted to its apparent emphasis on outcomes. This needs to be managed carefully. Often the outcome goal – 'to be painfree by next Friday' – is not under the control of the performer. The process goals of stretching and icing four times a day – which make the outcome more likely – may be less exciting and therefore less likely to be adhered to. The same processes in formulating goals should be undertaken. However I advise performers I work with not to fix on specific dates for healing events to have occurred. It is better to have safe rehabilitation, where the risks of reinjury are minimized and you are working with the natural healing, remodelling and strengthening processes.

Imagery and mental practice

Imagery allows the injured performer to review and maintain aspects of technique or tactics. Imagery specifically involves the visual system, which is important because vision tends to dominate in many sport skills. However there is a broader issue of mental practice, which has been shown to be beneficial. In particular, some interesting studies suggested that when a performer mentally rehearses a skill, there is some activity in the muscles which actually control the skill, thereby preventing the neural connections from breaking down. Another valuable application of imagery in injury rehabilitation relates to the 'healing imagery' described by Ievleva and Orlick (1991). In this type of imagery, the script guides performers to see, in their mind's eye, healing occurring in the injured tissue (for example, seeing the blood stream bringing oxygen and nutrients to the injury site, reducing swelling and seeing the old and damaged cells being removed). The script can go on to encourage the performer to 'feel' soft tissue or bone getting stronger (e.g., visualizing tissue as feeling as strong as steel as fibres bind together).

Healing imagery may also be effective due to the relaxation and calming effect. As noted above, this can reduce circulating cortisol and impact on the endocrine response associated with inflammation.

The role of the sport psychologist in working with injured performers

When athletes get injured, it is likely that their thoughts turn to the medical team rather than the sport psychologist. However, what this scene setting has shown is that with injury comes a great deal of psychological trauma which the medical team may not be willing or able to support the performer through. Most performers don't really engage with the possibility of injury before they become injured or learn about how to adjust to injury. They view injury as an unwelcome, unplanned-for and random event. Injury is almost inevitable and strategies for its management should be as routine as training plans. In my applied work I encourage performers to become their own psychologist in periods of injury as well as periods of performance. In that way they can understand more clearly what is going on in their thinking and emotions. I envisage a time in the future when there is a specialist area for psychologists working with injury-related trauma and rehabilitation.

Bibliography

Andersen, M.B., & Williams, J.M. (2008). A model of stress and athletic injury: prediction and prevention. *Journal of Sport and Exercise Psychology 1988* (10): 294–306.

Bramwell, S.T., Masuda, M., Wagner, N.N., & Holmes, T.H. (1975). Psychological factors in athletic injuries: development and application of the Social and Athletic Readjustment Rating Scale (SARRS). *Journal of Human Stress 1*: 6–20.

Brown. C. (2005). The psychology of recovery and rehab. In S. Murphy (Ed.), *The Sport Psych Handbook*. Human Kinetics.

Crossman, J., & Jamieson, J. (1985). Differences in perceptions of seriousness and disrupting effects of athletic injury as viewed by athletes and their trainer. *Perceptual and Motor Skills 61* (3): 1131–1134.

Fawkner, H.J., McMurray, N.E., & Summers, J.J. (1999). Athletic injury and minor life events: a prospective study. *Journal of Science and Medicine in Sport 2* (2): 117–127.

Finch, C.F., Ozanne-Smith, J., & Valuri, G. (1998). Sport and active recreation injuries in Australia: evidence from emergency department presentations. *British Journal of Sports Medicine 32*: 220–225.

Glaser, R. (1995). Slowing of wound healing by psychological stress. *Lancet 346*: 1194–1196.

Holmes, T.H., & Rahe, R.H. (1967). The social readjustment rating scale. *Journal of Psychosomatic Research, 11, 213.*

Ievleva, L., & Orlick, T. (1991). Mental links to enhanced healing: an exploratory study. *The Sport Psychologist 5*: 25–40.

Kubler-Ross, E. (1969). *On Death and Dying.* Scribner Publishers.

McDonald, S.A., & Hardy, C.J. (1990). Affective response patterns of the injured athlete: an exploratory analysis. *The Sport Psychologist 4*: 261–274.

Messner, M.A. (1992). *Power at Play: Sports and the Problem of Masculinity.* Beacon Press.

Nicholl, J.P., Coleman, P., & Williams, B.T. (1995). The epidemiology of sports and exercise related injury in the United Kingdom. *British Journal of Sports Medicine 29* (4): 232–238.

Passer, M.W., & Seese, M.D. (1983). Life stress and athletic injury: examination of positive versus negative events and three moderator variables. *Journal of Human Stress 9*: 11–16.

Stein, H. (1984). Brought to his knees. *Sport 63–66.*

Wiese-Bjornstal, D.M., Smith, A.M., Shaffer, S.M., & Morrey, M.A. (1998). *An integrated model of response to sport injury: psychological and sociological dynamics. Journal of Applied Sport Psychology 10*: 46–69.

Williams, J.M., & Andersen, M.B. (1998). Psychological antecedents of sports injury: review and critique of the stress and injury model. *Journal of Sport and Exercise Psychology 10*: 5–25.

Q62

What is the most important thing that a coach can do for an athlete who is injured in order to support that athlete?

The top priority for a newly injured performer is to get a fast and clear diagnosis. You will not be able to do this yourself, unless you are medically qualified. I urge coaches, teachers or parents not to make amateur diagnoses, no matter how experienced they are. Make it your business, as soon as you can after your appointment to a coaching role, to forge links with medical practitioners who can provide expertise in this area. It is inevitable that you will have a number of injured performers in your squad over the course of a season. Working with your medical practitioner (but not breaching confidentiality), look at patterns of injury and test the possibility that your coaching practice or competitive load is a causal factor in the injuries. Do all you are can not to establish a 'macho' culture of injury risk.

Once a diagnosis has been made, uncertainty is replaced by planning and open communication. Look at what the performer can still do. Can she maintain some aspects of fitness? Is she willing and/or able to take on another role whilst rehabilitating?

As the performer approaches returning to play, beware that physical and psychological readiness are not the same thing. Set up challenges that allow the performer to confirm her readiness. Go at the performer's pace.

Going deeper into the theory

Very few sport psychologists are specialists in injury. Most emphasize the development of performance enhancement skills in their work with individuals and teams. This is a mistake. As a practitioner you will encounter injury regularly and in my view it is a mistake to apply the same set of mental skills to rehabilitation as you would to performance. I recommend that practitioners engage with some of the excellent materials that have been written on the topic. Arvinen-Barrow and Walker's (2013) text is excellent and Heil and Podlog (2010) present a comprehensive account of the mental challenges of injury and rehabilitation.

Bibliography

Arvinen-Barrow, M., & Walker, N. (Eds.) (2013). *The Psychology of Sport Injury and Rehabilitation.* Routledge.
Heil, J., & Podlog, L. (2010). Injury and performance. In S. Murphy (Ed.), *The Oxford Handbook of Sport and Performance Psychology* (pp. 593–617). Oxford University Press.

Q63

How do we get players to be more accurate in self-assessment of injuries, as most will downplay their severity?

For me this really reinforces the importance of performers, coaches, teachers and parents having access to sports medicine support. Quick and accurate diagnosis removes all doubt and addresses the point you make that players will tend to operate on the optimistic bias – that the injury is less serious than it is in reality.

As a coach or teacher, you should educate players to take injuries seriously. Talk about immediate first aid – rest, ice, compression and elevation. Talk about the difference between the pain of heavy training – muscle soreness – and the pain of injury. Many coaches don't keep records of injuries among their athletes. It is wise to do this to try to identify any patterns and also check that it's not your practice which is leading to injury. Unfortunately (back in the real world!) sports medicine in the UK can be really difficult to access. Most people depend on their general practitioner, accident and emergency or minor injuries unit for a diagnosis. Sometimes this is excellent, the injury is taken seriously and the diagnosis is quick and accurate, and a referral to other health care professionals can be made. On the other hand, some medical practitioners have little time for sports injuries and the overall service is unsatisfactory. I strongly recommend coaches to take this aspect of their work very seriously. Once you have identified a good medical practitioner take great care of him or her, as this professional is a valuable asset to the organization.

Going deeper into the theory

It is important to note the often conflicting environment performers exist in. On the one hand, coaches, teachers and parents strive to protect performers from risk of injury. They aim to educate about injury and establish routines to prepare physically for training performance. They may monitor physiology to determine recovery and rest. Often in direct contrast to this is the ethic which promotes playing with and through pain: winners never quit – no pain, no gain.

Sport sociologists have examined how the norms and values of sport become internalized and encultured (e.g. Messner, 1990; Hughes and Coakley, 1991). Few researchers have resolved this interplay between the macho risk culture present in many sports and the preservation of performers' health. One positive line of research was presented by Safai (2003). In this work, looking at the sport ethic in Canadian university students, she identified a three-way relationship between the culture of risk promoted by the players and coaches and the culture of precaution promoted by the medical team. The third element is the resultant pragmatic culture of 'sensible risks'. However, it should be noted that, as the coaching team and players are highly motivated to practise the types of skills they will encounter in actual performance, sensible risks can sometimes have unintended negative outcomes. I have worked with several players who have suffered serious injuries in training or practice sessions. Their injuries were inflicted by team mates and often close friends. This can be a highly traumatic event for everyone concerned.

Bibliography

Hughes, R., & Coakley, J. (1991). Positive deviance among athletes: the implications of over conformity to the sport ethic. *Sociology of Sport Journal 4*: 307–327.

Messner, M. (1990). When bodies are weapons: masculinity and violence in sport. *International Review for the Sociology of Sport 25*: 203–219.

Safai, P. (2003). Healing the body in the 'culture of risk': examining the negotiation of treatment between sport medicine clinicians and injured athletes in Canadian intercollegiate sport. *Sociology of Sport Journal 20*: 127–146.

Q64

How do you best work with athletes who suffer a setback during rehabilitation from an original injury?

First let me clarify the term 'setback'. It is important because there is research to indicate that performers tend to overestimate the seriousness of an injury and underestimate the time it will take to rehabilitate when compared with the expert views of medical practitioners. A setback should not be seen in terms of time taken to rehabilitate. You should always be aware that healing processes vary from person to person and the transitions from rehabilitation back into training to competing are not necessarily the same for everyone. In this context we are talking about reinjury or a secondary injury which has occurred through the rehabilitation process.

Firstly, I advise caution when giving performers or coaches, teachers and parents fixed timelines for rehabilitation milestones. If you are forced into a situation, don't give a fixed date, give a realistic upper and lower limit. Reinforce that you are looking at symptoms rather than time.

Secondly, reinjury of the initial site is usually because of poor risk management. During rehabilitation it is essential that the injured athlete understands what the high-risk movements are – 'you are fine to exercise provided there is no changing of direction'.

Thirdly, encourage the performer to see the down time as an opportunity to develop other aspects of strength and conditioning, performance analysis or skills outside sport.

Finally, patience. You are working with Mother Nature. There is strong evidence to show that cortisol, a brain chemical associated with stress, actually slows the healing process.

Going deeper into the theory

Taylor and Taylor's (1997) return-to-sport model breaks the rehabilitation process into stages which can helpfully inform interventions. My personal preference is to go back a little before this and integrate aspects of the Brewer (2007) and Evans and Hardy (1997) grief/loss and stage models of injury. In these models the early stages post trauma are characterized by patterns of emotion such as disbelief, denial and isolation. Often in the initial posttrauma period players are experiencing these but are also in pain. They experience a profound sense of loss of the thing that gives life structure and purpose coupled with a great deal of time to think about it. It is important that this is addressed. Often the player's isolation is compounded by the attitude of a coach. The 'come back when you're fit' message may not be as common as it once was but it serves as a powerful message which may result in performers engaging in risky behaviours they believe will speed up recovery.

Taylor and Taylor's stage-based model identifies the initial return as the first phase of rehabilitation. This is when the healing is tested. It is essential that confidence in the site of injury is established before a transition to subsequent stages can be made. Recovery confirmation facilitates movement to physical and technical training which again needs to be risk-assessed. The transition to high-intensity and conditioned training allows graded exposure to competition-like conditions. Finally, there is a return to competition. Of all the stages this is the one which presents the greatest challenge. Players are often physically ready to compete, but psychologically they may be several weeks away. This is often because there are lingering concerns about reinjury or possibly images of finding themselves in the situation where the initial injury occurred. These should not be dismissed as they are encouraging the performer to think about non-task activity. Only when performers feel ready to maintain task focus do they become ready for selection.

Bibliography

Brewer, B.W. (2007). Psychology of sports injury rehabilitation. In G. Tenenbaum and R.C. Ecklund (Eds.), *Handbook of Sport Psychology* (3rd edn., pp. 404–424). John Wiley.

Evans, L., & Hardy, L. (1997). Sports injury and grief responses. A review. *Journal of Sport and Exercise Psychology 17*: 227–245.

Taylor, J., & Taylor, S. (1997). *Psychological Approaches to Sports Injury Rehabilitation*. Aspen.

Q65

What is the best way to give an athlete confidence again who is obviously not working on an injured area that is physically OK?

Physically there may be no reason why a performer cannot train with high intensity and return to competitive action. Physical healing and rehabilitation don't necessarily mean that the performer is ready mentally. My advice is to speak to the performer. Tell him what you are seeing: you feel he is avoiding testing the area of injury. Sensitively explore the reasons why this is happening. You need to make it clear that you have the player's best interests in mind and are not simply trying to rush him back into competition. Ask what the player needs from you or from training sessions to help clear these last hurdles to returning. Above all, go at the performer's pace. Rushing at this stage can be very destructive, both in terms of the player's recovery and also the coach–athlete relationship.

If you don't appear to be making headway I would advise referral to a psychology practitioner. There may be some issues that need to be addressed in confidence and away from the immediate training environment.

Going deeper into the theory

The issue of returning to training and competition has received attention from researchers in recent years. Findings indicate that there are many challenges in this period: heightened performance anxiety (Gould et al., 1997), concerns over reinjury (Walker et al., 2010), reduced physical self-efficacy (Andersen, 2001) concerns over performing at preinjury levels (Evans et al., 2000) and uncertainties about meeting the expectations of others (Taylor et al., 2003). There may also be a mismatch in the perceptions of athletes about rehabilitation and their coaches. Several studies have indicated that performers feel pressured to return to training and competition prematurely in order to hit external deadlines, such as competitions and training camps or to avoid negative evaluations. This can be compounded in professional performers coming towards the end of contract cycles or approaching funding decisions.

A useful line of theory around this which can be used to develop interventions is found in the work of Podlog and Eklund (2005, 2009, 2010). These researchers have applied self-determination theory to the motivational climate around returning performers. The development of intrinsic motives for return is associated with a range of benefits and contrast with extrinsic motives which appear more closely related to 'return concerns'.

Bibliography

Andersen, M.B. (2001). Return to action and prevention of future injury. In J. Crossman (Ed.), *Coping with Sports Injuries: Psychological Strategies for Rehabilitation*. Oxford University Press.

Evans, L., Hardy, L., & Flewming, S. (2000). Intervention strategies with injured athletes: an action research study. *The Sport Psychologist 14*: 188–206.

Gould, D., Udry, E., Bridges, D., & Beck, L. (1997). Stress sources encountered when rehabilitating from season ending ski-injuries. *The Sport Psychologist 11*: 361–378.

Podlog, L., & Eklund, R.C. (2005). Return to sport following serious injury. A retrospective examination of motivations and out-comes. *Journal of Sport Rehabilitation 14*: 201–214.

Podlog, L., & Eklund, R.C. (2009). High level athletes' perceptions of success following injury. *Psychology of Sport and Exercise 10*. 535–544.

Podlog, L., & Eklund, R.C. (2010). Returning to competition follow-ing a serious injury: the role of self-determination. *Journal of Sport Sciences 28*: 819–831.

Taylor, J., Stone, K.R., Mullin, M.J., Ellenbecker, T., & Walgenbach, A. (2003). *Comprehensive Sports Injury Management: From Examination of Injury to Return to Sport*. Pro-ed.

Walker, N., Thatcher, J., & Lavellee, D. (2010). A preliminary devel-opment of the Re-Injury Anxiety Inventory (RIAI). *Physical Therapy in Sport 11*: 23–29.

Q66

I am a physiotherapist working with elite performers. There is a big difference in how well performers adhere to their rehab programmes. Is there anything psychology can offer to get better adherence or compliance?

In medical literature a number of verbs are used to describe the extent to which someone receiving treatment engages fully with the pre-scribed course of action, taking medicines, changing behaviour or, as in this case, doing exercises which will ensure optimal healing and rehabilitation. Compliance feels quite a disempowering way of describing this interaction. Adherence is often used in the sport psychologist literature as it has a more active role for the patient receiving treatment. Adherence is the extent to which a person's behaviour coincides with advice or instructions from the health care provider to prevent, monitor or speed recovery from a disorder.

I would design an intervention including a number of strategies, often in combination, to boost adherence:

◆ injury education
◆ goal setting
◆ social support.

Often performers are surprisingly ignorant of how their body works and how an injury has affected tissue. Injury is a good opportunity for a performer to find out more about what has happened to the body to cause pain, inflammation and damage. The purpose of giving the injured athlete this information is to educate about how, by doing rehabilitative exercises and treatments, the performer can actively and positively enhance the healing and rehabilitation process. The individual may also learn how to prevent injury in the future. Be watchful for superadherers – ones who believe that if the therapist says, do an exercise eight times a day, then doing it 16 times or even more must be even better. I would be inclined to go through the risks of overadherence as part of the education process.

There is evidence that goal-setting interventions can boost adherence. Goal setting helps the performer see progress which can boost confidence in the rehabilitation process. It also helps performers view themselves as an active part in the process, rather than as a passive patient to whom things are done.

Recruiting social support can be very useful in increasing adherence to treatment. I have used family members and team mates as prompts to encourage performers to engage in their rehabilitation. An extension of this is to keep in contact with performers you have treated and ask them if they are willing to 'buddy' an injured performer. Using a 'model' who has successfully rehabilitated from an injury to support a performer who is currently in the early stages of the injury/recovery process can be very helpful.

Going deeper into the theory

Brewer (2010) has comprehensively summarized many of the key factors related to adherence to injury rehabilitation. Some personality characteristics appear to be linked to good adherence: athletes who are self-motivated, possess high levels of self-worth and have a well-established and robust athletic role were more likely to adhere to prescribed treatment. Combined with a high level of belief in the effectiveness of the treatment and a high level of self-efficacy in the execution of the rehabilitation exercises, these factors are associated with good adherence.

It is important to have a nuanced measure of adherence. Where a performer is attending a clinic, it is not sufficient simply to record whether that person attended or not; it is important to assess the effort and commitment with which the exercises were executed. This is more labour-intensive but because it doesn't rely on the self-report of the injured athlete but is more objective.

Bibliography

Brewer, B.W. (2010). Adherence to sport injury rehabilitation. In S.J. Hanrahan & M.B. Andersen (Eds.), *Routledge Handbook of Applied Sport Psychology: A Comprehensive Guide for Students and Practitioners* (pp. 233–241). Routledge.

Q67

When goal setting with an injured athlete on his return to action, how do you guard against disappointment if he doesn't reach his goal?

I encourage goal setting with injured performers, but where possible I avoid having specific dates or events in mind. The problem with having dates or events set as 'destinations' or outcome goals is that these dates can become so prominent and 'magical' in a player's mind he begins to neglect the day-to-day work which needs to be done to make sure that the player is fully rehabilitated in as short a period as possible. My approach is to work with the player and the medical team to identify specific periods in the rehabilitation process.

Phase 1

In this period the player may experience a range of negative emotions – anger, frustration, isolation and a sense of profound unfairness. This is compounded by the fact that structure is removed from the player's life and he has a great deal of time to think about what has happened. In this phase the day-to-day process goals are really to find meaningful activities which cope with the immediate challenges. Pain management is important, and the medical team should give clear advice about what activity can be safely undertaken. I have given players jobs or activities to undertake to act as a distraction and give some purpose to the day. These could be sport-related, such as watching video (although these can serve as a reminder to players that they are not able to participate) or unrelated, such as organizing an Itunes account or photograph album – the type of job that tends to fall off a 'to do' list.

Phase 2

This can be a difficult period to manage; often the player is now painfree. Without that reminder, the player may find it difficult to understand why he cannot be more active. It is a risky point in rehabilitation as tissue is healing and remodelling. Haste at this stage can cause problems later in the process. Working with medical support it may be possible to find some activity that can be undertaken which affords no risk to the injured area. This can be helpful. The day-to-day goals here may be to find contributions to the team – assisting coaching or reviewing video. In this phase I encourage players to develop a mental rehearsal routine.

Phase 3

At this stage, the medical support team will be comfortable with the player doing general, low-intensity activity. Return to physical activity should be graded and recovery between sessions should be monitored. Where possible, elements of game skills can be gradually introduced, such as ball carrying or dribbling. But risk needs to be assessed and managed. Mental rehearsal becomes more important at this stage. We are starting to orient the player towards return to competition. In many cases using imagery to revisit the competitive environment can prevent key skills becoming 'rusty'.

Phase 4

This is the immediate pre-return period. The player's physical and technical preparation is increasing in intensity. Where possible I spend time with players at this stage, to review training and assess their perceived readiness to return to play. I encourage players to keep the coach updated about their sense of readiness and whether they feel they need a graded return, working through lower teams, or are ready for a full return. In some sports return via the bench is not advised as an injury to another player in the first minute of a game may mean that the player is forced to play much longer than anticipated.

You can see from this that goal setting is being applied, but perhaps not in the way you envisaged. Process-type goals are more important than outcomes, dates or events.

Going deeper into the theory

This answer has applied Taylor and Taylor's (1997) return-to-sport model, integrating very clear process goals into the different phases. An example of this approach is Westbury (2009) – a case study from elite rugby, where an international player returned from a serious shoulder injury in a 100-day period. The phases were broken down into four roughly equal phases, each with clear aims and goals. The phased approach highlights the fact that players have different needs at the initial stage of injury, midway through rehabilitation and face a big mental challenge as they approach return to play.

A further line of theory worth exploring is the link between stress and the process of healing. Recent developments in psychoneuroimmunology (e.g. Kiecolt-Glaser et al., 1995) clearly demonstrate that there is a relationship between stress and delayed wound healing. Process goals, which aim to increase a sense of autonomy over the rehabilitation period and highlight daily progress, can help to reduce stress and thereby speed healing.

Bibliography

Kiecolt-Glaser, J.K., Marucha, P.T., Mercado, A.M., Malarky, W.B., & Glaser, R. (1995). Slowing of wound healing by psychological stress. *The Lancet 346* (8984): 1194–1196.

Taylor, J., & Taylor, S. (1997). *Psychological Approaches to Sports Injury Rehabilitation.* Aspen.

Westbury, T. (2009). A case study examining a gestalt approach to coping in Rugby Union. *Sport and Exercise Psychology Review 5* (2): 19–29.

Q68

What advice would you give to coaches of injured athletes who were/are on performance pathways but have a long-term injury which forces them off the pathway?

There is never a good time to be injured. However, it should be recognized that injury is an occupational hazard and that performers need to remain engaged in their personal development. The challenge for athletes on development pathways is that injury can feel like a complete personal catastrophe which is both unfair and cruel. Many of the emotional responses to injury may be magnified; there is profound denial, anger and frustration. This may give way, only to be replaced by a deep helplessness and even depression. Injured performers who lose a place on a pathway may lose funding and, ironically, their access to the high-quality sports medicine and science put in place to help them.

Your plan can be developed when the performer is healthy, rather than in a state of panic and emotional upset in the early stages of injury. Injury is a normal state for a performer – we do everything possible to avoid it but when it comes we engage a plan. It is not helpful to view it as a personal disaster.

As part of the plan we need to make sure that we have all the necessary information about the performance programme. Who needs to know about the injury? Are we able to access additional medical support? What are the key dates and competitions for the programme? My view is that keeping these channels of communication open is important for the athlete to remain on the governing body's radar.

Another part of the plan is for the athlete to engage in the stepped approach to rehabilitation outlined in other answers – starting with a clear diagnosis and then engaging in the progressive return to training, return to play and return to competition protocols. This process is not necessarily linear and there will be high points as milestones are achieved and lows where perhaps the performer pushes too hard too soon and fails to progress. Monitor these and reinforce the medical advice.

Some performers will experience profoundly negative or self-handicapping thinking about return to performance. It is a skilled job to challenge and restructure this. A coach should listen out for concerns about not being ready to return, this is likely to be derived from a fear that performance levels will not comparable with those prior to injury. For injuries longer than a few weeks it is inevitable that detraining will occur. Therefore the expectation to return at comparable performance levels is an irrational thought and should be challenged. Clarifying expectations and setting process and performance goals for return is an important part of the return-to-competition process.

When performers lose their place on the pathway, they often take this extremely personally. This is faulty thinking. Selectors have criteria and a fixed resource. Lines have to be drawn somewhere. It isn't personal – it is a challenge to show that they have made a mistake.

Going deeper into the theory

I would like to reinforce in this question that the psychologist, like every other member of the medical team, is working with the performer as an individual, not the injury or the present situation. There is no additional reason to expect someone on a talent pathway to be more challenging or to experience greater distress than any other injured performer. The individual might experience a heightened emotional response because he is not only injured but also sees his position, status or identity threatened. But equally the performer may experience relief from being able to withdraw temporarily from a highly pressured and performance-oriented environment.

In the case of this performer, it appears that he has been out of action for an extended period. The injury may be taking longer than expected to heal. The performer may be experiencing high levels of anxiety, either about reinjury or about not returning to preinjury performance levels. These may be prominent in the performer's thinking and should be carefully and sensitively worked through.

Bibliography

Heil, J., & Podlog, L. (2010). Injury and performance. In S. Murphy (Ed.), *The Oxford Handbook of Sport and Performance Psychology* (pp. 593–617). Oxford University Press.

Q69

My daughter is a gymnast. She has been diagnosed with a developmental bone condition. She doesn't want to stop competing but is often in considerable pain

You don't tell me the age of your daughter or specifically what the specialist has diagnosed. I am inferring that your daughter is in her early teens and has a condition related to her growth plates. My first advice for both you and your daughter is to speak to the specialist – you need a very clear overview of the risks of continuing to train and compete. Damaging a growth plate during puberty can be serious. You and your daughter need to be clear about the long-term implications of decisions taken now. My default is to be cautious; youngsters must realize that they will need their bones and joints in healthy working order for many years. Many young performers don't think in this way. They can only see to the next competition, and how important it is for them to be there and performing well.

I firmly believe that training with pain is not advisable. Pain is usually caused by some underlying damage. It is ill advised to 'push through it' and it is certainly not something a coach, parent or teacher should endorse without clear medical approval. In my view this is unlikely, but if the medical team are happy for your daughter to continue training and competing, then there are some things that can help.

Firstly, you need to work with her coach to make training sessions as efficient as possible. Rather than doing lots of repetition of activities which cause pain, focus on shorter bouts of high-quality training interspersed with activities which reduce the pain and discomfort.

Secondly, it is almost inevitable that the key aspects of the routine, the most technically challenging, will be the ones that cause the most discomfort. Experiencing pain will be inevitable. Have a very clear stop point for when the pain becomes too much. I suggest a simple ladder scale of 0 – no pain at all, through to 10 – the worst pain imaginable. Have a routine of asking, what is the pain right now? Agree that when the answer is 6, stop and recover. Don't start again until the pain score has dropped.

Finally, have regular pain management time-outs. Work on a routine in which when the pain becomes overwhelming you take a time out to calm yourself. Use a relaxation technique such as muscle relaxation or centring to lower your heart and breathing rates and allow the tension and discomfort to leave your body. Remind yourself that the medical team have approved your training and you are not doing further damage and in a few weeks you will be painfree again.

Going deeper into the theory

I cannot stress enough the importance of the ethical angle here. Before working with an athlete presenting with pain, I would seek assurances from the medical team that, by developing an intervention that allows her to continue to train and compete, I am not complicit in exacerbating an injury or risking longer-term damage.

The ethical issue extends to when you believe that the performer will continue to train and perform despite strong advice not to. In this case, the situation is complicated by the performer being a minor.

If a pain management intervention is indicated by the medical team, the work of Jensen (2010) and Heil (1993) is helpful. Jensen suggests developing pain management strategies around changing the thoughts, behaviours and sensory experiences of pain, using cognitive restructuring, conditioning and relaxation. Heil's approach is more prominently cognitive, drawing heavily on the literature around association – focusing on the cues from the task being executed, or dissociation, intentionally distracting yourself from the task. The challenge recognized by Heil is that the performer in pain has a double attentional challenge – focusing on skill execution whilst also focusing away from the painful stimulus. This approach usefully informs the mental skills intervention as it can account for the situation where pain is triggered when a skill is performed accurately, thereby reducing the likelihood of changing a pattern of movements which cause another injury through a modification in technique or compensatory movement.

Bibliography

Heil, J. (1993). *Psychology of Sport Injury.* Human Kinetics.
Jensen, M.P. (2010). A neuropsychological model of pain: research and clinical implications. *Journal of Pain 11*: 2–12.

Q70

How do you deal with performers who experience very severe psychological symptoms after an injury?

This can be a very challenging situation for a coach, teacher, parent or other sport science/sports medicine practitioner. Where is the line where professional competence ends and the ethical responsibility to refer a performer to a mental health specialist begins?

I tend to be conservative in my advice. It is usual for a performer to be very 'down' about an injury for a short period – a few days, perhaps a week. If the symptoms persist for longer, I would begin to be more active in my intervention, with a focus on moving to a more adaptive approach rehabilitation. At this point, I would be very attentive to what the performer is saying and doing. If she appears to be presenting with some of the more severe symptoms of anxiety, depression or posttraumatic stress, I would start to guide the performer towards more specialized mental health support.

I am attentive to the signs of posttraumatic stress, in particular vivid and persistent flashbacks to an incident where an injury has occurred. In my experience, this is not common. However knowing what to look out for is important, as it may begin several months after an injury has occurred.

Going deeper into the theory

This is a very important issue. It is easy to be preoccupied with the physical side of injury. Most sports medicine research is focused on causal factors, diagnosis and assessment, treatment and rehabilitation of physical aspects of injury, usually around the musculoskeletal system. In 2014 FifPro published a very significant study looking at mental illness in professional soccer players. Whilst some of these factors are based around responses to injury, many are not. The study gives a snapshot of the prevalence and seriousness of mental illness in football. In summary, in a sample of over 300 players, around one in four experienced clinical anxiety or depression, and almost one in five had adverse alcohol drinking habits. In addition, one in four reported unhealthy eating behaviours, including bulimia and binge eating. Not all of these will be linked with injury, but as I pointed out earlier, one of the challenges of injury is that performers have unscheduled down time – the loss of a valued activity and plenty of time to think about it.

FifPro also collected data on former players and found these adverse mental health indicators to be even more pronounced. In my view it is important for practitioners to keep eyes and ears open for signs of mental health issues and, without overstepping the boundaries, offer discreet advice to more clinical aspects of practice for which most sport psychologists are not qualified.

Bibliography

FifPro (2014). *Mental Illness in Professional Football*. Retrieved 14 July 2016 from: https://www.fifpro.org/en/news/study-mental-illness-in-professional-football.

Van Raalte, J.L. (2010). Referring clients to other professionals. In S.J. Hanrahan & M.B. Andersen (Eds.), *Routledge Handbook of Applied Sport Psychology: A Comprehensive Guide for Students and Practitioners* (pp. 205–213). Routledge.

Q71

Does the sport psychologist have a role in the management of concussion?

Concussion is a serious issue in sport and one that I think all support staff around performers have a role in preventing and, when it does occur, identifying and managing.

Psychologists can play their part by making themselves aware of the most recent updates of either their sport guidelines or the more generic guidelines for testing, such as the Sport Concussion Assessment Tool (SCAT) (Echemendia et al., 2017). Psychologists have an important role to play in making players aware of these guidelines and, more importantly, because the tests are only as good as the coaches, parents and teachers administering them (often at grassroots level of sport there is little or no independent medical cover), they may also have to act as the objective observer, ensuring that the principles of codes of practice are adhered to. This may result in the psychologist coming into conflict with a coach who wishes a player to continue. This is a test of the psychologist's adherence to his or her code of conduct or ethics. The psychologist should always act in the interest of the player, particularly when the coach doesn't appear to be.

There can be a difficult conversation to be had with a player who chooses to continue playing despite a concussive head injury.

Injury in general and concussion specifically are multidisciplinary issues. However, the medical team should have access to more specialized expertise than that offered by the psychologist. It is likely that the longer-term assessment and management of head injuries will be a clinical issue and therefore should be delivered by a psychologist with specialist qualifications and experience.

Going deeper into the theory

Heil and Podlog (2010) capture the essence of the challenge to the sport psychologist:

> Because head injury is a relatively common event, often occurring in the absence of medical personnel, it required grassroots attention. Given the significance of cognitive symptoms in head injury, the skill set and knowledge of the sport psychologist is well suited to identification and management.
>
> (Heil and Podlog, 2010, p. 602)

Heil and Podlog argue that sport psychologists should be trained at least to the level to enable them to be 'first responders' following a head injury.

Assessment of concussion is primarily based around cognitive factors: attention and concentration, cognitive processing speed, working memory, executive functioning and verbal fluency. However, it is important to establish baseline levels for these before an accurate assessment can be made. As concussion becomes more of an issue in many contact sports, it is highly likely that coaches will be required to assess players formally in a more systematic way. I think this is an important step in the right direction.

Bibliography

Echemendia, R.J., Meeuwisse, W., McCrory, P., et al. (2017) The Sport Concussion Assessment Tool, 5th edn. (SCAT5). *British Journal of Sports Medicine*. Published online first: 26 April 2017. doi: 10.1136/bjsports-2017-097506.

Heil, J., & Podlog, L. (2010). Injury and performance. In S. Murphy (Ed.), *The Oxford Handbook of Sport and Performance Psychology* (pp. 593–617). Oxford University Press.

White, P., Newton, J., Makdissi, M., Sullivan, J., Davis, G., McRory, P., Donaldson, A., Ewing, M., & Finch, C. (2013). Knowledge about sports-related concussion: is the message getting through to coaches and trainers? *British Journal of Sports Medicine48* (2): 119–124.

Pulling the threads together

As I conclude this chapter I recall an interview with Scottish international rugby union player, Rory Lamont. In 2013 he decided to retire from the game after failing to rehabilitate from his 16th operation in a 10-year professional career. The interview lifted the lid on a culture which coerced him and other players to play when injured. Players were mocked for reporting injury and frequently played on when they had very serious injuries. The culture of sport is all too quick to judge a player breaking the *omerta* around injury as being weak or that all Lamont's injury problems were in his head. This culture has to change. As the first generation of professional rugby union players retire from the game with a profound burden of injury to carry into the rest of their lives, sport science and sports medicine professionals need to reflect on their role in preventing injury and responding in a truly client-centred way.

Because there is never a good time to get injured and injury is almost always perceived as a loss of something valued, it is deeply psychological. Sports medicine has moved to recognize this. In some respects the applied sport psychology community has been slower to respond. Very few sport psychology practitioners would call themselves specialists in the area and those who are become so through necessity, working in performance enhancement contexts where injury rates are high. In time I would like to see applied sport psychology develop to acknowledge subspecialisms, the psychology of injury being one of the most pressing.

In the meantime, sport psychologists working with injured performers will frequently be working in collaboration with clinical colleagues, psychologists and medical and health care professionals. We need to learn from each other.

Injury is an occupational hazard but we should not view it fatalistically, as inevitable. In this chapter I hope to have achieved my aim in showing that many controllable factors influence whether a performer suffers an injury. For the parent, coach or teacher, this new knowledge should be used in the training methods, the implicit stresses and, importantly, the culture around a performer. We can also acknowledge that those in leadership roles with performers can help to protect performers from themselves.

When injuries do occur, the knowledge in this chapter will help those around the performer not just to be the physical first aider, but also to respond skilfully as a psychological first aider, recognizing the symptoms of adjustment and creating an environment where healing and rehabilitation can be optimized.

Mental skills have a role to play in this. The mental skills performers have developed to support and enhance performance can equally be applied to rehabilitation. This is another strong case for developing mental skills and competencies at an early stage in a performer's career.

X

Knowing when to stop: psychology and the transition out of sport

The public spectacle of players coping with the end of their career can be painful. Putting his personal life to one side, watching Tiger Woods' struggle undermines the memories we have of him dominating the world of golf. His body has been battered into submission and his game has become unrecognizable. What keeps him coming back and trying again? His case is very different from those of Serena Williams and Roger Federer. Even at the relatively old age (she was 34 years old when she won the Singles title at Wimbledon in 2016), she is still ranked in the top five in the world and continues to be highly motivated to add to her 22 major tournament victories. Similarly, Federer continues to play consistently well and at the age of 35 is ranked in the top ten in the world.

It is speculative but highly possible that Woods continues because he falls into the roughly one in five performers who experience a high degree of psychological distress over their transition out of sport. Federer remains a very good player, but he's not as good as he was. What will trigger his decision to leave the sport? How will he adjust?

The psychological challenge of life after sport

I introduced Scottish international rugby player Rory Lamont in the previous chapter. After a series of injuries, in 2013, Lamont decided to call time on his career. You would expect a player with the profile Lamont enjoyed in England, Scotland and France to move seamlessly on to the next phase of his life. But an interview published in *The Sunday Times* on 1 May 2016 showed that nothing could be further from the truth. His psychological state declined, he became reclusive and experienced profound depression, including thoughts of suicide. Physically he declined; unable to eat, he lost 25 kg.

What happened?

Lamont spoke about the culture of professional rugby, the macho 'hype', where you adopt the role of the superathlete, part of a team, invulnerable and 'bullet-proof'. But this culture was just masking insecurities. When he left professional rugby all these insecurities became apparent. Lamont's life lost its structure and purpose. To make matters worse, his work raising the important question of concussion in rugby brought him into direct conflict with his former employers, the Scottish Rugby Union. His integrity was questioned, adding further to his overwhelming sense of isolation. He felt like he was consigned to the scrap heap, and with further medical treatment required post retirement he found himself waking up each morning in pain, angry, frustrated, but with nothing to do and no energy to plan his own future.

In the interview Lamont described symptoms readily compatible with a diagnosis of clinical depression; of particular concern were the suicidal thoughts. Although he was never formally diagnosed with depression, the fact that he was not supported or referred to a mental health professional whilst injured but still playing indicates a lack of holistic care. As he entered a retirement he was wholly unprepared for, it became even more serious.

Lamont spent 3 years adjusting to retirement; now there are signs that he is mentally in a better place to move on to a happy and fulfilling life. Physically, he still has much mending to do. He will probably carry the scars, both physical and mental, of his elite status for the rest of his life.

Lamont is not alone. Clarke Carlisle, the former Blackpool and Burnley defender went on to chair the Professional Footballers' Association in England. Carlisle finished playing in 2013 and in December 2014, whilst suffering depression, attempted to take his own life by stepping out in front of a lorry.

These are not isolated cases. There are many other high-profile sport performers who face profound psychological struggles at the conclusion of their careers. In this chapter I will examine the psychological impact of retirement and particularly focus on what performers can do to make the transition out of sport a positive one.

Retirement and mental health

In the past 5 years there have been a number of important developments which have served to raise awareness of the link between retirement and declines in mental health. Clarke Carlisle, the former player mentioned above, has been in the forefront of these.

One of the most prominent was the initiative by Mind – a very prominent mental health charity in the UK (Mind, 2017). This is a well-designed and comprehensive project aimed at raising awareness about mental health in elite sport, using high-profile performers as case studies and addressing the stigma of mental illness.

The social psychology of retirement

In the developed world the idea of retirement is a relatively recent one. Due to low life expectancy and the absence of any social benefits, until the late 19th century people worked until death. Now, as life expectancy grows, people feel physically able to maintain the affirming role of employment until much later. Unless your job is sport. There are outliers: Sir Stanley Matthews turned out for Stoke City in the First Division of the English League at the age of 50 and cricketer Brian Close played his final first-class innings at the age of 55. But these achievements are of a bygone age. Today the longevity of a player's career is determined by the physical demands of the sport. A rugby player can lengthen his career by carefully limiting the number of games played each season, but for most by the time they reach their mid-30s the repeated collisions have taken their toll and they are likely to be being outperformed by younger players, who inevitably recover quicker. Endurance sports, such as running and rowing, demand such heavy training loads that retirement is a wise long-term health decision. Over 25 years of training have left Paula Radcliffe with a chronic foot injury. Each mile of repeated foot strikes – in heavy training she ran over 100 miles a week for months on end – brought injuries she will carry for the rest of her life.

Retirement from sport is rarely a simple process. The research differentiates performers for whom the decision is a chosen one from those forced to retire through deselection or injury. There are no clear statistics on what proportion of players make the choice to end their career, but in all cases the implications are the same – to withdraw from an activity which has given day-to-day life meaning and structure from childhood.

Grove et al. (1997) suggested that around one performer in five experiences distress during the process of retiring from sport.

A small minority will have stories like Lamont and Carlisle. At the other end of the spectrum, many performers will have very positive experiences, where new challenges are set and a new identity is established outside the sport. It is important to distil down both sets of experiences to identify what can be done to maximize the positive and, where possible, avoid the negative.

Retirement – a grieving process or necessary and positive transition?

Early research linked the retirement process from sport with the emotional grieving process we looked at in Chapter IX, on injury. The stages have been criticized by researchers and applied practitioners. The emotional sequence of shock, denial, anger, bargaining, depression and acceptance does help researchers and practitioners understand the emotional complexity of the experience.

Deselection, injury and a chosen withdrawal are offered as the three main reasons for disengagement from sport. These in themselves are not the factors which determine a performer's psychological well-being around retirement. For many the big hurdles to overcome are psychosocial – the extent to which performers viewed themselves as performers, their sporting identity. They also lose a structure to their lives and social contact with people with whom they have shared a very significant part of their emotional lives. Often it is the social contact with team mates that, at least in the short term, feels irreplaceable. The 'double whammy' is that, by withdrawing from regular training, players are not getting their neurochemical 'fix' of endorphins, dopamine and serotonin. As a result the world seems a bleaker, less exciting, less engaging and more stressful place.

Another approach to retirement comes the work of Danish et al. (1995). This emphasizes continuous growth and development throughout the life of the performer. It views retirement as a predictable event which should be prepared for and supported. Lavellee (2005) has published work indicating that, when performers were supported through the retirement process, using preretirement assessment of their personality, the types of career or education opportunities they would like to move into and an audit of the skills developed in their playing career, the transition is more goal-oriented and constructive.

Knowing when to quit: preparation and working through

Sport is an uncertain business. As they prepare to train or play on any given day, most players will not consciously consider the fact that, in that session or game, they may receive an injury which ends their career. Even as they get older the reality that their time in the game is coming to an end may be ignored. Performance levels may be dropping, contract negotiations may become more difficult and the feeling that the body is not recovering as it once was are all indicators of an inevitable day, but still it prompts little action.

There is often a 'spike' of retirements following an Olympic or other major games or tournament. Players who are fortunate to have a choice will often retire from competition at a point when a major goal has been achieved. This can be an important aspect of the 'account-making' process. Leaving sport following a major achievement allows performers some breathing space, buffering the negative emotion that will almost inevitably follow. They are losing something valued, but on their terms and at a moment when they believe they could not have achieved more. Despite losing something which gave their lives structure and meaning for many years, they are exercising choice in a way a player who is injured out of sport or deselected cannot.

Having a fixed date in mind for retirement allows the performer to make preparations and to anticipate some of the challenges ahead. Leaving sport and making transitions into employment or education can pose significant challenges, for example, sport retirees may be much older than others in their immediate peer group. They may have different values and approaches to life and work.

I recommend the use of mentors to help in this process. Mentorship, developing a supportive relationship with someone who has successfully made the transition out of sport, can be extremely useful. The mentor will have lived through many of the same situations and be in a position to offer practical help. This is the kind of support that is now offered by many sport organizations.

Many performers believe that, as they leave sport, remaining involved through coaching is a good option. In my work with performers I have encountered examples where this has been the correct decision. The player has gone on to build a career as a highly effective coach. On the flip side, for several performers I have worked with it has proved to be a negative decision, both for the former player, who received a daily reminder that he is no longer playing, and for the players he coaches – the retiree had such high standards that none of the performers he coached were ever perceived to be good or committed enough.

The role of sport psychologist is to support the decision-making process and help the performer work through the often profoundly challenging emotional adjustment. Planning and mentoring can prepare the performer for the day, but in most cases there is still a sense of loss. Creating some space for performers to tell their story and helping them manage the emotional aftermath are important in preventing the kind of bleak story we heard from Rory Lamont. Retirement is a new beginning.

Bibliography

Danish, S.J., Petitpas, A.J., & Hale, B.D. (1995). Psychological interventions: a life development model. In Murphy, S.M. (Ed.), *Sport Psychology Interventions* (pp. 19–38). Human Kinetics.

Grove, J.R., Lavallee, D., & Gordon, S. (1997). Coping with retirement from sport: the influence of athletic identity. *Journal of Applied Sport Psychology, 9* (2), 191–203.

Lavellee, D. (2005). The effect of a life development intervention on sports career transition adjustment. *The Sport Psychologist, 19*, 193–202.

Mind. (2017). *Performance Matters: Mental Health in Elite Sport.* Retrieved from: http://www.mind.org.uk/media/1085139/Mental-Health-and-Elite-Sport.pdf?ctald=/about-us/our-policy-work/sport-physical-activity-and-mental-health/professionals in sport/slices/prof-sport/.

Q72

How do you know when it's time to hang up your boots?

Every performer is different. There can be all kinds of triggers: some recognize small but critical declines in performance, some have achieved all they want to achieve, some have opportunities outside the sport that they want to pursue, some have simply stopped enjoying what they are doing. The key thing is that the more the decision can be conscious and worked through, the more likely it is to be a successful transition.

One of the exercises I do with players contemplating retirement is a simple decisional balance sheet, where we look at the pros and cons of continuing to play and the pros and cons of retiring. It is important that this doesn't become simply a counting process – there are more pros for retiring so I must retire; each item on the list has a weighting or value to it. For example, the changes in financial terms due to a drop in income may need some planned adjustments. The more comprehensive the decisional balance, the clearer performers become of their motivations and the push/pull factors operating on their decision.

Once this exercise has been worked through, performers are in a stronger position to set goals and clarify the challenges for the next step in their lives, anticipating the potential pitfalls and putting in place the types of support they may require to overcome them.

Former players who have worked through the transition out of sport can also be useful in mentoring those considering retirement.

Going deeper into the theory

I have borrowed the idea of decisional balance from another area of psychology. In the behavioural change literature in health psychology, the stages-of-change model (Prochaska et al., 1992) identifies the process of change as proceeding from precontemplation (not thinking about change), through contemplation (thinking about change) into preparation (preparing for change) and then into action (enacting a change). I feel that this line of theory fits well into the process of retirement from sport. In this process decisional balance is a process of weighing up the advantages and disadvantages of particular actions.

Motivational interviewing is a technique which is often applied in this context. Originally developed as a technique for changing damaging and addictive behaviour, motivational interviewing is now applied in many areas of positive behavioural change, such as the adoption of a health-enhancing physically active lifestyle. It is a cognitively based counselling approach which aims to clarify the objectives of the behavioural change, whilst also addressing and working to remove potential barriers (Miller and Rollnick, 1991).

Bibliography

Miller, W.R., & Rollnick, S. (1991). *Motivational Interviewing: Preparing People to Change Addictive Behavior*. Guilford Press.

Prochaska, J.O., DiClemente, C.C., & Norcross, J.C. (1992). In search of how people change. Applications to addictive behaviours. *American Psychology 47*: 1102.

Q73

I am a former professional player. I've decided not to coach at a pro level but move down and coach at a lower level and work at the same time. I'm finding that I am expecting too much from the players I work with. They are good but don't have the skills or commitment that I'm used to in the professional game. What do you suggest I do?

What motivates you to coach? I think you might be well served to explore this in more depth and make sure that you are doing the right thing for yourself in remaining this close to the game.

What has led you not to want to coach at the professional level? Is it a pragmatic choice or a forced one?

Your answers to these questions will provide a framework for how we might proceed. I am aware that I'm doing some 'mind reading' but suspect that at the end of a playing career many players feel the need, possibly even obligation, 'to give something back' to the game they love and that has given them a living. This is very laudable and the game appreciates them for it. But it might *not* be the right decision for them. They can become stuck in a role which doesn't allow them to develop as people or somewhat paradoxically may not benefit the players they coach.

There can be a huge chasm, physically, technically and mentally, between the professional game and its closest amateur or semi-professional rung. Put very bluntly, professionals are paid to train and the whole environment allows them to focus on just that. Amateurs or semiprofessional players can be paid to play, and may be very professional in their outlook, but ultimately they are juggling a whole lot of other pressures and demands. As a coach you can demand the highest possible standards for a few hours in the week and for a game on Saturday. To expect more may lead to the kind of frustration you are experiencing.

You may need to modify your approach. Talk to the players about how to develop a more committed and professional approach both as individuals and as a team. If you are still motivated to coach them, look at ways in which you can develop them as players in their unique situations rather than comparing them to a professional equivalent.

Going deeper into the theory

I am fascinated by the decision of former players to coach. Looking through the prism of lifespan development, what is driving them? Is it an entirely new challenge? Is it an extension of a playing career? Is it the oft-cited desire 'to give something back'?

Erikson (1950) presented a model of lifespan development built around virtues or stages. The desire to 'give something back' to society or, in this case, sport fits into the seventh stage – one usually linked to middle adulthood. It is interesting that people in this stage of development are driven to create or nurture things that will outlast them, often by parenting children or contributing to positive changes that benefit other people. Erikson called this generativity and contrasted it with stagnation, where individuals fail to make their mark on the world and as a result feel unconnected with their community or society as a whole.

This desire to connect, contribute and care may be at the heart of many coaches' motivation. However, for some former players, remaining in the game may not be the best way of achieving this. By constantly comparing their playing days with those whom they coach they may experience regret at the mistakes they made, bitterness about how their career turned out and a sense that they have wasted their time. It may be better for them to move to new areas of interest, or possibly, if they wish to coach, to move into a new sport without the associated 'baggage'.

Bibliography

Erikson, E.H. (1950). *Childhood and Society*. Norton.

Q74

I've been a national-level gymnast since I was 12 years old. I'm 15 now and want to quit but I'm getting a lot of pressure to stay in the sport, from my coach, my parents and other gymnasts. What should I do?

This is an unfortunate, but common and complicated story. There is some ground-setting work to do before we can make progress on this. As a young person under the age of 16 it would not be appropriate to meet a sport psychologist in private, without your parent or guardian present. However, with your parent present you may feel inhibited to tell your story as you wish to. Therefore I would like to meet with your parents before I meet with you and them together to establish some ground rules for our work. The main one is to listen to your full story before making any judgement.

However, you also need to listen to theirs and see the situation through their eyes. They will have seen you progress to where you are now; they will have seen your hard work and sacrifice. They may also have made sacrifices to get you to training and competition and spent of lot of money travelling and staying away from home to support you. They may not understand your reasons for wanting to give up your sport. It might be a difficult and emotionally distressing conversation. However, we do need to 'go there' in order to make progress.

Once some ground work has been done and we have arrived at a situation where you, your parents and I can have an open discussion, my aim is to create a pressure-free environment where we can work through the same type of decisional balance conversation I have outlined above.

As you know, gymnastics is a highly intensive sport, but not one that you can readily return to, at your current level of performance, after a break. The time window for elite performance is quite small. Working with your coach, it might be possible to schedule a break to rest and test whether you have intrinsic motivation to return and continue your career. That is an option you may want to explore.

I suspect that, quite reasonably, you want to experience the life of a 'normal' teenager. You have probably seen what your non-gymnast friends are doing and feel that you are missing out. Keep this in perspective; elite sport is something that most of your peers will never experience. You will have a lot of years to catch up on more 'normal' social life once you retire.

Going deeper into the theory

Gymnastics is a sport that boys and girls often enter at a very young age, reach the peak of their performance very young (although there is more regulation around this now) and also frequently retire from at a young age. Some research (e.g. Warrinder and Lavellee, 2008) has identified particular issues around retirement of female gymnasts during adolescence. For teenagers outside sport, this period is one when a sense of personal identity is established; for those within sport, the identity is closely allied to their sporting role. To leave the sport may intensify the challenge of building a coherent sense of self and a place in the social world. If there is also conflict with close family and coaches, all of whom were previously strong and trusted pillars within the developing child's social world, this can be a deeply traumatic experience for the child (Chase, 2010).

Warrinder and Lavellee (2008) also reported that withdrawal from the training environment led to physiological changes, for example, triggering puberty, weight gain and changes in physical appearance, which may also provoke negative changes in how the person perceives her physical self.

Finally, there is a strong ethical angle to this question. My view is that all sport psychology consultations with children should be with parents or chaperones present. Interestingly, this is not an issue which appears in many research projects which have sought to deliver mental skills interventions to young performers under the age of 16.

Bibliography

Chase, M. (2010). Children. In S.J. Hanrahan & M.B. Andersen (Eds.), *Routledge Handbook of Sport Psychology*. Routledge.

Warrinder, K., & Lavellee, D. (2008). The retirement experiences of elite female gymnasts: self identity and the physical self. *Journal of Applied Sport Psychology 20* (3): 301–317.

Q75

I'm a masters runner. I'm 65 years young. I have a chronic injury, and every time I practise or perform I experience pain. I have been advised by my doctor to retire from running. But I just don't want to! Is there mentally anything I can do to help?

It looks like you are doing everything mentally already! You are highly motivated to continue and have found ways to manage the pain you experience and keep doing what you love.

- ◆ On a simple ladder scale of 0 to 10, where is the pain at present?
- ◆ Where does it get to when you train and race?
- ◆ What are you currently doing to manage the pain?
    - ✓ Physically?
    - ✓ Mentally?
    - ✓ Pharmacologically?
- ◆ Are there any ways we can tweak what you are doing in these areas to manage the situation better without risking any further injury or side-effects?
- ◆ Can you persist with your management of the pain in the longer term?
- ◆ What do you think you will need to change for you to heed your doctor's advice?

More broadly, I would want to explore the reasons why it has to be running. You can remain active by doing other things.

What I'm trying to get at are the reasons why the runner is motivated to continue despite clear and present threats to health, both through the injury and possibly the long-term use of anti-inflammatory or analgesic drugs. Once that has been resolved we are in a much better position to identify strategies which achieve the personal goals of the runner whilst limiting the risk of further injury.

Going deeper into the theory

There has been surprisingly little research focussed specifically on masters or age group performers. This is surprising as masters or age group sport is growing very rapidly at present. In the same way as I can see a subspecialty area in injury, I can also see a subspeciality in older performers, who often remain very competitive until late in life.

The small amounts of research that have been done reveal motivational differences between male and female performers. Males appear more extrinsically motivated towards tangible signs of achievement, winning races and receiving medals, whilst females appear more intrinsically motivated to continue to train and compete, focusing particularly on the social connectedness of training with a group and forming a close bond with fellow competitors or a coach (Medic et al., 2006).

This research also indicated that around 80% of masters performers had unaccomplished goals in their sport. These motivate the performer to continue training and competing. Whilst goal setting is an important and useful tool, it may be necessary to look at the types of goals that performers are creating for themselves and restructure them into more process and performance goals rather than emphasizing only outcomes.

In many sports competition for masters performers is divided into 5-year age brackets. For some performers there may be added incentive to train hard in the year before moving up an age group, in order to take advantage of relative age benefit (Medic et al., 2009).

Finally, it should be noted that around 10% of masters performers stated that they would never stop training and competing under any circumstances. These individuals are highly motivated but may lack objectivity about the physical cost of their commitment in ways which parallel a dependence on exercise (Hausenblas and Symons-Down 2000).

Bibliography

Hausenblas, H.A., & Symons-Downs, D. (2000). How much is too much? The development and validation of the exercise dependence scale. *Psychology and Health 17*: 387–404.

Medic, N., Starkes, J.L., Young, B.W., & Weir, P.L. (2006). Motivations for sport and goal orientations in masters athletes. Do masters swimmers differ from masters runners? *Journal of Sport and Exercise Psychology 28* (suppl): S132.

Medic, N., Starkes, J.L., Weir, P.L, Young, B.W., & Grove, J.L. (2009). Relative age effect in masters sport. Replication and extension. *Research Quarterly for Sport and Exercise 80*: 669–675.

Pulling the threads together

Reviewing the material in this chapter I note a rather negative tone. There seems to be a great deal of emphasis on how not to retire from sport, rather than looking at the positives that moving from one phase of life to another can yield.

I think the emphasis on the negative comes from two fundamental points. Firstly, frequently performers' identity is so bound up in their sport that they define themselves and others define them according to sport and their achievements within it. This makes moving out and moving on a significant process, requiring time and support. The second fundamental is that, for most performers, involvement in sport began at such a young age and has been so absorbing that is difficult to envisage a life without it. This leads to a lack of perspective about how and when it will end. I think this is true for both amateur and professional performers. There will come a time when age, injury, deselection or other demands mean that the nature of involvement will change. There are options, such as 'giving back' through coaching or other roles within the sport, but I think these need to be approached with care – they are not the panacea they sometimes appear.

In retirement, performers frequently report a sense of unfinished business, of goals unachieved. In my view this is a powerful reason for performers working with a sport psychologist in preparation for retirement. Being able to anticipate this and working to set goals which can mitigate against it can be extremely valuable.

For elite performers, preparation and support as early as possible in the pre-retirement process should be comprehensive; players need detraining programmes, they need practical help with finances, education and employment. They may need ongoing medical support.

For the grassroots performer, the transitions may not be so psychologically profound but there may be a loss of the social aspect of the sport, the recognition of achievement, the management of injury or support following deselection. Some thought needs to go into finding adequate replacements. It may be impossible to recapture the excitement of preparing for a big game or event – even a bad day in sport is better than a good day in the office! But we must try to soften the blow.

XI

Three things: one final pull of the threads

Applied sport psychology is a predominantly 'talking' intervention. As such it can be quite alien to action-oriented sports people. In an effort to address this I will usually finish a session with an athlete with an exercise designed to turn the talk into action aimed at achieving positive change.

A useful way of doing this, and gaining feedback from the performer, is to do a 'three things' exercise. Tell me three things that you are going to begin to do as a result of our meeting. In this section of the book I will make three suggestions based on each of the chapters: these are my perceptions, you may take something entirely different away.

Chapter II: Do I need sport psychology?

♦ Recognize that sport psychology and psychiatry are not the same thing. Remember Bradley Wiggins' change of mind!
♦ Be open-minded about the possible benefits of sport psychology in performance. There are no miracles but probably some 'low-hanging fruit'.
♦ Spend half an hour with a sport psychologist – it will probably be more beneficial than innumerable self-help books.

Chapter III: Motivation – making sense of the will to win

♦ Where is your sense of purpose? Why am I doing this?
♦ Reflect on the motivational climate you prefer – do prizes, incentives and recognition motivate you? Or do you look for mastery of skills? It is possibly a bit of both. Remember, mastery is within your control in a way that winning is not: aim to be a little better today than you were yesterday.
♦ Motivation to prepare is more important than motivation to win. If you are not committed to excellence in training,

there is someone training somewhere in the world who is, and when you meet that person s/he will beat you.

Chapter IV: Can sport psychology stop me being sick with nerves before I perform?

♦ Think about what your ideal emotional 'temperature' is. Do you prefer to run hot on excitement and emotion or cold? Develop strategies to increase the 'temperature' to psyche yourself up, and decrease it to calm yourself down.

♦ Develop practices which put your skills under pressure in match-like scenarios and situations.

♦ Most pressure is self-generated. Examine the 'faulty' thinking which tends to provoke nerves.

Chapter V: Choking, ball watching and 'sledging' – applying the science of attention to staying focused in sport performance

♦ Here-and-now focus. Work hard to 'park' errors in the past and not to anticipate or 'crystal ball' the future. Maintain a focus on the job at hand. In pauses tune into your next job, not the one that's just gone.

♦ Have a well-developed 'BS' filter. In sport, there is a great deal of opinion presented as fact – a BS filter helps you to screen out the unhelpful and just focus on what is relevant and helpful.

♦ Think about your ideal preperformance and pre-execution of skills routines. Understand what distracts you the most. Is it the internal distraction of your inner perfectionist? Or the external noise around you – the environment, team mates and the audience? Either way have strategies for tuning in and tuning out.

Chapter VI: It's all about having a positive mental attitude – isn't it?

(I'm allowing myself four points on this one!)

◆ Competence in executing skills is more important than confidence. Train to become competent and skilled. Test and refine the skills in game-like simulations. You build competence through effective practice and reconnecting with executing skills accurately and efficiently. You build confidence by reconnecting with success. Don't dwell on error – it is merely the byproduct of developing competence.

◆ Are you Teflon or Velcro? Do mistakes slip easily away as you move on to the next phase of training or performance (Teflon), or do they get stuck, and you just can't get free of them (Velcro)?

◆ Your inner voice – bring it on, thriving on pressure. Remember everyone is probably more nervous than you.

◆ Relax and let the skills out – your body knows how to play the game. Quieten your thoughts and anxieties and let it out.

Chapter VII: Team spirit: accident or design?

◆ Decide what type of team you want to be. Is social cohesion more important than task cohesion?

◆ Clarify expectations, norms and responsibilities. Leaders aim to create a culture of everyday excellence.

◆ Communication, based on respect, honesty and trust, is critical. Make it safe for people to ask questions and be vulnerable. This is not a sign of weakness.

Chapter VIII: Children and youth sport: the mind of a child is not a vessel to be filled, it is a fire to be kindled

- ◆ As a coach, teacher or parent be aware of the motivational climate you are creating.
- ◆ Deliberate play is more important than deliberate practice in the early stages of learning a sport. Maximize 'ball at feet' immersion in gaining skills.
- ◆ Avoid early specialization.

Chapter IX: The psychology of sport injury: there are two types of performer – those who are currently injured and those who will become injured

- ◆ Have an injury plan – starting with diagnosis, find an injury buddy.
- ◆ Be aware of the negative impact of stress both on causing injury and slowing recovery. Find out more about stress management.
- ◆ Be particularly aware of the return-to-play protocols, in particular around the reintroduction of contact. Address and manage specific concerns about returning to play – worries about performance levels and fears of reinjury.

Chapter X: Knowing when to stop: psychology and the transition out of sport

- ◆ If possible, plan and prepare a long way in advance. Retirement should be on your mind throughout your career. Take advantage of all opportunities offered to secure your future, financially, education-wise and in terms of careers.

- ◆ Decisional balance – work through the pros and cons of retirement. You may not retire; you may transition to another sport or another role within the sport. The more actively you engage with this, the better.
- ◆ Look for social support. Despite the feelings of isolation and despair, you are not alone. Look for social support and accept it if it is offered.

These are my 'take-aways' – look for your own!

Applied sport psychology has much to offer, at every level of sport. As I've worked my way through the construction of this project I have become very sensitive to the fine balance between doing justice to my academic colleagues who are publishing excellent research and engaging the sporting community, many of whom will never have met a sport psychologist. Somehow we have got to get these two communities together, more often and more closely. This is my humble contribution.

Recommended reading

Andersen, M. (2000). *Doing Sport Psychology*. Human Kinetics.

Andersen, M., & Hanrahan, S. (2012). *Routledge Handbook of Applied Sport Psychology: A Comprehensive Guide for Students and Practitioners*. Routledge.

Bull, S., & Shambrook, C. (2005). *Soccer, The Mind Game*. Reedswain.

Halliwell, W., Orlick, T., Ravizza, K., & Rotella, B. (2003). *Consultant's Guide to Excellence for Sport and Performance Enhancement*. Zone of Excellence.

Hardy, L., Jones, J., & Gould, D. (1996). *Understanding Psychological Preparation for Sport: Theory and Practice of Elite Performers*. Wiley.

Hemmings, B., & Holder, T. (2009). *Applied Sport Psychology: A Case Based Approach*. Wiley.

Jennings, K.E. (1993). *Mind in Sport: Directing Energy Flow Into Success*. Kenwyn: Juta.

Orlick, T. (2015). *In Pursuit of Excellence*. Human Kinetics.

Robinson, J. (2013). *Mind Training for Swimming Fast*. CreateSpace Independent Publishing Platform.

Syer, J., & Connolly, C. (1998). *Sporting Body, Sporting Mind: An Athlete's Guide to Mental Training*. Simon & Schuster.

Williams, J. (2015). *Applied Sport Psychology: Personal Growth to Peak Performance* (5th edn.). McGraw-Hill.

Index

Locators in **bold** refer to tables and those in *italics* to figures. Alphabetisation is word-by-word.